EVERYMAN'S LIBRARY

821

TRAVEL & TOPOGRAPHY

Everyman, I will go with thee, and be thy guide,
In thy most need to go by thy side

DANIEL DEFOE (FOE), born in St Giles about 1661. Joined Monmouth's army, 1685; William III's, 1688. Employed in the Glass Duty Office, 1695–9, and then settled down to journalism and pamphleteering. He died in 1731.

DANIEL DEFOE

A TOUR THROUGH ENGLAND AND WALES

IN TWO VOLUMES · VOLUME TWO

INTRODUCTION BY
G. D. H. COLE

LONDON   J. M. DENT & SONS LTD
NEW YORK   E. P. DUTTON & CO INC

60:735

CONTENTS

VOLUME TWO

A TOUR
IN CIRCUITS, THROUGH ENGLAND AND WALES

LETTER VI

CONTAINING A DESCRIPTION OF PART OF THE COUNTIES OF MIDDLESEX, HERTFORD, BUCKS, OXFORD, WILTS, SOMERSET, GLOUCESTER, WARWICK, WORCESTER, HEREFORD, MONMOUTH, AND THE SEVERAL COUNTIES OF SOUTH AND NORTH-WALES

I HAVE spent so much time, and taken up so much room in my description of London, and the adjacent parts, that I must be the more cautious, at least, as to needless excursions in the country near it.

The villages round London partake of the influence of London, so much, that it is observ'd as London is encreased, so they are all encreased also, and from the same causes.

I have taken notice of this in my first setting out, and particularly in the counties of Essex, Kent, and Surrey; and as the same appears to an extreme in Middlesex: I shall only give some discriptions, and say the less of the reason of it.

Hackney and Bromley are the first villages which begin the county of Middlesex, east; for Bow as reckon'd to Stepney, is a part of the great mass. This town of Hackney is of a great extent, containing no less than 12 hamlets or separate villages, tho' some of them now join, viz.

Church-street,	Well-street,
Hummerton,	Cambridge-Heath,
Wyck-House,	Shacklewell,
Grove-street,	Dalstone,
Clapton,	Kingsland,
Mare-street,	Newington.

I

All these, tho' some of them are very large villages, make up but one parish (viz.) of Hackney.

All these, except the Wyck-house, are within a few years so encreas'd in buildings, and so fully inhabited, that there is no comparison to be made between their present and past state: Every separate hamlet is encreas'd, and some of them more than treble as big as formerly; Indeed as this whole town is included in the bills of mortality, tho' no where joining to London, it is in some respects to be call'd a part of it.

This town is so remarkable for the retreat of wealthy citizens, that there is at this time near a hundred coaches kept in it; tho' I will not join with a certain satyrical author, who said of Hackney, that there were more coaches than Christians in it.

Newington, Tottenham, Edmonton, and Enfield stand all in a line N. from the city; the encrease of buildings is so great in them all, that they seem to a traveller to be one continu'd street; especially Tottenham and Edmonton, and in them all, the new buildings so far exceed the old, especially in the value of them, and figure of the inhabitants, that the fashion of the towns are quite altered.

At Tottenham we see the remains of an antient building called the Cross, from which the town takes the name of High-Cross. There is a long account of the antiquities of this place lately published, to which I refer, antiquities as I have observed, not being my province in this work, but a description of things in their present state.

Here is at this town a small but pleasant seat of the Earl of Colerain, in Ireland; his lordship is now on his travels, but has a very good estate here extending from this town to Muzzle-hill, and almost to High-gate.

The first thing we see in Tottenham is a small but beautiful house, built by one Mr. Wanly, formerly a goldsmith, near Temple Bar; it is a small house, but for the beauty of the building and the gardens, it is not outdone by any of the houses on this side the country.

There is not any thing more fine in their degree, than most of the buildings this way; only with this observation, that they are generally belonging to the middle sort of mankind, grown wealthy by trade, and who still taste of London; some of them live both in the city, and in the country at the same time: yet many of these are immensely rich.

High-gate and Hamstead are next on the north-side; At the

first is a very beautiful house built by the late Sir William Ashurst, on the very summit of the hill, and with a view from the very lowest windows over the whole vale, to the city: And that so eminently, that they see the very ships passing up and down the river for 12 or 15 miles below London. The Jews have particularly fixt upon this town for their country retreats, and some of them are very wealthy; they live there in good figure, and have several trades particularly depending upon them, and especially, butchers of their own to supply them with provisions kill'd their own way; also, I am told, they have a private synagogue here.

As the county does not extend far this way, I take no notice of smaller towns; nor is there any thing of note but citizens houses for several miles; except that in the chase, at Enfield is a fine lodge formerly possest by the Earl of Denbigh: Now we are told that General Pepper is fixt ranger of the chase, and resides there.

This chase was once a very beautiful place, and when King James I. resided at Theobalds, which he loved for the pleasure of his hunting; it was then very full of deer, and all sorts of game; but it has suffered several depredations since that, and particularly in the late Protector's usurpation, when it was utterly stript, both of game, and timber, and let out in farms to tenants, for the use of the publick.

After the Restoration, it was reassumed, and laid open again; Woods and groves were every where planted, and the whole chase stored with deer: But the young timber which indeed began to thrive, was so continually plundered, and the deer-stealers have so harass'd the deer, and both perhaps by those who should have preserved it, as well as by others, that the place was almost ruined for a forrest, and little but hares and bushwood was to be found in it. But now we hear, that by the vigilance of General Pepper, the chase is much recovered, and likely to be a place fit for the diversion of a prince, as it has been before.

At a village a little farther north, called Totteridge, Mr. Charleton of the Ordnance Office, has a very delicious seat, the house new built, and the gardens extremely fine: In the same town the old Earl of Anglesey had also a house, but not extraordinary for any thing more than a rural situation, very retired, but yet very agreeable.

The Mineral Waters, or Barnet Wells, are a little beyond this house, on the declivity of a hill; they were formerly in great request, being very much approved by physicians; but of late, they began to decline, and are now almost forgotten: Other waters at Islington, and at Hamstead having grown popular in their stead.

Hampstead indeed is risen from a little country village, to a city, not upon the credit only of the waters, tho' 'tis apparent, its growing greatness began there; but company increasing gradually, and the people liking both the place and the diversions together; it grew suddenly populous, and the concourse of people was incredible. This consequently raised the rate of lodgings, and that encreased buildings, till the town grew up from a little village, to a magnitude equal to some cities; nor could the uneven surface, inconvenient for building, uncompact, and unpleasant, check the humour of the town, for even on the very steep of the hill, where there's no walking twenty yards together, without tugging up a hill, or stradling down a hill, yet 'tis all one, the buildings encreased to that degree, that the town almost spreads the whole side of the hill.

On the top of the hill indeed, there is a very pleasant plain, called the Heath, which on the very summit, is a plain of about a mile every way; and in good weather 'tis pleasant airing upon it, and some of the streets are extended so far, as that they begin to build, even on the highest part of the hill. But it must be confest, 'tis so near heaven, that I dare not say it can be a proper situation, for any but a race of mountaineers, whose lungs have been used to a rarity'd air, nearer the second region, than any ground for 30 miles round it.

It is true, this place may be said to be prepared for a summer dwelling, for in winter nothing that I know can recommend it: 'Tis true, a warm house, and good company, both which are to be had here, go a great way to make amends for storms, and severity of cold.

Here is a most beautiful prospect indeed, for we see here Hanslop Steeple one way, which is within eight miles of Northampton, N.W. to Landown-Hill in Essex another way, east, at least 66 miles from one another; the prospect to London, and beyond it to Bansted Downs, south; Shooters-Hill, S.E. Red-Hill, S.W. and Windsor-Castle, W. is also uninterrupted: Indeed due north, we see no farther than to Barnet, which is not above six miles; but the rest is sufficient.

At the foot of this hill is an old seat of the Earls of Chester-fields, called Bellsize; which for many years had been neglected, and as it were forgotten: But being taken lately by a certain projector to get a penny, and who knew by what handle to take the gay part of the world, he has made it a true house of pleasure; Here, in the gardens he entertained the company with all kind of sport, and in the house with all kinds of game, to say no more of it: This brought a wonderful concourse of people to the place, for they were so effectually gratified in all sorts of diversion, that the wicked part at length broke in, till it alarm'd the magistrates, and I am told it has been now in a manner suppress'd by the hand of justice.

Here was a great room fitted up with abundance of dexterity for their balls, and had it gone on to a degree of masquerading as I hear was actually begun, it would have bid fair to have had half the town run to it: One saw pictures and furniture there beyond what was to have been expected in a meer publick house; and 'tis hardly credible how it drew company to it; But it could not be, no British government could be supposed to bear long with the liberties taken on such publick occasions: So as I have said, they are reduc'd, at least restrain'd from liberties which they could not preserve by their prudence.

Yet Hampstead is not much the less frequented for this. But as there is (especially at the Wells) a conflux of all sorts of company, even Hampstead itself has suffered in its good name; and you see sometimes more gallantry than modesty: So that the ladies who value their reputation, have of late more avoided the wells and walks at Hampstead, than they had formerly done.

I could not be at Hampstead, and not make an excursion to Edgworth, a little market town, on the road to St. Albans; I say to St. Albans, because 'tis certain, that this was formerly the only or the main road from London to St. Albans; being the famous high road, call'd Watling-street, which in former times reached from London to Shrewsbury, and on towards Wales.

The remains of this road are still to be seen here, and particularly in this, (viz.) That from Hide-Park Corner, just where Tyburn stands, the road makes one straight line without any turning, even to the very town of St. Albans. In this road lyes the town of Edgworth, some will have it that it was built by King Edgar the Saxon monarch, and called by his name, and so will have the town called Edgar, and that it was built as a garrison on the said Watling-street, to preserve the high-way from thieves: But all this I take to be fabulous, and without authority.

Near this town, and which is the reason for naming it, the present Duke of Chandos has built a most magnificent palace or mansion house, I might say, the most magnificent in England: It is erected where formerly stood an old seat belonging to Sir Lancelot Lake, whose son and successor struggled hard to be chosen representative for the county, but lost it, and had a great interest and estate hereabouts.

This palace is so beautiful in its situation, so lofty, so majestick the appearance of it, that a pen can but ill describe it, the pencil not much better; 'tis only fit to be talk'd of upon the very spot, when the building is under view, to be consider'd in all its parts.

The fronts are all of freestone, the columns and pilasters are lofty and beautiful, the windows very high, with all possible ornaments: The pilasters running flush up to the cornish and architrave, their capitals seems as so many supporters to the fine statues which stand on the top, and crown the whole; in a word, the whole structure is built with such a profusion of expence, and all finish'd with such a brightness of fancy, goodness of judgment; that I can assure you, we see many palaces of sovereign princes abroad, which do not equal it, which yet pass for very fine too either within or without. And as it is a noble and well contriv'd building; so it is as well set out, and no ornament is wanting to make it the finest house in England. The plaistering and guilding is done by the famous Pargotti an Italian, said to be the finest artist in those particular works now in England. The great salon or hall is painted by Paolucci, for the duke spared no cost to have every thing as rich as possible. The pillars supporting the building are all of marble: The great staircass is the finest by far of any in England; and the steps are all of marble, every step being of one whole piece, about 22 foot in length.

Nor is the splendor which the present duke lives in at this place, at all beneath what such a building calls for, and yet, so far is the duke from having exhausted himself by this prodigy of a building; that we see him since that laying out a scheme, and storing up materials for building another house for his city convenience, on the north side of the new square, call'd Oxford or Cavendish Square, near Maribone; and if that is discontinued it seems to be so, only because the duke found an opportunity to purchase another much more to his advantage; namely, the Duke of Ormond's house in St. James's Square.

It is in vain to attempt to describe the beauties of this building at Cannons; the whole is a beauty, and as the firmament is a glorious mantle filled with, or as it were made up of a concurrence of lesser glories the stars; so every part of this building adds to the beauty of the whole. The avenue is spacious and majestick, and as it gives you the view of two fronts, join'd as it were in one, the distance not admitting you to see the angle, which is in the centre; so you are agreeably drawn in, to think the front of the house almost twice as large as it really is.

And yet when you come nearer you are again surprized, by seeing the winding passage opening as it were a new front to the eye, of near 120 feet wide, which you had not seen before, so that you are lost a while in looking near hand for what you so evidently saw a great way off. Tho' many of the palaces in Italy are very large fine buildings, yet I venture to say, not Italy it self can show such a building rais'd from the common surface, by one private hand, and in so little a time as this; For Cannons as I was inform'd, was not three years a building and bringing the gardens and all, to the most finish'd beauty we now see it in.

The great palaces in Italy, are either the work of sovereign princes, or have been ages in their building; one family laying the design, and ten succeeding ages and families being taken up, in carrying on the building: But Cannons had not been three years in the duke's possession, before we saw this prodigy rise out of the ground, as if he had been resolv'd to merit that motto which the French king assum'd, He saw, and it was made.

The building is very lofty, and magnificent, and the gardens are so well designed, and have so vast a variety, and the canals are so large, that they are not to be out done in England; possibly the Lord Castlemains at Wanstead, may be said to equal but can not exceed them.

The inside of this house is as glorious, as the outside is fine; the lodgings are indeed most exquisitely finish'd, and if I may call it so, royally furnish'd; the chapel is a singularity, not only in its building, and the beauty of its workmanship, but in this also, that the duke maintains there a full choir, and has the worship perform'd there with the best musick, after the manner of the chappel royal, which is not done in any other noble man's chappel in Britain; no not the Prince of Wales's, though heir apparent to the crown.

Nor is the chapel only furnish'd with such excellent musick, but the duke has a set of them to entertain him every day at dinner.

The avenues and vista's to this house are extreamly magnificent, the great walk or chief avenue is near a mile in length, planted with two double rows of trees, and the middle walk broad enough for a troop of horse to march in front; in the middle way there is a large basin or fountain of water, and the coaches drive round it on either side; there are three other avenues exceeding fine, but not so very large; the beauty of them all will double, with time, when the trees may be grown, like those of New-Hall, in Essex.

Two things extreamly add to the beauty of this house, namely, the chapel, and the library; but I cannot enlarge, having taken up so much room in the view of this house, as must oblige me to abate in others, to whom I am willing to do what justice I can.

In his gardens and out-houses the duke keeps a constant night-guard, who take care of the whole place, duly walk the rounds, and constantly give the hour to the family at set appointed places and times; so that the house has some waking eyes about it, to keep out thieves and spoilers night and day. In a word, no nobleman in England, and very few in Europe, lives in greater splendour, or maintains a grandeur and magnificence, equal to the Duke of Chandos.

Here are continually maintained, and that in the dearest part of England, as to house expences, not less than one hundred and twenty in family, and yet a face of plenty appears in every part of it; nothing needful is with-held, nothing pleasant is restrained; every servant in the house is made easy, and his life comfortable; and they have the felicity that it is their lord's desire and delight that it should be so.

But I am not writing panegyrick. I left Cannons with regret, the family all gay, and in raptures on the marriage of the Marquiss of Caernarvon, the dukes eldest son, just then celebrated with the Lady Katharine Talmash daughter of the Earl of Dysert which marriage adds to the honour and estate also, of the family of Chandos.

Two mile from hence, we go up a small ascent by the great road, which for what reason I know not, is there call'd Crab Tree Orchard, when leaving the Street Way on the right, we enter a spacious heath or common call'd Bushy-Heath, where, again, we have a very agreeable prospect.

I cannot but remember, with some satisfaction, that having two foreign gentlemen in my company, in our passing over this heath, I say I could not but then observe, and now remember it with satisfaction, how they were surprized at the beauty of this prospect, and how they look'd at one another, and then again turning their eyes every way in a kind of wonder, one of them said to the other, That England was not like other country's, but it was all a planted garden.

They had there on the right hand, the town of St. Albans in their view; and all the spaces between, and further beyond it, look'd indeed like a garden. The inclos'd corn-fields made one grand parterre, the thick planted hedge rows, like a wilderness or labyrinth, divided in espaliers; the villages interspers'd, look'd like so many several noble seats of gentlemen at a distance. In a word, it was all nature, and yet look'd all like art; on the left hand we see the west-end of London, Westminster-Abbey, and the Parliament-House, but the body of the city was cut off by the hill, at which Hampstead intercepted the sight on that side.

More to the south we had Hampton Court, and S.W. Windsor, and between both, all those most beautiful parts of Middlesex and Surrey, on the bank of the Thames, of which I have already said so much, and which are indeed the most agreeable in the world.

At the farther end of this heath, is the town of Bushy, and at the end of the town, the Earl of Essex has a very good old seat, situate in a pleasant park, at Cashiobery; a little farther, is the town of Hemstead, noted for an extraordinary corn-market, and at Ashridge, near Hemstead, is an antient mansion house of the Duke of Bridge-water, both these are old built houses, but both shew the greatness of the antient nobility, in the grandeur and majesty of the building, and in the well-planted parks, and high grown woods, with which they are surrounded, than which, there are few finer in England.

St. Albans is the capital town, tho' not the county town of Hertfordshire, it has a great corn market, and is famous for its antient church, built on the ruins, or part of the ruins of the most famous abbey of Verulam; the greatness of which, is to be judg'd by the old walls, which one sees for a mile before we come to town.

In this church as some workmen were digging for the repairs of the church, they found some steps which led to a door in a very thick stone wall, which being opened, there was discover'd an arched stone vault, and in the middle of it a large coffin near 7 foot long, which being open'd, there was in it the corps of a man, the flesh not consum'd, but discolour'd; by the arms and other paintings on the wall, it appear'd that this must be the body of Humphry Duke of Gloucester, commonly call'd, the good Duke of Gloucester, one of the sons of Henry IV. and brother to King Henry V. and by the most indisputable authority, must have lain buried there 277 years.

Viz. It being in the 26th of Hen. VI. 1477.

But I must travel no farther this way, till I have taken a journey west from London, and seen what the country affords that way; the next towns adjacent to London, are, Kensington, Chelsea, Hammersmith, Fulham, Twickenham, &c. all of them near, or adjoyning to the river of Thames, and which, by the beauty of their buildings, make good the north shore of the river, answerable, to what I have already describ'd.

Kensington cannot be nam'd without mentioning the king's palace there; a building which may now be call'd entirely new, tho' it was originally an old house of the Earl of Nottingham's of whom the late King William bought it, and then enlarg'd it as we see; some of the old building still remaining in the center of the house.

The house it self fronts to the garden three ways, the gardens being now made exceeding fine, and enlarged to such a degree, as to reach quite from the great road to Kensington town, to the Acton road north, more than a mile. The first laying out of these gardens was the design of the late Queen Mary, who finding the air agreed with, and was necessary to the health of the king, resolved to make it agreeable to her self too, and gave the first orders for enlarging the gardens: the author of this account, having had the honour to attend her majesty, when she first viewed the ground, and directed the doing it, speaks this with the more satisfaction.

The late Queen Anne compleated what Queen Mary began, and delighted very much in the place; and often was pleased to make the green house which is very beautiful, her summer supper house.

But this house has lost much of its pleasantness on one account, namely, that all the princes that ever might be said to single it out for their delight, had the fate to dye in it; namely, King William, Prince George of Denmark, and lastly, Queen Anne her self; since which it has not been so much in request, King George having generally kept his summer, when in England, at Hampton Court.

As this palace opens to the west, there are two great wings built, for lodgings for such as necessarily attend the court, and a large port cocher at the entrance, with a postern and a stone gallery on the south side of the court which leads to the great stair-case.

This south wing was burnt down by accident, the king and queen being both there, the queen was a little surprized at first, apprehending some treason, but King William a stranger to fears smil'd at the suggestion, chear'd her majesty up, and being soon dress'd, they both walked out into the garden, and stood there some hours till they perceived the fire by the help that came in, and by the diligence of the foot guards, was gotten under foot.

It is no wonder if the Court being so much at Kensington, that town has encreased in buildings, so I do not place that to the same account as of the rest; On the south side of the street over against the palace, is a fair new large street, and a little way down a noble square full of very good houses, but since the Court has so much declin'd the palace, the buildings have not much encreased.

South of this town stands Chelsea, a town of palaces, and which by its new extended buildings seems to promise itself to be made one time or other a part of London, I mean London in its new extended capacity, which if it should once happen, what a monster must London be, extending (to take it in a line) from the farther end of Chelsea, west, to Deptford-Bridge east, which I venture to say, is at least eleven miles.

Here is the noblest building, and the best foundation of its kind in the world, viz. for the entertainment of maimed and old soldiers. If we must except the hospital call'd Des Invalids at Paris, it must be only that the number is greater there, but I pretend to say that the oeconomy of the invalids there, is not to compare with this at Chelsea; and as for the provisions, the lodging and attendance given, Chelsea infinitely exceeds that at Paris. Here the poor men are lodg'd, well cloathed, well furnish'd, and well fed, and I may say there are thousands of poor families in England who are said to live well too, and do not feed as the soldiers there are fed; and as for France, I may add, they know nothing there what it is to live so. The like may be said of the invalid sea men at the hospital of Greenwich.

Near this hospital or college, is a little palace, I had almost call'd it a paradise, of the late earl of Ranelagh. It is true that his lordship was envied for the work, but had it been only for the beauties of the building, and such things as these, I should have been hardly able to censure it, the temptation wou'd have been so much; In a word, the situation, the house, the gardens, the pictures, the prospect, and the lady, all is such a charm; who could refrain from coveting his neighbours . . . . &c.

It is impossible to give an account of all the rest of England in this one volume, while London and its adjacent parts, take up one half of it: I must be allowed therefore to abate the description of private houses and gardens, in which (this part especially) so abounds, that it would take up two or three volumes equal to this, to describe the county of Middlesex only.

Let it suffice to tell you that there's an incredible number of fine houses built in all these towns, within these few years, and that England never had such a glorious show to make in the world before; In a word, being curious in this part of my enquiry, I find two thousand houses which in other places wou'd pass for palaces, and most, if not all the possessors whereof, keep coaches in the little towns or villages of the county of Middlesex, west of London only; and not reckoning any of the towns within three miles of London; so that I exclude Chelsea, Kensington, Knights-Bridge, Marybon, and Paddington; as for Hampstead, that lying north of London, is not concerned in the reckoning, for I reckon'd near a thousand more such in the towns north of London, within the county of Middlesex, and exclusive of Hackney, for Hackney I esteem as part of London itself as before: among all these three thousand houses I reckon none but such, as are built since the year 1666, and most of them since the Revolution.

Among these, that is to say, among the first two thousand new foundations, there are very many houses belonging to the nobility, and to persons of quality, (some of whom) have been in the ministry; which excel all the rest. Such as the Lord Peterborough's at Parsons Green; Lord Hallifax at Bushy Park, near Hampton Court; the late Earl of Marr, Earl of Bradford, Earl of Strafford, Earl of Shrewsbury, Earl of Burlington, Earl of Falconberg, Lady Falkland, Lord Brook, Lord Dunbarr, Moses Hart, Mr. Barker, Sir Stephen Fox, Sir Thomas Frankland, General Wettham, Sir Godfrey Kneller, Secretary Johnson's, and others. This last is a seat so exquisitely finish'd, that his majesty was pleased to dine there, to view the delightful place, and honour it with his presence, that very day, that I was writing this account of it. The king was pleased to dine in the green house, or rather in a pleasant room which Mr. Johnson built, joyning to the green house; from whence is a prospect every way into the most delicious gardens; which indeed for the bigness of them are not out-done in any part of the world. Here is a compleat vineyard, and Mr. Johnson who is a master of gardening, perhaps the greatest master now in England, has given a testimony that England notwithstanding the changeable air and uncertain climate, will produce most excellent wines, if due care be taken in the gardening or cultivating, as also in the curing and managing part; and without due care in these, not France it self will do it.

Sir Stephen Fox's house at Chiswick is the flower of all the private gentlemens palaces in England. Here when the late King William, who was an allowed judge of fine buildings, and of gardening also, had seen the house and garden, he stood still on the terras for near half a quarter of an hour without speaking one word, when turning at last to the Earl of Portland, the king said, This place is perfectly fine, I could live here five days.[1]

In the village of Hammersmith, which was formerly a long scattering place, full of gardeners grounds, with here and there an old house of some bulk: I say, in this village we see now not only a wood of great houses and palaces, but a noble square built as it were in the middle of several handsome streets, as if the village seem'd enclin'd to grow up into a city.

Here we are told they design to obtain the grant of a market, tho' it be so near to London, and some talk also of building a fine stone bridge over the Thames; but these things are yet but in embryo, tho' it is not unlikely but they may be both accomplished in time, and also Hammersmith and Chiswick joyning thus, would in time be a city indeed.

I have now ranged the best part of Middlesex, a county made rich, pleasant, and populous by the neighbourhood of London: The borders of the county indeed have three market towns; which I shall but just mention, Stanes, Colebrook, and Uxbridge: This last, a pleasant large market town, famous in particular, for having abundance of noble seats of gentlemen and persons of quality in the neighbourhood: But I can not describe all the fine houses, it would be endless. This town is also famous in story, for being the town where an attempt was in vain made in the late war, to settle the peace of these nations, by a treaty; Some say both sides were sincerely inclin'd to peace; some say neither side; all I can say of it is, in the words of blessed St. Paul, Sathan hindred. There are but three more market towns in the county, viz. Brentford, Edgworth and Enfield.

On the right hand as we ride from London to Uxbridge, or to Colebrook, we see Harrow, a little town on a very high hill, and is therefore call'd Harrow on the Hill: The church of this

[1] *N.B.* This was an expression the king used on no occasion, but such, as where the places were exquisitely fine, and particularly pleased him: and it was not observ'd that ever his majesty said it of any place in England, but of this, and of Burleigh-House by Stamford in Lincolnshire, the seat of the Earl of Exeter.

town standing upon the summit of the hill, and having a very handsome and high spire, they tell us, King Charles II. ridiculing the warm disputes among some critical scripturallists of those times, concerning the visible church of Christ upon earth; us'd to say of it, that if there was e'er a visible church upon earth, he believ'd this was one.

About Uxbridge, and all the way from London, as we do every where this way, we saw a great many very beautiful seats of the nobility and gentry, too many I say to enter upon the description of here.

From hence, we proceeded on the road towards Oxford; but first turned to the right to visit Aylesbury. This is the principal market town in the county of Bucks; tho' Buckingham a much inferior place, is call'd the county town: Here also is held the election for Members of Parliament, or Knights of the Shire for the county, and county goal, and the assizes. It is a large town, has a very noble market for corn, and is famous for a large tract of the richest land in England, extended for many miles round it, almost from Tame, on the edge of Oxfordshire, to Leighton in Bedfordshire, and is called from this very town, the Vale of Aylesbury. Here it was that conversing with some gentlemen, who understood country affairs, for all the gentlemen hereabouts are graziers, tho' all the graziers are not gentlemen; they shew'd me one remarkable pasture-field, no way parted off or separated, one piece of it from another; I say, 'tis one enclosed field of pasture ground, which was let for 1400l. per ann. to a grazier, and I knew the tenant very well, whose name was Houghton, and who confirm'd the truth of it.

It was my hap formerly, to be at Aylesbury, when there was a mighty confluence of noblemen and gentlemen, at a famous horse race at Quainton-Meadow, not far off, where was then the late Duke of Monmouth, and a great many persons of the first rank, and a prodigious concourse of people.

I had the occasion to be there again in the late queen's reign; when the same horse race which is continu'd yearly, happen'd again, and then there was the late Duke of Marlborough, and a like concourse of persons of quality; but the reception of the two dukes was mightily differing, the last duke finding some reasons to withdraw from a publick meeting, where he saw he was not like to be used as he thought he had deserved.

The late Lord Wharton, afterwards made duke, has a very good dwelling at Winchenden, and another much finer nearer Windsor, call'd Ubourn. But I do not hear that the present duke has made any additions, either to the house or gardens; they were indeed admirably fine before, and if they are but kept in the same condition, I shall think the dukes care cannot be reproach'd.

Were there not in every part of England at this time so many fine palaces, and so many curious gardens, that it would but be a repetition of the same thing to describe them; I should enter upon that task with great chearfulness here, as also at Clifden, the Earl of Orkney's fine seat built by the late D. of Buckingham, near Windsor, and at several other places, but I proceed: We went on from Aylesbury to Thame or Tame, a large market town on the River Thames: This brings me to mention again The Vale of Aylesbury; which as I noted before, is eminent for the richest land, and perhaps the richest graziers in England: But it is more particularly famous for the head of the River Thame or Thames, which rises in this vale near a market town call'd Tring, and waters the whole vale either by itself or the several streams which run into it, and when it comes to the town of Tame, is a good large river.

At Tring abovenam'd is a most delicious house, built *à la moderne*, as the French call it, by the late Mr. Guy, who was for many years Secretary of the Treasury, and continued it till near his death; when he was succeeded by the late Mr. Lowndes. The late King William did Mr. Guy the honour to dine at this house, when he set out on his expedition to Ireland, in the year 1690, the same year that he fought the battle of the Boyn; and tho' his Majesty came from London that morning, and resolved to lye that night at Northampton, yet he would not go away without taking a look at the fine gardens, which are perhaps the best finish'd in the worst situation of any in England. This house was afterwards bought by Sir William Gore, a merchant of London; and left by him to his eldest son, who now enjoys it.

There was an eminent contest here between Mr. Guy, and the poor of the parish, about his enclosing part of the common to make him a park; Mr. Guy presuming upon his power, set up his pales, and took in a large parcel of open land, call'd Wiggington-Common; the cottagers and farmers oppos'd it, by their complaints a great while; but finding he went on with his work, and resolv'd to do it, they rose upon him, pull'd down his banks, and forced up his pales, and carried away the wood, or set it on a heap and burnt it; and this they did several times, till he was oblig'd to desist; after some time he began again, offering to treat with the people, and to give them any equivalent for it: But that not being satisfactory, they mobb'd him again. How they accommodated it at last, I know not; but I see that Mr. Gore has a park, and a very good one but not large: I mention this as an instance of the popular claim in England; which we call right of commonage, which the poor take to be as much their property, as a rich man's land is his own.

But to return to the Vale of Aylesbury. Here the great and antient family of Hampden flourish'd for many ages, and had very great estates: But the present heir may (I doubt) be said, not to have had equal success with some of his ancestors.

From Thame, a great corn market, the Thame joins the other branch call'd also the Thames, at a little town call'd Dorchester. I observe that most of our historians reject the notion that Mr. Cambden makes so many flourishes about, of the marriage of Thame and Isis; that this little river was call'd the Thame, and the other, the Isis; and that being join'd, they obtain'd the united name of Thamisis: I say they reject it, and so do I. At this little town of Dorchester was once the seat of the bishoprick of Lincoln.

From hence I came to Oxford, a name known throughout the learned world; a city famous in our English history for several things, besides its being an university.

1. So eminent for the goodness of its air, and healthy situation; that our Courts have no less than three times, if my information is right, retir'd hither, when London has been visited with the pestilence; and here they have always safe.

2. It has also several times been the retreat of our princes, when the rest of the kingdom has been embroil'd in war and rebellion; and here they have found both safety and support; at least, as long as the loyal inhabitants were able to protect them.

3. It was famous for the noble defence of religion, which our first reformers and martyrs made here, in their learned and bold disputations against the Papists, in behalf of the Protestant religion; and their triumphant closing the debates, by laying down their lives for the truths which they asserted.

4. It was likewise famous for resisting the attacks of arbitrary power, in the affair of Magdalen College, in King James's time; and the Fellows laying down their fortunes, tho' not their lives, in defence of liberty and property.

This, to use a scripture elegance, is that city of Oxford; the greatest (if not the most antient) university in this island of Great-Britain; and perhaps the most flourishing at this time, in men of polite learning, and in the most accomplish'd masters, in all sciences, and in all the parts of acquir'd knowledge in the world.

I know there is a long contest, and yet undetermin'd between the two English universities, about the antiquity of their foundation; and as they have not decided it themselves, who am I? and what is this work? that I should pretend to enter upon that important question, in so small a tract?

It is out of question, that in the largeness of the place, the beauty of situation, the number of inhabitants, and of schollars, Oxford has the advantage. But fame tells us, that as great and applauded men, as much recommended, and as much recommending themselves to the world, and as many of them have been produced from Cambridge, as from Oxford.

Oxford has several things as a university, which Cambridge has not; and Cambridge ought not to be so meanly thought of, but that it has several things in it, which cannot be found in Oxford. For example,

The theater, the museum, or chamber of rarities, the Bodleian Library, the number of colleges, and the magnificence of their buildings are on the side of Oxford, yet Kings College Chappel, and College, is in favour of Cambridge; for as it is now edifying, it is likely to be the most admir'd in a few years of all the colleges of the world.

I have said something of Cambridge; I'll be as brief about Oxford as I can: It is a noble flourishing city, so possess'd of all that can contribute to make the residence of the scholars easy and comfortable, that no spot of ground in England goes beyond it. The situation is in a delightful plain, on the bank of a fine navigable river, in a plentiful country, and at an easy distance from the capital city, the port of the country.

The city itself is large, strong, populous, and rich; and as it is adorn'd by the most beautiful buildings of the colleges, and halls, it makes the most noble figure of any city of its bigness in Europe.

To enter into the detail or description of all the colleges, halls, &c. would be to write a history of Oxford, which in so little a compass as this work can afford, must be so imperfect, so superficial, and so far from giving a stranger a true idea of the place; that it seems ridiculous, even to think it can be to any ones satisfaction. However, a list of the names and establishments of the colleges may be useful, so take them as follows, according to the seniority of their foundation.

A List of the Colleges and Halls in the City of Oxford,
plac'd according to the respective Dates of their
Foundations

1. *University College*

This college was properly the university it self for about 345
years; being as they tell us, founded by King Alfred in the year
872; the old building on which the college now stands was
erected by that king; after which viz. anno 1217. William
Bishop of Durham, form'd it into a regular house and built
the college, which however was for a long time call'd sometimes
the college, sometimes the university, and by some the college
of the university, there being at that time no other; till at
length other colleges rising up in the same city; this was call'd
University College, that is, the college which was the old
university. It maintained at the end of Queen Elizabeth's reign.

1 Master,	
8 Fellows,	
1 Bible clark,	In all 69.
Students,	
and Servants.	

2. *Baliol College*

Founded by John Baliol, father to John Baliol King of
Scotland, and by Dame Der Verguilla his wife, who enlarged
the foundation after her husbands decease. It maintained at
the end of King James the 1st's reign,

1 Master,	
12 Fellows,	
13 Schollars,	In all 136.
4 Exhibitioners,	
Students, and	
Servants.	

3. *Merton College*

Founded by William de Merton, Lord Chancellour to King
Henry III. afterwards Bishop of Rochester. *N.B.* This college
was first erected at Maldon in Surrey, near Kingston, anno 1260.

and translated to Oxford ten years after, by the same founder.
It maintains

1	Warden,	
21	Fellows,	
13	Schollars,	In all 79.
	Students, and	
	Servants.	

4. *Excester College*

Founded by Walter Stapleton Bishop of Excester, and Lord
High Treasurer to King Edward II. afterwards beheaded by
Queen Isabella mother to King Edward III. It was first call'd
Stapleton-Hall, but afterwards on the benefaction of other
inhabitants of Excester and of the county of Devon, it was
made a college. It maintained in the time of King James 1st,

1	Rector,	
23	Fellows,	
	Commoners,	In all 200.
	Students, and	
	other Servants	

5. *Oriel College*

Founded by King Edward II. anno 1327. but some say
Adam Brown the king's almoner and who was the first provost,
was also the founder, only that being afraid to be call'd to an
account for so great wealth, he put the fame of it upon the
king after his death. It had only a provost, 10 fellows, with
some servants, at its first institution, but encreasing by subsequent benefactions, it maintained in King James's time who
also incorporated the college,

1	Provost,	
18	Fellows,	
12	Exhibitioners,	In all 105.
	Commoners, and	
	Servants.	

6. *Queen's College*

Founded anno 1340. by Robert Eglesfield a private clergyman, only domestick chaplain to Queen Phillippa, Edward the 3d's queen; 'tis said the land it stood on was his own inheritance, and he built the house at his own charge; but begging her majesty to be the patroness of his charity, he call'd it Queens Hall, recommending the scholars at his death, to her majesty and the Queens of England her successors: He dyed before it was finish'd, having settled only 12 fellows, whereas he intended 70 schollarships besides, representing all together Christ his 12 apostles, and his 70 disciples; but this pious design of the good founder was so well approved on all hands, that it was presently encreased by several royal benefactors, and is now one of the best colleges in the university; also it is lately rebuilt, the old building being wholly taken down and the new being all of free stone, containing two noble squares with piazza's, supported by fine pillars; the great hall, the library, and a fine chappel, all contained in the same building, so that it is without comparison the most beautiful college in the university.

7. *New College*

Founded anno 1379. by William of Wickham Bishop of Winchester, the same who is said to have built Windsor Castle, for King Edward III; rebuilt the cathedral church at Winchester, and the fine school there, the scholars of which are the nursery to this fine college. He instituted here and they still remain,

1 Warden,	
70 Fellows,	
10 Chaplains	
16 Choiristers,	In all 135.
1 Organist,	
3 Clarks,	
1 Sexton,	
Students, &c.	

N.B. This college is very rich.

8. *Lincoln College*

Founded anno 1420. by Richard Hemming Arch-Bishop of York, but left it imperfect; the foundation was finish'd by

Thomas Rotherham Bishop of Lincoln, 59 years after. It maintains

$$\left.\begin{array}{rl} 1 & \text{Warden,} \\ 14 & \text{Fellows,} \\ 2 & \text{Chaplains,} \\ 4 & \text{Scholars,} \\ & \text{Commoners, and} \\ & \text{Servants.} \end{array}\right\} \quad \text{In all 72.}$$

9. *All-Souls College*

Founded anno 1437. by Henry Chichley Arch-Bishop of Canterbury, also Cardinal Pool was a great benefactor to it afterwards. It maintains

$$\left.\begin{array}{rl} 1 & \text{Warden,} \\ 40 & \text{Fellows,} \\ 2 & \text{Chaplains,} \\ 3 & \text{Clarks,} \\ 6 & \text{Choiristers,} \\ & \text{Students, and} \\ & \text{Servants.} \end{array}\right\} \quad \text{In all 65.}$$

10. *Magdalen College*

Founded 1459, by William Wainfleet Bishop of Winton, who built it in the stately figure we now see it in, very little having been added; and what has been rebuilt, has kept much to the founders first design; except a new appartment added by one Mr. Clarke a private gentleman, who serv'd many years in Parliament for the university; this new building is exceeding fine; as is now also, the library, towards which, another private gentleman, namely, Colonel Codrington, gave ten thousand pounds, and a good collection of books. It maintains

$$\left.\begin{array}{rl} 1 & \text{President,} \\ 40 & \text{Fellows,} \\ 30 & \text{Deans,} \\ 4 & \text{Chaplains,} \\ 3 & \text{Clarks,} \\ 16 & \text{Choristers,} \\ 3 & \text{Readers,} \\ 2 & \text{Humanists,} \\ & \text{Commoners, and} \\ & \text{Servants.} \end{array}\right\} \quad \text{In all 151.}$$

11. *Brason-Nose College*

First founded by William Smith Bishop of Lincoln, anno.
1512. but finish'd by Richard Sutton, Esq; a Cheshire gentleman,
who perfected the buildings of the house; and both together
gave considerably large revenues. It has also had great benefactors since, so that it now maintains

> 1 Principal,
> 20 Fellows,
> Scholars, } In all 182.
> Commoners, and
> Servants.

12. *Corpus-Christi College*

Founded anno 1516. by Richard Fox Bishop of Winchester,
who also endow'd it very liberally; and Hugh Oldham Bishop
of Excester, advanc'd the best part of the building. It maintains

> 1 President,
> 20 Fellows,
> 20 Scholars,
> 2 Chaplains,
> 6 Clarks, } In all 61.
> 2 Choiristers,
> Commoners, and
> Servants.

13. *Christ-Church College*

Founded anno 1524. by Cardinal Woolsey. 'Tis said he
suppres'd 40 monasteries to build this magnificent college, but
the king having demolish'd the cardinal, he could not finish it;
so the king carried on the work, and establish'd the church to
be the cathedral of the diocess of Oxford, ann. 1519. The
revenues of this college are exceeding great, it is the largest
college in the university, and the buildings are very noble and
well finish'd, all of free-stone. It maintains

1	Dean,	
8	Canons,	
8	Chaplains,	
8	Choiristers,	
8	Singing-Men,	In all 224.
1	Organist,	
24	Alms-Men,	
	Students,	
	Commoners, and	
	Servants.	

The royal school at Winchester, is the nursery of this college, sending as some say, 25 scholars hither every 3 months.

14. *Trinity College*

Founded anno 1518. by Tho. Hatfield Bishop of Durham, and it was then call'd Durham College; but the bishop not living, Sir Thomas Pope carried on his design; and having seen the first foundation suppress'd, because it was a provision for monks, &c. he restor'd it and endow'd it, dedicating it to the undivided Trinity, anno 1556. as it is to this day. It maintains

1	President,	
12	Fellows,	
12	Scholars,	In all 123.
	Students, and	
	Servants.	

15. *St. John's College*

First founded by Arch-Bishop Chichley, anno 1437. and call'd Bernards College; but being suppress'd as a house of religion in the reign of King Henry VIII. it was again founded as a college by Sir Thomas White a wealthy citizen and merchant of London, who new built the house, and richly endow'd it, to maintain as it now does,

1	President,	
50	Fellows,	
	and Scholars,	
1	Chaplain,	In all 123.
1	Clark,	
	Students, and	
	Servants.	

16. *Jesus College*

The foundation of this college is corruptly assign'd to Hugh Paice, Esq; a Welch gentleman, who was indeed a benefactor to the foundation, and particularly gave 600*l*. towards erecting the fabrick of the college; as did afterwards Sir Eubule Thitwall, who was principal; and this last in particular gave 8 fellowships, and 8 scholarships: But Queen Elizabeth was the foundress of this college, and endow'd it for a principal, adding 8 fellowships, and 8 scholarships. This Mr. Speed confirms, as also Mr. Dugdale, and it appears by the present endowment. By which it maintains

1 Principal,	
16 Fellows,	
16 Scholars,	In all 105.
Students, and	
Servants.	

17. *Wadham College*

Founded anno 1613. by Nicolas Wadham, Esq; and Dorothy his wife, and sister to the Lord Petre of Essex; they endow'd it with its whole maintenance, by which at this day it maintains

1 Warden,	
15 Fellows,	
15 Scholars,	
2 Chaplains,	In all 125.
2 Clarks,	
Students, and	
Servants.	

As therefore I did in the speaking of Cambridge, I shall now give a summary of what a traveller may be suppos'd to observe in Oxford, *en passant*, and leave the curious inquirer to examine the histories of the place, where they may meet with a compleat account of every part in the most particular manner, and to their full satisfaction.

There are in Oxford 17 colleges, and seven halls, some of these colleges as particularly, Christ Church, Magdalen, New College, Corpus Christi, Trinity, and St. John's will be found to be equal, if not superior to some universities abroad; whether we consider the number of the scholars, the greatness of their revenues, or the magnificence of their buildings.

I thought my self oblig'd to give a more particular account of the colleges here, than I have done of those at Cambridge; because some false and assuming accounts of them have been publish'd by others, who demand to be credited, and have impos'd their accounts upon the world, without sufficient authority.

Besides the colleges, some of which are extremely fine and magnificent; there are some publick buildings which make a most glorious appearance: The first and greatest of all is the theatre, a building not to be equall'd by any thing of its kind in the world; no, not in Italy itself: Not that the building of the theatre here is as large as Vespasian's or that of Trajan at Rome; neither would any thing of that kind be an ornament at this time, because not at all suited to the occasion, the uses of them being quite different.

We see by the remains that those amphitheatres, as they were for the the exercise of their publick shews, and to entertain a vast concourse of people, to see the fighting of the gladiators, the throwing criminals to the wild beasts, and the like, were rather great magnificent bear-gardens, than theatres, for the actors of such representations, as entertain'd the polite part of the world; consequently, those were vast piles of building proper for the uses for which they were built.

What buildings were then made use of in Rome for the fine performances of ------ who acted that of Terence, or who wrote that, we can not be certain of; but I think I have a great deal of reason to say, they have no remains of them, or of any one of them at Rome; or if they are, they come not near to this building.

The theatre at Oxford prepared for the publick exercises of the schools, and for the operations of the learned part of the English world only, is in its grandeur and magnificence, infinitely superiour to any thing in the world of its kind; it is a finish'd piece, as to its building, the front is exquisitely fine, the columns and pilasters regular, and very beautiful; 'tis all built of free-stone: The model was approv'd by the best masters of architecture at that time, in the presence of K. Charles II. who was himself a very curious observer, and a good judge; Sir Christopher Wren was the director of the work, as he was the person that drew the model: Archbishop Sheldon, they tell us, paid for it, and gave it to the university: There is a world of decoration in the front of it, and more beautiful additions, by way of ornament, besides the antient inscription, than is to be seen any where in Europe; at least, where I have been.

The Bodleian Library is an ornament in it self worthy of Oxford, where its station is fix'd, and where it had its birth. The history of it at large is found in Mr. Speed, and several authors of good credit; containing in brief, that of the old library, the first publick one in Oxford, erected in Durham now Trinity College, by Richard Bishop of Durham, and Lord Treasurer to Ed. III. it was afterward joined to another, founded by Cobham Bishop of Worcester, and both enlarg'd by the bounty of Humphry Duke of Gloucester, founder of the divinity schools: I say, these libraries being lost, and the books embezzled by the many changes and hurries of the suppressions in the reign of Hen. VIII. the commissioner appointed by King Edw. VI. to visit the universities, and establish the Reformation; found very few valuable books or manuscripts left in them.

In this state of things, one Sir Thomas Bodley, a wealthy and learned knight, zealous for the encouragement both of learning and religion, resolv'd to apply, both his time, and estate, to the erecting and furnishing a new library for the publick use of the university.

In this good and charitable undertaking, he went on so successfully, for so many years, and with such a profusion of expence, and obtain'd such assistances from all the encouragers of learning in his time, that having collected books and manuscripts from all parts of the learned world; he got leave of the university, (and well they might grant it) to place them in the old library room, built as is said, by the good Duke Humphry.

To this great work, great additions have been since made in books, as well as contributions in money, and more are adding every day; and thus the work was brought to a head, the 8th of Nov. 1602, and has continued encreasing by the benefactions of great and learned men to this day: To remove the books once more and place them in beauty and splendor suitable to so glorious a collection, the late Dr. Radcliff has left a legacy of 40000*l.* say some, others say not quite so much, to the building a new repository or library for the use of the university: This work is not yet built, but I am told 'tis likely to be such a building as will be greater ornament to the place than any yet standing in it.

I shall say nothing here of the benefactions to this library. Unless I had room to mention them all, it would be both partial and imperfect. And as there is a compleat catalogue of the books preparing, and that a list of the benefactors and what books they gave, will be speedily publish'd; it would be needless to say any thing of it here.

Other curious things in Oxford are, the museum, the chamber of rarities, the collection of coins, medals, pictures and antient inscriptions, the physick-garden, &c.

The buildings for all these are most beautiful and magnificent, suitable for the majesty of the university, as well as to the glory of the benefactors.

It is no part of my work to enter into the dispute between the two universities about the antiquity of their foundation: But this I shall observe for the use of those who insist, that it was the piety of the Popish times to which we owe the first, institution of the university it self, the foundation and endowment of the particular colleges, and the encouragement arising to learning from thence, all which I readily grant; but would have them remember too, that tho' those foundations stood as they tell us eight hundred years, and that the Reformation as they say, is not yet of 200 years standing, yet learning has more encreas'd and the universities flourish'd more; more great scholars been produc'd, greater libraries been raised, and more fine buildings been erected in these 200 years than in the 800 years of Popery; and I might add, as many great benefactions have been given, notwithstanding this very momentous difference; that the Protestant's gifts are meerly acts of charity to the world, and acts of bounty, in reverence to learning and learned men, without the grand excitement of the health of their souls, and of the souls of their fathers, to be pray'd out of purgatory and get a ready admission into heaven, and the like.

Oxford, had for many ages the neighbourhood of the Court, while their kings kept up the royal palace at Woodstock; which tho' perhaps it was much discontinu'd, for the fate of the fair Rosamond, mistress to Henry Fitz Empress, or Henry II. of which history tells us something, and fable much more; yet we after find that several of the kings of England made the house and park at Woodstock, which was always fam'd for its pleasant situation, the place of their summer retreat for many years. Also for its being a royal palace before, even beyond the certainty of history, there is abundant reason to believe it; nay some will have it to have been a royal house before Oxford was an university. Dr. Plott allows it to have been so ever since King Alfred; and a manuscript in the Cotton Library confirms it; and that King Henry I. was not the founder of it, but only rebuilt it: And as for Henry II. he built only some additions; namely, that they call'd the Bower, which was a building in the garden (or labyrinth,) for the entertainment and security of his fair mistress, of whose safety he was it seems very careful. Notwithstanding which the queen found means to come at her, and as fables report, sent her out of the way by poison.

The old buildings are now no more, nor so much as the name, but the place is the same and the natural beauty of it indeed, is as great as ever.

It is still a most charming situation, and 'tis still disputable after all that has been laid out, whether the country round gives more lustre to the building, or the building to the country. It has now chang'd masters, 'tis no more a royal house or palace for the king; but a mark of royal bounty to a great, and at that time powerful subject, the late Duke of Marlborough.

The magnificence of the building does not here as at Canons, at Chatsworth, and at other palaces of the nobility, express the genius and the opulence of the possessor, but it represents the bounty, the gratitude, or what else posterity pleases to call it, of the English Nation, to the man whom they delighted to honour: Posterity when they view in this house the trophies of the Duke of Marlborough's fame, and the glories of his great atchievements will not celebrate his name only; but will look on Blenheim House, as a monument of the generous temper of the English Nation; who in so glorious a manner rewarded the services of those who acted for them as he did: Nor can any nation in Europe shew the like munificence to any general, no nor the greatest in the world; and not to go back to antient times, not the French nation to the great Luxemberg, or the yet greater Turenne: Nor the emperor to the great Eugene, or to the yet greater Duke of Lorrain; whose inimitable conduct saved the imperial city of Vienna, and rescued the whole house of Austria; retook the whole kingdom of Hungary, and was victorious in seaventeen pitch'd battles. I say none of these ever receiv'd so glorious a mark of their country's favour.

Again, It is to be consider'd, that not this house only, built at the nation's expence, was thus given; but lands and pensions to the value of above one hundred thousand pounds sterl. and honours the greatest England can bestow: These are all honours indeed to the duke, but infinitely more to the honour of the nation.

The magnificent work then is a national building, and must

for ever be call'd so. Nay, the dimensions of it will perhaps call
upon us hereafter, to own it as such in order to vindicate the
discretion of the builder, for making a palace too big for any
British subject to fill, if he lives at his own expence.

Nothing else can justify the vast design, a bridge or *ryalto*
rather, of one arch costing 20000*l*. and this, like the bridge at
the Escurial in Spain, without a river. Gardens of near 100
acres of ground. Offices fit for 300 in family. Out-houses fit for
the lodgings of a regiment of guards, rather than of livery
servants. Also the extent of the fabrick, the avenues, the salons,
galleries, and royal apartments; nothing below royalty and a
prince, can support an equipage suitable to the living in such a
house: And one may without a spirit of prophecy, say, it seems
to intimate, that some time or other Blenheim may and will
return to be as the old Woodstock once was, the palace of
a king.

I shall enter no farther into the description, because 'tis yet
a house unfurnish'd, and it can only be properly said what it is
to be, not what it is: The stair-case of the house is indeed very
great, the preparations of statues and paintings, and the ornament both of the building and finishing and furnishing are also
great, but as the duke is dead, the duchess old, and the heir
abroad, when and how it shall be all perform'd, requires more
of the gift of prophecy than I am master of.

From Woodstock I could not refrain taking a turn a little
northward as high as Banbury to the banks of the Charwell,
to see the famous spot of ground where a vigorous rencounter
happen'd between the Royalists in the grand Rebellion, and the
Parliament's forces, under Sir William Waller; I mean at
Croprady Bridge, near Banbury. It was a vigorous action, and
in which the king's forces may be said fairly to out-general
their enemies, which really was not always their fate: I had the
plan of that action before me, which I have had some years,
and found out every step of the ground as it was disputed on
both sides by inches, where the horse engaged and where the
foot; where Waller lost his cannon, and where he retired; and
it was evident to me the best thing Waller cou'd do, (tho'
superiour in number) was to retreat as he did, having lost half
his army.

From thence, being within eight miles of Edge-Hill, where
the first battle in that war happen'd, I had the like pleasure
of viewing the ground about Keinton, where that bloody battle
was fought; it was evident, and one could hardly think of it

without regret, the king with his army had an infinite advantage by being posted on the top of the hill, that he knew that the Parliament's army were under express orders to fight, and must attack him lest his majesty who had got two days march of them, should advance to London, where they were out of their wits for fear of him.

The king I say knowing this, 'tis plain he had no business but to have intrench'd, to fight upon the eminence where he was posted, or have detach'd 15000 men for London, while he had fortify'd himself with a strong body upon the hill: But on the contrary, his majesty scorning to be pursued by his subjects, his army excellently appointed, and full of courage, not only halted, but descended from his advantages and offer'd them battle in the plain field, which they accepted.

Here I cannot but remark that this action is perhaps the only example in the world, of a battle so furious, so obstinate, manag'd with such skill, every regiment behaving well, and doing their duty to the utmost, often rallying when disorder'd, and indeed fighting with the courage and order of veterans; and yet not one regiment of troops that had ever seen the face of an enemy, or so much as been in arms before. It's true, the king had rather the better of the day; and yet the rebel army though their left wing of horse was entirely defeated, behav'd so well, that at best it might be call'd a drawn battle; and the loss on both sides was so equal, that it was hard to know who lost most men.

But to leave the war, 'tis the place only I am taking notice of. From hence I turn'd south, for I was here on the edge both of Warwickshire, and Gloucestershire: But I turned south, and coming down by and upon the west side of Oxfordshire, to Chipping-Norton, we were shew'd Roll-Richt-Stones, a second Stone-Henge; being a ring of great stones standing upright, some of them from 5 to 7 foot high.

I leave the debate about the reason and antiquity of this antient work to the dispute of the learned, who yet cannot agree about them any more than about Stone-Henge in Wiltshire. Cambden will have them be a monument of victory, and the learned Dr. Charleton is of the same mind. Mr. Cambden also is willing to think that they were erected by Rollo the Dane, because of the town of Rollwright, from which they are call'd Rolle Right or Rolle Richt Stones. Aiston wou'd have them to be a monument of the dead, perhaps kill'd in battle; and that a great stone 9 foot high, at a distance, was over a king; and 5 other great ones likewise at a distance, were great commanders and the like.

The ingenious and learned Dr. Plot wou'd have us think it was a cirque or ring for their field elections of a king, something like the Dyetts on horseback in Poland; that they met in the open field to choose a king, and that the persons in competition were severally placed in such a cirque, surrounded by the suffrages or voters; and that when they were chosen, the person chosen was inaugurated here.

Thus I leave it as I find it: for antiquity as I have often said is not my business in this work; let the occasion of those stones be what it will, they are well worth notice; especially to those who are curious in the search of antiquity.

We were very merry at passing thro' a village call'd Bloxham, on the occasion of a meeting of servants for hire, which the people there call a Mop; 'tis generally in other places vulgarly call'd a Statute, because founded upon a statute law in Q. Elizabeth's time for regulating of servants. This I christn'd by the name of a Jade-Fair, at which some of the poor girls began to be angry, but we appeas'd them with better words.

I have observ'd at some of these fairs, that the poor servants distinguish themselves by holding something in their hands, to intimate what labour they are particularly qualify'd to undertake; as the carters a whip, the labourers a shovel, the wood men a bill, the manufacturers a wool comb, and the like. But since the ways and manners of servants are advanc'd as we now find them to be, those Jade Fairs are not so much frequented as formerly, tho' we have them at several towns near London; as at Enfield, Waltham, Epping, &c.

Here we saw also the famous parish of Brightwell, of which it was observed, that there had not been an alehouse nor a dissenter from the church, nor any quarrel among the inhabitants that rise so high as to a suit of law within the memory of man. But they could not say it was so still, especially as to the alehouse part; tho' very much is still preserved, as to the unity and good neighbourhood of the parishioners, and their conformity to the church.

Being now on the side of Warwickshire, as is said before, I still went south, and passing by the four Shire Stones, we saw where the counties of Oxford, Warwick, and Gloucester joyn all in a point; one stone standing in each county, and the fourth touching all three.

Hence we came to the famous Cotswold-Downs, so eminent

for the best of sheep, and finest wool in England: It was of the breed of these sheep. And fame tells us that some were sent by King Rich. I. into Spain, and that from thence the breed of their sheep was raised, which now produce so fine a wool, that we are oblig'd to fetch it from thence, for the making our finest broad cloaths; and which we buy at so great a price.

In viewing this part of England, and such things as these, and considering how little notice other writers had taken of them, it occur'd to my thoughts that it wou'd be a very useful and good work, if any curious observer would but write an account of England, and oblige himself to speak of such things only, as all modern writers had said nothing of, or nothing but what was false and imperfect. And there are doubtless so many things, so insignificant, and yet so omitted, that I am persuaded such a writer would not have wanted materials; nay, I will not promise that even this work, tho' I am as careful as room for writing will allow, shall not leave enough behind, for such a gleaning to make it self richer than the reapings that have gone before; and this not altogether from the meer negligence and omissions of the writers, as from the abundance of matter, the growing buildings, and the new discoveries made in every part of the country.

Upon these downs we had a clear view of the famous old Roman high-way, call'd the Fosse, which evidently crosses all the middle part of England, and is to be seen and known (tho' in no place plainer than here,) quite from the Bath to Warwick, and thence to Leicester, to Newark, to Lincoln, and on to Barton, upon the bank of Humber.

Here it is still the common road, and we follow'd it over the downs to Cirencester. We observ'd also how several cross roads as antient as it self, and perhaps more antient, joyn'd it, or branch'd out of it; some of which the people have by antient usage tho' corruptly call'd also Fosses, making the word Fosse as it were a common name for all roads. For example,

The Ackemanstreet which is an antient Saxon road leading from Buckinghamshire through Oxfordshire to the Fosse, and so to the Bath; this joyns the Fosse between Burford and Cirencester. It is worth observing how this is said to be call'd Ackeman's Street; namely, by the Saxon way of joyning their monosyllables into significant words, as thus, *ackman* or *achman*, a man of aching limbs, in English a *cripple* travelling to the Bath for cure: So Achmanstreet was the road or street for diseased people going to the Bath; and the city of Bath was on the same

account call'd Achmanchester, or the city of diseased people;
or, *Urbs Ægrotorum hominum.* Thus much for antiquity.

There are other roads or fosses which joyn this grand high-
way, viz. Grinnes Dike, from Oxfordshire, Wattle Bank, or
Aves Ditch from ditto. and the Would Way, call'd also the
Fosse crossing from Gloucester to Cirencester.

In passing this way we very remarkably cross'd four rivers
within the length of about 10 miles, and enquiring their names,
the country people call'd them every one the Thames, which
mov'd me a little to enquire the reason, which is no more than
this; namely, that these rivers, which are, the Lech, the Coln,
the Churn, and the Isis; all rising in the Cotswould Hills and
joyning together and making a full stream at Lechlade near
this place, they become one river there, and are all call'd
Thames, or vulgarly Temms; also beginning there to be navigable, you see very large barges at the key, taking in goods
for London, which makes the town of Lechlade a very populous
large place.

On the Churne one of those rivers stands Cirencester, or
Ciciter for brevity, a very good town, populous and rich, full
of clothiers, and driving a great trade in wool; which as likewise
at Tetbury, is brought from the midland counties of Leicester,
Northampton, and Lincoln, where the largest sheep in England
are found, and where are few manufactures; it is sold here in
quantities, so great, that it almost exceeds belief: It is generally
bought here by the clothiers of Wiltshire and Gloucestershire,
for the supply of that great clothing trade; of which I have
spoken already: They talk of 5000 packs in a year.

As we go on upon the Fosse, we see in the vale on the left
hand, the antient town of Malmsbury, famous for a monastary,
and a great church, built out of the ruins of it; and which
I name in meer veneration to that excellent, and even best of
our old historians Gulielmus Malmsburiensis, to whom the
world is so much oblig'd, for preserving the history and
antiquities of this kingdom.

We next arriv'd at Marshfield, a Wiltshire clothing town,
very flourishing and where we cross'd the great road from
London to Bristol, as at Cirencester, we did that from London,
to Gloucester; and in the evening keeping still the Fosse-Way,
we arriv'd at Bath.

My description of this city would be very short, and indeed it
would have been a very small city, (if at all a city) were it not for
the hot baths here, which give both name and fame to the place.

The antiquity of this place, and of the baths here, is doubtless very great, tho' I cannot come in to the inscription under the figure, said to be of a British king, placed in that call'd the King's Bath, which says that this King Bladud, (Mr. Cambden calls him Blayden, or Blaydon Clyoth; that is, the south-sayer) found out the use of these baths, 300 years before our Saviour's time. I say, I cannot come into this, because even the discovery is ascribed to the magick of the day, not their judgment in the physical virtue of minerals, and mineral-waters.

The antiquities of this place are farther treated of by Mr. Cambden, as the virtues of the waters, are, by several of the learned members of that faculty, who have wrote largely on that subject; as particularly, Dr. ——, Dr. Baynard, Dr. —— and others.

There remains little to add, but what relates to the modern customs, the gallantry and diversions of that place, in which I shall be very short; the best part being but a barren subject, and the worst part meriting rather a satyr, than a description.

It has been observ'd before, that in former times this was a resort hither for cripples, and the place was truly *Urbs Ægrotorum Hominum*: And we see the crutches hang up at the several baths, as the thank-offerings of those who have come hither lame, and gone away cur'd. But now we may say it is the resort of the sound, rather than the sick; the bathing is made more a sport and diversion, than a physical prescription for health; and the town is taken up in raffling, gameing, visiting, and in a word, all sorts of gallantry and levity.

The whole time indeed is a round of the utmost diversion. In the morning you (supposing you to be a young lady) are fetch'd in a close chair, dress'd in your bathing cloths, that is, stript to the smock, to the Cross-Bath. There the musick plays you into the bath, and the women that tend you, present you with a little floating wooden dish, like a bason; in which the lady puts a handkerchief, and a nosegay, of late the snuff-box is added, and some patches; tho' the bath occasioning a little perspiration, the patches do not stick so kindly as they should.

Here the ladies and the gentlemen pretend to keep some distance, and each to their proper side, but frequently mingle here too, as in the King and Queens Bath, tho' not so often; and the place being but narrow, they converse freely, and talk, rally, make vows, and sometimes love; and having thus amus'd themselves an hour, or two, they call their chairs and return to their lodgings.

The rest of the diversion here, is the walks in the great church, and at the raffling shops, which are kept (like the cloyster at Bartholomew Fair,) in the churchyard, and ground adjoyning. In the afternoon there is generally a play, tho' the decorations are mean, and the performances accordingly; but it answers, for the company here (not the actors) make the play, to say no more. In the evening there is a ball, and dancing at least twice a week, which is commonly in the great town hall, over the market-house; where there never fails in the season to be a great deal of very good company.

There is one thing very observable here, which tho' it brings abundance of company to the Bath, more than ever us'd to be there before; yet it seems to have quite inverted the use and virtue of the waters, (viz.) that whereas for seventeen hundred or two thousand years, if you believe King Bladud, the medicinal virtue of these waters had been useful to the diseased people by bathing in them, now they are found to be useful also, taken into the body; and there are many more come to drink the waters, than to bathe in them; nor are the cures they perform this way, less valuable than the outward application; especially in colicks, ill digestion, and scorbutick distempers.

This discovery they say, is not yet above fifty years old, and is said to be owing to the famous Dr. Radcliff, but I think it must be older, for I have my self drank the waters of the Bath above fifty years ago: But be it so, 'tis certain, 'tis a modern discovery, compar'd to the former use of these waters.

As to the usefulness of these waters to procure conception, and the known story of the late King James's queen here, the famous monument in the Cross-Bath gives an account of it. Those that are enclin'd to give faith to such things, may know as much of it at the Santa Casa of Loretto, as here; and in Italy I believe it is much more credited.

There is nothing in the neighbourhood of this city worth notice, except it be Chipping-Norton-Lane, where was a fight between the forces of King James II. and the Duke of Monmouth, in which the latter had plainly the better; and had they push'd their advantage, might have made it an entire victory. On the N.W. of this city up a very steep hill, is the King's Down, where sometimes persons of quality who have coaches go up for the air: But very few people care to have coaches here, it being a place where they have but little room to keep them, and less to make use of them. And the hill up to the Downs is so steep, that the late Queen Anne was extremely frighted in going up, her coachman stopping to give the horses breath, and the coach wanting a dragstaff, run back in spight of all the coachman's skill; the horses not being brought to strain the harness again, or pull together for a good while, and the coach putting the guards behind it into the utmost confusion, till some of the servants setting their heads and shoulders to the wheels, stopt them by plain force.

When one is upon King-Down, and has pass'd all the steeps and difficulties of the ascent, there is a plain and pleasant country for many miles, into Gloucestershire, and two very noble palaces, the one built by Mr. Blathwait, late Secretary of War; and the other is call'd Badminton, the mansion of the most noble family of the Dukes of Beaufort, the present duke being under age. The lustre and magnificence of this palace is magnify'd by the surprise one is at, to see such a house in such a retreat, so difficult of access, at least this way, so near to so much company, and yet, so much alone.

Following the course of the river Avon, which runs thro' Bath, we come in ten miles to the city of Bristol, the greatest, the richest, and the best port of trade in Great Britain, London only excepted.

The merchants of this city not only have the greatest trade, but they trade with a more entire independency upon London, than any other town in Britain. And 'tis evident in this particular, (viz.) That whatsoever exportations they make to any part of the world, they are able to bring the full returns back to their own port, and can dispose of it there.

This is not the case in any other port in England. But they are often oblig'd to ship part of the effects in the ports abroad, on the ships bound to London; or to consign their own ships to London, in order both to get freight, as also to dispose of their own cargoes.

But the Bristol merchants as they have a very great trade abroad, so they have always buyers at home, for their returns, and that such buyers that no cargo is too big for them. To this purpose, the shopkeepers in Bristol who in general are all wholesale men, have so great an inland trade among all the western counties, that they maintain carriers just as the London tradesmen do, to all the principal countries and towns from Southampton in the south, even to the banks of the Trent north; and tho' they have no navigable river that way, yet they drive a very great trade through all those counties.

Add to this, That, as well by sea, as by the navigation of two great rivers, the Wye, and the Severn, they have the whole trade of South-Wales, as it were, to themselves, and the greatest part of North-Wales; and as to their trade to Ireland, it is not only great in it self, but is prodigiously encreas'd in these last thirty years, since the Revolution, notwithstanding the great encrease and encroachment of the merchants at Liverpool, in the Irish trade, and the great devastations of the war; the kingdom of Ireland it self being wonderfully encreas'd since that time.

The greatest inconveniences of Bristol, are, its situation, and the tenacious folly of its inhabitants; who by the general infatuation, the pretence of freedoms and priviledges, that corporation-tyranny, which prevents the flourishing and encrease of many a good town in England, continue obstinately to forbid any, who are not subjects of their city sovereignty, (that is to say, freemen,) to trade within the chain of their own liberties; were it not for this, the city of Bristol, would before now, have swell'd and encreas'd in buildings and inhabitants, perhaps to double the magnitude it was formerly of.

This is evident by this one particular; There is one remarkable part of the city where the liberties extend not at all, or but very little without the city gate. Here and no where else, they have an accession of new inhabitants; and abundance of new houses, nay, some streets are built, and the like 'tis probable wou'd have been at all the rest of the gates, if liberty had been given. As for the city itself, there is hardly room to set another house in it, 'tis so close built, except in the great square, the ground about which is a little too subject to the hazard of inundations: So that people do not so freely enlarge that way.

The Tolsey of this city, (so they call their Exchange where their merchants meet,) has been a place too of great business, yet so straighten'd, so crowded, and so many ways inconvenient, that the merchants have been obliged to do less business there, than indeed the nature of their great trade requires; They have therefore long solicited, a sufficient authority of Parliament, empowering them to build a Royal Exchange; by which, I mean a place suitable and spatious, fit for the accommodation of the merchants, and for the dispatch of business; and to be impowered to pull down the adjacent buildings for that purpose: But there is not much progress yet made in this work, tho' if finish'd, it would add much to the beauty of the city of Bristol.

The Hot Well, or, the water of St. Vincents Rock, is not in the city, but at the confluence of the two little rivers, and on the north side of the stream. It is but a few years since this spring lay open at the foot of the rock, and was covered by the salt water at every tide, and yet it preserved both its warmth and its mineral virtue entire.

The rock tho' hard to admiration, has since that been work'd down, partly by strength of art, and partly blown in pieces by gunpowder, and a plain foundation made for building a large house upon it, where they have good apartments for entertaining diseased persons. The well is secur'd, and a good pump fix'd in it, so that they have the water pure and unmix'd from the spring it self.

The water of this well possess'd its medicinal quality no doubt from its original, which may be as antient as the Deluge. But what is strangest of all is, that it was never known before; it is now famous for being a specifick in that otherwise incurable disease the diabetes; and yet was never known to be so, 'till within these few years; namely, thirty years, or thereabout.

There are in Bristol 21 parish churches, many meeting-houses, especially Quakers, one (very mean) cathedral, the reason of which, may be, that it is but a very modern bishoprick. It is supposed they have an hundred thousand inhabitants in the city, and within three miles of its circumference; and they say above three thousand sail of ships belong to that port, but of the last I am not certain.

'Tis every remarkable, That this city is so plentifully supply'd with coals, tho' they are all brought by land carriage, that yet they are generally bought by the inhabitants, laid down at their doors, after the rate of from seven to nine shillings per chaldron.

The situation of the city is low, but on the side of a rising hill. The ground plat of it is said very much to resemble that of old Rome, being circular, with something greater diameter one way than another, but not enough to make it oval: And the river cutting off one small part, as it were, a sixth, or less from the rest.

The bridge over the Avon is exceeding strong, the arches very high, because of the depth of water, and the buildings so close upon it, that in passing the bridge, you see nothing but an entire well built street. The tide of flood rises here near 6 fathom, and runs very sharp.

They draw all their heavy goods here on sleds, or sledges without wheels, which kills a multitude of horses; and the pavement is worn so smooth by them, that in wet-weather the streets are very slippery, and in frosty-weather 'tis dangerous walking.

From this city I resolv'd to coast the marshes or border of Wales, especially South-Wales, by tracing the rivers Wye, and Lug, into Monmouth and Herefordshire. But I chang'd this resolution on the following occasion; namely, the badness and danger of the ferries over the Severn, besides, having formerly travers'd these counties, I can without a re-visit, speak to every thing that is considerable in them, and shall do it in a letter by itself. But in the mean time, I resolv'd to follow the course of the famous river Severn, by which I should necessarily see the richest, most fertile, and most agreeable part of England; the bank of the Thames only excepted.

From Bristol West, you enter the county of Gloucester, and keeping the Avon in view, you see King Road, where the ships generally take their departure, as ours at London do from Graves-End; and Hung Road, where they notify their arrival, as ours for London do in the Downs: The one lyes within the Avon, the other, in the open sea or the Severn; which is there call'd the Severn Sea. Indeed great part of Bristol is in the bounds of Gloucestershire, tho' it be a county of itself. From hence going away a little north west, we come to the Pill, a convenient road for shipping, and where therefore they generally run back for Ireland or for Wales. There is also a little farther, an ugly, dangerous, and very inconvenient ferry over the Severn, to the mouth of Wye; namely, at Aust; the badness of the weather, and the sorry boats, at which, deterr'd us from crossing there.

As we turn north towards Gloucester, we lose the sight of the Avon, and in about two miles exchange it for an open view of the Severn Sea, which you see on the west side, and which is as broad as the ocean there; except, that you see two small islands in it, and that looking N.W. you see plainly the coast of South Wales; and particularly a little nearer hand, the shore of Monmouthshire. Then as you go on, the shores begin to draw towards one another, and the coasts to lye parallel; so that the Severn appears to be a plain river, or an *æstuarium*, somewhat like the Humber, or as the Thames is at the Nore, being 4 to 5 and 6 miles over; and to give it no more than its just due, a most raging, turbulent, furious place. This is occasion'd by those violent tides call'd the Bore, which flow here sometimes six or seven foot at once, rolling forward like a mighty wave: So that the stern of a vessel shall on a sudden be lifted up six or seven foot upon the water, when the head of it is fast a ground.

After coasting the shore about 4 miles farther, the road being by the low salt marshes, kept at a distance from the river: We came to the ferry call'd Ast Ferry, or more properly Aust Ferry, or Aust Passage, from a little dirty village call'd Aust; near which you come to take boat.

This ferry lands you at Beachly in Monmouthshire, so that on the out-side 'tis call'd Aust Passage, and on the other side, 'tis call'd Beachly-Passage. From whence you go by land two little miles to Chepstow, a large port town on the river Wye. But of that part I shall say more in its place.

When we came to Aust, the hither side of the Passage, the sea was so broad, the fame of the Bore of the tide so formidable, the wind also made the water so rough, and which was worse, the boats to carry over both man and horse appear'd (as I have said above) so very mean, that in short none of us car'd to venture: So we came back, and resolv'd to keep on the road to Gloucester. By the way we visited some friends at a market-town, a little out of the road, call'd Chipping-Sodbury, a place of note for nothing that I saw, but the greatest cheese market in all that part of England; or, perhaps, any other, except Atherstone, in Warwickshire.

Hence we kept on north, passing by Dursley to Berkley-Castle; the antient seat of the Earls of Berkley, a noble tho' antient building, and a very fine park about it. The castle gives title to the earl, and the town of Dursly to the heir apparent; who during the life of his father, is call'd the Lord Dursley. I say nothing of the dark story of King Edward II. of England; who, all our learned writers agree, was murther'd in this castle: As Richard II. was in that of Pontefract, in Yorkshire; I say I take no more notice of it here, for history is not my present business: 'Tis true, they show the apartments where they say that king was kept a prisoner: But they do not admit that he was kill'd there. The place is rather antient, than pleasant or healthful, lying low, and near the water; but 'tis honour'd by its present owner, known to the world for his many services to his country, and for a fame, which our posterity will read of, in all the histories of our times.

From hence to Gloucester, we see nothing considerable, but a most fertile, rich country, and a fine river, but narrower as you go northward, 'till a little before we come to Gloucester it ceases to be navigable by ships of burthen, but continues to be so, by large barges, above an hundred miles farther; not reckoning the turnings and windings of the river: Besides that, it receives several large and navigable rivers into it.

Gloucester is an antient middling city, tolerably built, but not fine; was fortify'd and stood out obstinately against its lord King Charles the 1st, who besieged it to his great loss in the late Rebellion, for which it had all its walls and works demolish'd; for it was then very strong: Here is a large stone bridge over the Severn, the first next the sea; and this, and the cathedral is all I see worth recording of this place. Except that the late eminent and justly famous Sir Thomas Powel, commonly call'd Judge Powel, one of the judges of the King's Bench Court; and contemporary with Sir John Holt lived and dyed in this city, being one of the greatest lawyers of the age.

The cathedral is an old venerable pile, with very little ornament within or without, yet 'tis well built; and tho' plain, it makes together, especially the tower, a very handsome appearance. The inhabitants boast much of its antiquity, and tell us, that a bishop and preachers were plac'd here, in the very infancy of the Christian religion; namely, in the year 189. But this I take *ad referendum*. The cathedral they tell us, has been three times burnt to the ground.

The first Protestant bishop of this church, was, that truly reverend and religious Dr. John Hooper, set up by King Edward VI. and afterwards martyr'd for his religion in the Marian tyranny: Being burnt to death in the cimitary of his own cathedral.

The whispering place in this cathedral, has for many years pass'd for a kind of wonder; but since, experience has taught us the easily comprehended reason of the thing: And since there is now the like in the church of St. Paul, the wonder is much abated. However, the verses written over this whispering place, intimate, that it has really past for something miraculous; and as the application rather shows religion, than philosophy in the author, the reader may not like them the worse.

> Doubt not, that God who sits on high,
>   Thy secret prayers can hear;
> When a dead wall thus cunningly,
>   Conveys soft whispers to thine ear.

From Gloucester we kept the east shore of the Severn, and in twelve miles came to Tewksbury, a large and very populous town situate upon the river Avon, this is call'd the Warwickshire Avon, to distinguish it from the Avon at Bristol and others, for there are several rivers in England of this name; and some tell us that *avona* was an old word in the British tongue signifying a river.

This town is famous for a great manufacture of stockings, as are also, the towns of Pershore, and Evesham, or Esham; on the same river.

The great old church at Tewksbury may indeed be call'd the largest private parish church in England; I mean, that is not a collegiate or cathedral church. This town is famous for the great, and as may be said, the last battle, fought between the two houses of Lancaster and York, in which Edward IV. was conqueror; and in, or rather after which, Prince Edward the only surviving son of the House of Lancaster, was kill'd by the cruel hands of Richard the king's brother; the same afterwards Richard III. or Crookback Richard. In this place begins that fruitful and plentiful country which was call'd the Vale of Esham, which runs all along the banks of the Avon, from Tewksbury to Pershore, and to Stratford upon Avon, and in the south part of Warwickshire; and so far, (viz. to Stratford,) the river Avon is navigable.

At this last town, going into the parish church, we saw the monument of old Shakespear, the famous poet, and whose dramatick performances so justly maintain his character among the British poets; and perhaps will do so to the end of time. The busto of his head is in the wall on the north side of the church, and a flat grave-stone covers the body, in the isle just under him. On which grave-stone these lines are written.

> Good friend, for Jesus's sake, forbear
> To move the dust that resteth here.
> Blest be the man that spares these stones,
> And curst be he, that moves my bones.

The navigation of this river Avon is an exceeding advantage to all this part of the country, and also to the commerce of the city of Bristol. For by this river they drive a very great trade for sugar, oil, wine, tobacco, iron, lead, and in a word, all heavy goods which are carried by water almost as far as Warwick; and in return the corn, and especially the cheese, is brought back from Gloucestershire and Warwickshire, to Bristol.

This same vale continuing to extend it self in Warwickshire, and under the ridge of little mountains call'd Edge-Hill, is there call'd the vale of Red-Horse. All the grounds put together, make a most pleasant corn country, especially remarkable for the goodness of the air, and fertility of the soil.

Gloucestershire must not be pass'd over, without some account of a most pleasant and fruitful vale which crosses part of the country, from east to west on that side of the Cotswold, and which is call'd Stroud-Water; famous not for the finest cloths only, but for dying those cloths of the finest scarlets, and other grain colours that are any where in England; perhaps in any part of the world: Here I saw two pieces of broad cloth made, one scarlet, the other crimson in grain, on purpose to be presented, the one to His Majesty King George, and the other to the prince; when the former was Elector of Hanover, and the latter, electoral prince: And it was sent to Hanover, presented accordingly, and very graciously accepted. The cloth was valued including the colour, at 45s. per yard: Indeed it was hardly to be valued, nothing so rich being ever made in England before, at least as I was informed.

The clothiers lye all along the banks of this river for near 20 miles, and in the town of Stroud, which lyes in the middle of it, as also at Paynswick, which is a market-town at a small distance north. The river makes its way to the Severn about 5 miles below Gloucester.

From Tewkesbury we went north 12 miles, to Worcester, all the way still on the bank of the Severn; and here we had the pleasing sight of the hedge-rows, being fill'd with apple trees and pear trees, and the fruit so common, that any passenger as they travel the road may gather and eat what they please; and here, as well as in Gloucestershire, you meet with cyder in the publick-houses sold as beer and ale is in other parts of England, and as cheap.

Here we saw at a distance, in a most agreeable situation, the mansion or seat of Sir John Packington, a barronet of a very antient family; and for so long from father to son knight of the shire for the county, that it seems as if it were hereditary to that house.

On the other side of the Severn at --- and near the town of Bewdly the Lord Foley has a very noble seat suitable to the grandeur of that rising family.

Worcester is a large, populous, old, tho' not a very well built city; I say not well built because the town is close and old, the houses standing too thick. The north part of the town is more extended and also better built. There is a good old stone bridge over the Severn, which stands exceeding high from the surface of the water. But as the stream of the Severn is contracted here by the buildings on either side, there is evident occasion sometimes for the height of the bridge, the waters rising to an incredible height in the winter-time.

It narrowly escap'd burning, but did not escape plundering at the time when the Scots army commanded by King Ch. II. in person, was attack'd here by Cromwel's forces; 'twas said some of the Royalist's officers themselves, propos'd setting the city on fire, when they saw it was impossible to avoid a defeat, that they might the better make a retreat; which they propos'd to do over the Severn, and so to march into Wales: But that the king, a prince from his youth, of a generous and merciful disposition would by no means consent to it.

I went to see the town-house, which afforded nothing worth taking notice of, unless it be how much it wants to be mended with a new one; which the city, they say, is not so much enclin'd, as they are able and rich to perform. I saw nothing of publick notice there, but the three figures, (for they can hardly be call'd statues) of King Charles I. King Charles II. and Queen Anne.

The cathedral of this city is an antient, and indeed, a decay'd building; the body of the church is very mean in its aspect, nor did I see the least ornament about it, I mean in the outside. The tower is low, without any spire, only four very small pinnacles on the corners; and yet the tower has some little beauty in it more than the church itself, too; and the upper part has some images in it, but decay'd by time.

The inside of the church has several very antient monuments in it, particularly some royal ones; as that of King John, who lyes interr'd between two sainted bishops, namely, St. Oswald, and St. Woolstan. Whether he ordered his interment in that manner, believing that they should help him *up* at the last call, and be serviceable to him for his salvation I know not; it is true they say so, but I can hardly think the king himself so ignorant, whatever the people might be in those days of superstition; nor will I say but that it may be probable, they may all three go together at last (as it is) and yet, without being assistant to, or acquainted with one another at all.

Here is also a monument for that famous Countess of Salisbury, who dancing before, or with K. Edward III. in his great hall at Windsor, dropt her garter, which the king taking up, honoured it so much as to make it the denominating ensign of his new order of knighthood, which is grown so famous, and is call'd the *most Noble* Order of the Garter: What honour, or that any honour redounds to that most noble order, from its being so deriv'd from the garter of a --- For 'tis generally agreed, she was the king's mistress, I will not enquire.

Certainly the Order receives a just claim to the title of *most noble*, from the honour done it, by its royal institution; and its being compos'd of such a noble list of the kings and princes as have been entred into it: I say, certainly this order has a just title to that of *noble*, and *most noble* too; yet I cannot but think that the king might have found out a better trophy to have fix'd it upon, than that lady's garter. But this by the way: here lyes the lady that's certain, and a very fine monument she has, in which one thing is more ridiculous than all that went before, (viz.) That about the monument, there are several angels cut in stone, strewing garters over the tomb, as if that passage, which at best had something a little obscene in it, I mean of the kings taking up the lady's garter, and giving such honours to it, was also a thing to be celebrated by angels, *in perpetuam rei memoriam*.

Besides this, here is the monument or the body of Prince Arthur, eldest son to King Henry VII. who was married, but died soon after; and his wife Katharine Infanta of Spain, was afterwards married to, and after 20 years wedlock divorced from King Henry VIII.

Upon the prince's tomb stone is this inscription.

HERE lyes the body of Prince Arthur, the eldest son of King Henry VII. who dyed at Ludlow, in the year 1502. and in the seventeenth year of his father's reign.

There are several other antient monuments in this church, too many to be set down here: They reckon up 99 Bishops of this diocess, beginning at the year 980, out of which catalogue they tell us have been furnish'd to the world, 1 Pope, 4 Saints, 7 High-Chancellors of England, 11 Arch-Bishops, 2 Lord Treasurers of England, 1 Chancellor to the Queen, 1 Lord President of Wales, and 1 Vice President: Their names are as follows.

1 *Pope.* (*viz.*)
Julius de Medicis, call'd
    Clement VII.

4 *Saints.*
St. Egwin.
St. Dunstan.
St. Oswald.
St. Wolstan.

11 *Archbishops.*
St. Dunstan.
St. Oswald
Adulf.
St. Wolstan.
Aldred.
Grey.
Bourcher.
Wittelry.

11 *Archbishops (continued).*

Heath.
Sands.
Whitgift.

7 *Chancellors*
of England.

De Ely.
Giffard.
Reynolds.
Thoresby.
Barnett.
Alcock.
Heath.

1 *President.*

Heath.

1 *Vice-President.*

Whitgift.

2 *Lord Treasurers.*

Reynolds.
Wakefield.

1 *Chancellor to a Queen.*

Simon.

This city is very full of people, and the people generally esteem'd very rich, being full of business, occasion'd chiefly by the cloathing trade, of which the city and the country round carries on a great share, as well for the Turkey trade as for the home trade.

The salt springs in this county which were formerly esteem'd as next to miraculous, have since the discovery of the mines of rock salt in Lancashire, Cheshire, &c. lost all of wonder that belong'd to them, and much of the use also; the salt made there being found to be much less valuable than what is now made of the other. So I need say little to them.

Near this city are the famous Maulvern Hills, or Mauvern Hills, seen so far every way. In particular, we saw them very plainly on the Downs, between Marlborough and Malmsbury; and they say they are seen from the top of Salisbury steeple, which is above 50 miles.

There was a famous monastery at the foot of these hills, on the S.W. side, and the ruins are seen to this day; the old legend of wonders perform'd by the witches of Mauvern, I suppose they mean the religieuse of both kinds, are too merry, as well as too antient for this work.

They talk much of mines of gold and silver, which are certainly to be found here, if they were but look'd for, and that Mauvern wou'd out do Potosi for wealth; but 'tis probable if there is such wealth, it lies too deep for this idle generation to find out, and perhaps to search for.

There are three or four especial manufactures carried on in this country, which are peculiar to it self, or at least to this county with the two next adjoyning; namely, Chester, and Warwick.

1. Monmouth cups sold chiefly to the Dutch seamen, and made only at Beawdly.

2. Fine stone potts for the glass-makers melting their metal, of which they make their fine flint glass, glass plates, &c. not to be found any where but at Stourbridge in this county, the same clay makes crucibles and other melting pots.

3. The Birmingham iron works: The north indeed claims a share or part of this trade, but it is only a part.

4. Kidderminster stuffs call'd Lindsey Woolseys, they are very rarely made any where else.

At Stourbridge also they have a very great manufacture for glass of all sorts.

From Worcester I took a tour into Wales, which tho' I mentioned above, it was not at the same time with the rest of my journey; my account I hope will be as effectual.

In passing from this part of the country to make a tour through Wales, we necessarily see the two counties of Hereford and Monmouth, and for that reason I reserv'd them to this place, as I shall the counties of Chester and Salop to my return.

A little below Worcester the Severn receives a river of a long course and deep chanel, call'd the Teme, and going from Worcester we past this river at a village call'd Broadways; from whence keeping a little to the north, we come to Ludlow-Castle, on the bank of the same river. On another journey I came from Stourbridge, famous for the clay for melting pots as above; thence to Kidderminster, and passing the Severn at Bewdley we came to Ludlow, on the side of Shropshire.

In this course we see two fine seats not very far from the Severn, (viz.) the Lord Foley's, and the Earl of Bradford's, as we had before a most delicious house, belonging to the Lord Conway, now in the family of the late famous Sir Edward Seymour. Indeed this part of the county, and all the county of Salop is fill'd with fine seats of the nobility and gentry, too many so much as to give a list of, and much less to describe.

The castle of Ludlow shows in its decay, what it was in its flourishing estate: It is the palace of the Princes of Wales, that is, to speak more properly, it is annex'd to the principality of Wales; which is the appanage of the heir apparent, and this is his palace in right of his being made Prince of Wales.

The situation of this castle is most beautiful indeed; there is a most spacious plain or lawn in its front, which formerly continu'd near two miles; but much of it is now enclosed. The country round it is exceeding pleasant, fertile, populous, and the soil rich; nothing can be added by nature to make it a place fit for a royal palace: It only wants the residence of its princes, but that is not now to be expected.

The castle itself is in the very perfection of decay, all the fine courts, the royal apartments, halls, and rooms of state, lye open, abandoned and some of them falling down; for since the Courts of the President and Marches are taken away, here is nothing to do that requires the attendance of any publick people; so that time, the great devourer of the works of men, begins to eat into the very stone walls, and to spread the face of royal ruins upon the whole fabrick.

The town of Ludlow is a tolerable place, but it decays to be sure with the rest: It stands on the edge of the two counties, Shropshire, and Worcestershire, but is itself in the first; 'tis on the bank of the Teme, over which it has a good bridge, and it was formerly a town of good trade; the Welch call this town Lye Twysoe, which is in English, the Prince's Court. Mr. Cambden calls the river Teme the Tem'd, and another river which joyns it just at this town, the Corve, whence the rich flat country below the town is call'd Corvesdale.

King Henry VIII. established the Court of the President here, and the Council of the Marches and all causes of *nisi prius*, or of civil right were try'd here, before the Lord President and Council; but this Court was entirely taken away by Act of Parliament in our days, and this, as above, tends to the sensible decay of the town as well as of the castle.

From Ludlow we took our course due south to Lemster, or Leominster, a large and good trading town on the River Lug. This river is lately made navigable by Act of Parliament, to the very great profit of the trading part of this country, who have now a very great trade for their corn, wool, and other products of this place, into the river Wye, and from the Wye, into the Severn, and so to Bristol.

Leominster has nothing very remarkable in it, but that it is a well built, well inhabited town: The church which is very large, has been in a manner rebuilt, and is now, especially in the inside, a very beautiful church. This town, besides the fine wool, is noted for the best wheat, and consequently the finest bread; whence Lemster Bread, and Weobly Ale, is become a proverbial saying.

The country on our right as we came from Ludlow is very

fruitful and pleasant, and is call'd the Hundred of Wigmore, from which the late Earl of Oxford at his creation, took the title of Baron of Wigmore: And here we saw two antient castles, (viz.) Brampton-Brian, and Wigmore-Castle, both belonging to the earl's father, Sir Edward Harley; Brampton is a stately pile, but not kept in full repair, the fate of that antient family not permitting the rebuilding it as we were told was intended. Yet it is not so far decay'd as Ludlow, nor is it abandoned, or like to be so, and the parks are still very fine, and full of large timber.

We were now on the borders of Wales, properly so call'd; for from the windows of Brampton-Castle, you have a fair prospect into the county of Radnor, which is, as it were, under its walls; nay, even this whole county of Hereford, was, if we may believe antiquity, a part of Wales, and was so esteem'd for many ages. The people of this county too, boast that they were a part of the antient Silures, who for so many ages withstood the Roman arms, and who could never be entirely conquer'd. But that's an affair quite beyond my enquiry. I observ'd they are a diligent and laborious people, chiefly addicted to husbandry, and they boast, perhaps, not without reason, that they have the finest wool, and best hops, and the richest cyder in all Britain.

Indeed the wool about Leominster, and in the Hundred of Wigmore observ'd above, and the Golden Vale as 'tis call'd, for its richness on the banks of the river Dove, (all in this county) is the finest without exception, of any in England, the South Down wool not excepted: As for hops, they plant abundance indeed all over this county, and they are very good. And as for cyder, here it was, that several times for 20 miles together, we could get no beer or ale in their publick houses, only cyder; and that so very good, so fine, and so cheap, that we never found fault with the exchange; great quantities of this cyder are sent to London, even by land carriage tho' so very remote, which is an evidence for the goodness of it, beyond contradiction.

One would hardly expect so pleasant, and fruitful a country as this, so near the barren mountains of Wales; but 'tis certain, that not any of our southern counties, the neighbourhood of London excepted, comes up to the fertility of this county, as Gloucester furnishes London with great quantities of cheese, so this county furnishes the same city with bacon in great quantities, and also with cyder as above.

From Lemster it is ten miles to Hereford, the chief city, not of this county only, but of all the counties west of Severn: 'Tis a large and a populous city, and in the time of the late Rebellion, was very strong, and being well fortify'd, and as well defended, supported a tedious and very severe siege; for besides the Parliament's Forces, who could never reduce it, the Scots army was call'd to the work, who lay before it, 'till they laid above 4000 of their bones there, and at last, it was rather taken by the fate of the war, than by the attack of the besiegers.

Coming to Hereford, we could not but enquire into the truth of the story so famous, that the Reverend Dr. Gibson had mentioned it in his continutaion of Cambden; of the removing the two great stones near Sutton, which the people confirm'd to us. The story is thus,

Between Sutton and Hereford, is a common meadow call'd the Wergins, where were plac'd two large stones for a water-mark; one erected upright, and the other laid a-thwart. In the late Civil Wars, about the Year 1652, they were remov'd to about twelve score paces distance, and no body knew how; which gave occasion to a common opinion, That they were carried thither by the Devil. When they were set in their places again, one of them requir'd nine yoke of oxen to draw it.

Not far from Lidbury, is Colwal; near which, upon the waste, as a countryman was digging a ditch about his cottage, he found a crown or a coronet of gold, with gems set deep in it. It was of a size large enough to be drawn over the arm, with the sleeve. The stones of it are said to have been so valuable, as to be sold by a jeweller for fifteen hundred pounds.

It is truly an old, mean built, and very dirty city, lying low, and on the bank of Wye, which sometimes incommodes them very much, by the violent freshes that come down from the mountains of Wales; for all the rivers of this county, except the Driffin-Doe, come out of Wales.

The chief thing remarkable next to the cathedral, is the college, which still retains its Foundation Laws, and where the residentiaries are still oblig'd to celibacy, but otherwise, live a very happy, easy, and plentiful life; being furnish'd upon the foot of the foundation, besides their ecclesiastical stipends.

The great church is a magnificent building, however ancient, the spire is not high, but handsome, and there is a fine tower at the west end, over the great door or entrance. The choir is very fine, tho' plain, and there is a very good organ: The revenues of this bishoprick are very considerable, but lye under some abatement at present, on account of necessary repairs.

There are several monuments in it of antient bishops, but no

other of note. Between Leominster and this city, is another
Hampton Court, the seat of the Lord Conningsby, who has also
a considerable interest in the north part of this county; a
person distinguishing himself in the process or impeachment
against the late Earl of Oxford, his neighbour; who, to his no
small disappointment, escap'd him. There is nothing remarkable
here that I could observe: But the name putting me in mind
of another Hampton Court, so much beyond it, that the house
seems to be a foil to the name; the house was built by Rowland
Lenthall, Esq; who was Guard de Robe to Henry IV. so that it
is old enough, if that may recommend it, and so is its master.

From Hereford keeping the bank of Wye as near as we could,
we came to Ross, a good old town, famous for good cyder, a
great manufacture of iron ware, and a good trade on the River
Wye, and nothing else as I remember, except it was a monstrous
fat woman, who they would have had me gone to see. But I had
enough of the relation, and so I suppose will the reader, for
they told me she was more than three yards about her wast;
that when she sat down, she was oblig'd to have a small stool
plac'd before her, to rest her belly on, and the like.

From hence we came at about 8 miles more into Monmouthshire, and to the town of Monmouth. It is an old town situate
at the conflux of the Wye and of Munnow, whence the town
has its name; it stands in the angle where the rivers joyn, and
has a bridge over each river, and a third over the River Trothy,
which comes in just below the other.

This town shews by its reverend face, that it is a place of
great antiquity, and by the remains of walls, lines, curtains,
and bastions, that it has been very strong, and by its situation
that it may be made so again: This place is made famous, by
being the native place of one of our most antient historians
Jeoffry of Monmouth. At present 'tis rather a decay'd than a
flourishing town, yet, it drives a considerable trade with the
city of Bristol, by the navigation of the Wye.

This river having as I said, just received two large streams,
the Mynevly or Munno, and the Trother, is grown a very noble
river, and with a deep chanel, and a full current hurries away
towards the sea, carrying also vessels of a considerable burthen
hereabouts.

Near Monmouth the Duke of Beaufort has a fine old seat,
call'd Troy; but since the family has had a much finer palace
at Badminton, near the Bath; this tho' a most charming
situation seems to be much neglected.

Lower down upon the Wye stands Chepstow, the sea port for all the towns seated on the Wye and Lug, and where their commerce seems to center. Here is a noble bridge over the Wye: To this town ships of good burthen may come up, and the tide runs here with the same impetuous current as at Bristol; the flood rising from six fathom, to six and a half at Chepstow Bridge. This is a place of very good trade, as is also Newport, a town of the like import upon the River Uske, a great river, tho' not so big as Wye, which runs thro' the center of the county, and falls also into the Severn Sea.

This county furnishes great quantities of corn for exportation, and the Bristol merchants frequently load ships here, to go to Portugal, and other foreign countries with wheat; considering the mountainous part of the west of this county, 'tis much they should have such good corn, and so much of it to spare; but the eastern side of the county, and the neighbourhood of Herefordshire, supplies them.

I am now at the utmost extent of England west, and here I must mount the Alps, traverse the mountains of Wales, (and indeed, they are well compar'd to the Alps in the inmost provinces;) But with this exception, that in abundance of places you have the most pleasant and beautiful valleys imaginable, and some of them, of very great extent, far exceeding the valleys so fam'd among the mountains of Savoy, and Piedmont.

The two first counties which border west upon Monmouthshire, are Brecknock, and Glamorgan, and as they are very mountainous, so that part of Monmouthshire which joyns them, begins the rising of the hills. Kyrton-Beacon, Tumberlow, Blorench, Penvail, and Skirridan, are some of the names of these horrid mountains, and are all in this shire; and I could not but fansy my self in view of Mount Brennus, Little Barnard, and Great Barnard, among the Alps. When I saw Plinlimmon Hill, and the sources of the Severn on one side of it, and the Wye and Rydall on the other: it put me in mind of the famous hill, call'd ---- in the cantons of Switzerland, out of which the Rhine rises on one side, and the Rhosne, and the Aa on the other. But I shall give you more of them presently.

We now entered South Wales: The provinces which bear the name of South Wales, are these, Glamorgan, Brecknock, Radnor, Caermarthen, Pembroke, and Cardigan. We began with Brecknock, being willing to see the highest of the mountains, which are said to be hereabouts; and indeed, except I had still an idea of the height of the Alps, and of those mighty mountains of America, the Andes, which we see very often in the South-Seas, 20 leagues from the shore: I say except that I had still an idea of those countries on my mind, I should have been surprized at the sight of these hills; nay, (as it was) the Andes and the Alps, tho' immensely high, yet they stand together, and they are as mountains, pil'd upon mountains, and hills upon hills; whereas sometimes we see these mountains rising up at once, from the lowest valleys, to the highest summits which makes the height look horrid and frightful, even worse than those mountains abroad; which tho' much higher, rise as it were, one behind another: So that the ascent seems gradual, and consequently less surprising.

Brecknockshire is a meer inland county, as Radnor is; the English jestingly (and I think not very improperly) call it Breakneckshire: 'Tis mountainous to an extremity, except on the side of Radnor, where it is something more low and level. It is well watered by the Wye, and the Uske, two rivers mentioned before; upon the latter stands the town of Brecknock, the capital of the county: The most to be said of this town, is what indeed I have said of many places in Wales, (viz.) that it is very antient, and indeed to mention it here for all the rest, there are more tokens of antiquity to be seen every where in Wales, than in any particular part of England, except the counties of Cumberland, and Northumberland. Here we saw Brecknock-Mere, a large or long lake of water, two or three miles over; of which, they have a great many Welch fables, not worth relating: The best of them is, that a certain river call'd the Lheweni runs thro' it, and keeps its colour in mid-chanel distinguish'd from the water of the lake, and as they say, never mingles with it. They take abundance of good fish in this lake, so that as is said of the river Thysse in Hungary; they say this lake is two thirds water, and one third fish. The country people affirm, there stood a city once here, but, that by the judgment of Heaven, for the sin of its inhabitants, it sunk into the earth, and the water rose up in the place of it. I observe the same story is mentioned by Mr. Cambden with some difference in the particulars: I believe my share of it, but 'tis remarkable, that Mr. Cambden having lost the old city Loventium, mentioned by Ptolemy to be hereabouts, is willing to account for it, by this old story.

It was among the mountains of this county that the famous Glendower shelter'd himself, and taking arms on the deposing Richard II. proclaimed himself Prince of Wales; and they shew

us several little refuges of his in the mountains, whither he
retreated, and from whence, again, he made such bold
excursions into England.

Tho' this county be so mountainous, provisions are exceeding
plentiful, and also very good all over the county; nor are these
mountains useless, even to the city of London, as I have noted
of other counties; for from hence they send yearly, great herds
of black cattle to England, and which are known to fill our fairs
and markets, even that of Smithfield it self.

The yellow mountains of Radnorshire are the same, and their
product of cattle is the same; nor did I meet with any thing
new, and worth noticing, except monuments of antiquity,
which are not the subject of my enquiry: The stories of Vorti-
gern, and Roger of Mortimer, are in every old woman's mouth
here. There is here a great cataract or water fall of the River
Wye, at a place call'd Rhayadr Gwy in Welch, which signifies
the Cataract or Water Fall of the Wye, but we did not go to
see it, by reason of a great flood at that time, which made the
way dangerous: There is a kind of desart too, on that side,
which is scarce habitable or passable, so we made it our north
boundary for this part of our journey, and turn'd away to
Glamorganshire.

Entring this shire, from Radnor and Brecknock, we were
saluted with Monuchdenny-Hill on our left, and the Black-
Mountain on the right, and all a ridge of horrid rocks and
precipices between, over which, if we had not had trusty guides,
we should never have found our way; and indeed, we began to
repent our curiosity, as not having met with any thing worth
the trouble; and a country looking so full of horror, that we
thought to have given over the enterprise, and have left Wales
out of our circuit: But after a day and a night conversing thus
with rocks and mountains, our guide brought us down into a
most agreeable vale, opening to the south, and a pleasant
river running through it, call'd the Taaffe; and following the
course of this river, we came in the evening to the antient
city of Landaff, and Caerdiff, standing almost together.

Landaff is the seat of the episcopal see, and a city; but
Cardiff which is lower on the river, is the port and town of
trade; and has a very good harbour opening into the Severn
Sea, about 4 miles below the town. The cathedral is a neat
building, but very antient; they boast that this church was
a house of religious worship many years before any church
was founded in England, and that the Christian religion flourish'd

here in its primitive purity, from the year 186, till the Pelagian heresy overspread this country; which being afterwards rooted out by the care of the orthodox bishop, they plac'd St. Dobricius as the first bishop in this town of Landaff, then call'd Launton: 'Tis observable, that though the Bishop of Landaff was call'd an arch-bishop, yet the cathedral church was but 28 foot long, and 10 foot broad, and without any steeple or bells; notwithstanding which the 3 first bishops were afterwards sainted, for their eminent holiness of life, and the miracles they wrought; nor had they any other cathedral from the year 386, to the year 1107, when Bishop Urban built the present church, with some houses for the clergy adjoyning, in the nature of a cloyster.

Tho' the church is antient, yet the building is good, and the choir neat, and pretty well kept; but there are no monuments of note in it, except some so antient, that no inscription can be read, to give any account of.

The south part of this country is a pleasant and agreeable place, and is very populous; 'tis also a very good, fertile, and rich soil, and the low grounds are so well cover'd with grass, and stock'd with cattle, that they supply the city of Bristol with butter in very great quantities salted and barrell'd up, just as Suffolk does the city of London.

The chief sea port is Swanzey, a very considerable town for trade, and has a very good harbour: Here is also a very great trade for coals, and culmn, which they export to all the ports of Sommerset, Devon, and Cornwal, and also to Ireland itself; so that one sometimes sees a hundred sail of ships at a time loading coals here; which greatly enriches the country, and particularly this town of Swanzey, which is really a very thriving place; it stands on the River Tawye, or Taw: 'Tis very remarkable, that most of the rivers in this county chime upon the letters T, and Y, as Taaf, Tawy, Tuy, Towy, Tyevy.

Neath is another port, where the coal trade is also considerable, tho' it stands farther within the land. Kynfig Castle, is now the seat and estate of the Lord Mansel, who has here also a very royal income from the collieries; I say royal, because equal to the revenues of some sovereign princes, and which formerly denominated Sir Edward Mansel, one of the richest commoners in Wales; the family was enobled by Her late Majesty Queen Anne.

In this neighbourhood, near Margan Mynydd, we saw the famous monument mentioned by Mr. Cambden, on a hill, with the inscription, which the people are so terrify'd at, that no body will care to read it; for they have a tradition from father to son, that whoever ventures to read it, will dye within a month. We did not scruple the adventure at all, but when we came to try, the letters were so defac'd by time, that we were effectually secur'd from the danger; the inscription not being any thing near so legible, as it seems it was in Cambdens time.

The stone pillar is about 4 or 5 foot high, and 1 foot thick, standing on the top of this hill; there are several other such monuments in Radnorshire, and other counties in Wales, as likewise in Scotland we saw the like: But as I have always said, I carefully avoid entering into any discourses of antiquity, as what the narrow compass of these letters will not allow.

Having thus touch'd at what is most curious on this coast, we pass'd thro' the land of Gowre, and going still west, we came to Caermarthen, or Kaer-Vyrdhin, as the Welsh call it, the capital of the county of Kaermardhinshire.

This is an antient but not a decay'd town, pleasantly situated on the River Towy, or Tovy, which is navigable up to the town, for vessels of a moderate burthen. The town indeed is well built, and populous, and the country round it, is the most fruitful, of any part of all Wales, considering that it continues to be so for a great way; namely, thro' all the middle of the county, and a great way into the next; nor is this county so mountainous and wild, as the rest of this part of Wales: but it abounds in corn, and in fine flourishing meadows, as good as most are in Britain, and in which are fed, a very great number of good cattle.

The chancery, and exchequer of the principality, was usually kept at this town, till the jurisdiction of the Court and Marches of Wales was taken away. This town was also famous for the birth of the old Brittish prophet Merlin, of whom so many things are fabled, that indeed nothing of its kind ever prevail'd so far, in the delusion of mankind, and who flourish'd in the year 480: And here also the old Britains often kept their parliament or assemblies of their wise men, and made their laws. The town was fortify'd in former times, but the walls are scarcely to be seen now, only the ruins of them.

Here we saw near Kily-Maen Ibwyd, on a great mountain, a circle of mighty stones, very much like Stone-henge in Wiltshire, or rather like the Rollrych Stones in Oxfordshire; and tho' the people call it Bruarth Arthur, or King Arthur's Throne, we see no reason to believe that King Arthur knew any thing of it, or that it had any relation to him.

We found the people of this county more civiliz'd and more curteous, than in the more mountainous parts, where the disposition of the inhabitants seems to be rough, like the country: But here as they seem to converse with the rest of the world, by their commerce, so they are more conversible than their neighbours.

The next county west, is Pembrokeshire, which is the most extreme part of Wales on this side, in a rich, fertile, and plentiful country, lying on the sea coast, where it has the benefit of Milford Haven, one of the greatest and best inlets of water in Britain. Mr. Cambden says it contains 16 creeks, 5 great bays, and 13 good roads for shipping, all distinguish'd as such by their names; and some say, a thousand sail of ships may ride in it, and not the topmast of one be seen from another; but this last, I think, merits confirmation.

Before we quitted the coast, we saw Tenbigh, the most agreeable town on all the sea coast of South Wales, except Pembroke, being a very good road for shipping, and well frequented: Here is a great fishery for herring in its season, a great colliery, or rather export of coals, and they also drive a very considerable trade to Ireland.

From hence, the land bearing far into the sea, makes a promontory, call'd St. Govens Head or Point. But as we found nothing of moment was to be seen there, we cross'd over the isthmus to Pembroke, which stands on the E. shore of the great haven of Milford.

This is the largest and richest, and at this time, the most flourishing town of all S. Wales: Here are a great many English merchants, and some of them men of good business; and they told us, there were near 200 sail of ships belong'd to the town, small and great; in a word, all this part of Wales is a rich and flourishing country, but especially this part is so very pleasant, and fertile, and is so well cultivated, that 'tis call'd by distinction, Little England, beyond Wales.

This is the place also made particularly famous for the landing of King Henry VII, then Duke of Richmond: From hence, being resolv'd to see the utmost extent of the county west, we ferry'd over the haven as ---- and went to Haverford, or by some call'd Haverford-West; and from thence to St. Davids, or St. Taffys, as the Welch call it. Haverford is a better town than we expected to find, in this remote angle of Britain; 'tis strong, well built, clean, and populous.

From hence to St. Davids, the country begins to look like

Wales again, dry, barren, and mountainous; St. Davids is not a bishop's see only, but was formerly an arch-bishop's, which they tell us, was by the Pope transferr'd to Dole in Britany, where it still remains.

The venerable aspect of this cathedral church, shews that it has been a beautiful building, but that it is much decay'd. The west end or body of the church is tolerably well; the choir is kept neat, and in tollerable repair, the S. isle without the choir, and the Virgin Mary's Chappel, which makes the E. end of the church, are in a manner demolish'd, and the roofs of both fallen in.

There are a great many eminent persons bury'd here, besides such, whose monuments are defac'd by time: There is St. Davids monument, to whom the church is dedicated, the monument of the Earl of Richmond, as also of the famous Owen Tudor; there are also four antient monuments of Knights Templars, known by their figures lying cross legg'd; but their names are not known, and there are six several monuments of bishops, who ruled this church, besides St. David.

This St. David they tell us was uncle to King Arthur, that he lived to 146 years of age, that he was bishop of this church 65 years, being born in the year 496, and dyed ann. 642; that he built 12 monasteries, and did abundance of miracles.

There was a very handsome house for the bishop, with a college, all built in a close by themselves, but they are now turn'd to ruins.

Here the weather being very clear, we had a full view of Ireland, tho' at a very great distance: The land here is call'd St. Davids Head, and from hence, there has some time ago, gone a passage boat constantly between England and Ireland, but that voiture is at present discontinued. They reckon up 112 bishops of this see, since it begun, to the year 1712.

The last bishop but two, was Dr. Thomas Watson, of whom the world has heard so much, being depriv'd after a long debate, on a charge of simony; whether justly, or not, I shall not enquire, but he bestow'd great sums on charitable designs, and is still (living) enclined as I am told, to do much more.

From hence we turn'd N. keeping the sea in our W. prospect, and a rugged mountainous country on the E. where the hills even darken'd the air with their heighth; as we went on, we past by Newport, on the River Nevern, a town having a good harbour, and consequently a good trade with Ireland.

Here we left Pembrokeshire, and after about 22 miles, came

to the town of Cardigan, an old and well inhabited town, on the River Tivy: 'Tis a very noble river indeed, and famous for its plenty of the best and largest salmon in Britain.

The country people told us, that they had beavers here, which bred in the lakes among the mountains, and came down the stream of Tivy to feed; that they destroy'd the young frye of salmon, and therefore the country people destroy'd them; but they could shew us none of them, or any of their skins, neither could the countrymen describe them, or tell us that they had ever seen them; so that we concluded they only meant the otter, till I found after our return, that Mr. Cambden mentions also, that there were beavers seen here formerly.

This town of Cardigan was once possess'd by the great Robert Fitz-Stephen, who was the first Britain that ever attempted the conquest of Ireland; and had such success with a handful of men, as afterwards gave the English a footing there, which they never quitted afterwards, till they quite reduc'd the country, and made it, as it were, a province of England.

The town is not large, has been well fortify'd, but that part is now wholly neglected. It has a good trade with Ireland, and is enrich'd very much, as is all this part of the country, by the famous lead mines, formerly discover'd by Sir Carbery Price, which are the greatest, and perhaps the richest in England; and particularly as they require so little labour and charge to come at the oar, which in many places lyes within a fathom or two of the surface, and in some, even bare to the very top.

Going N. from the Tyvy about 25 miles, we came to Abrystwyth, that is to say, the town at the mouth of the River Ystwyth. This town is enrich'd by the coals and lead which is found in its neighbourhood, and is a populous, but a very dirty, black, smoaky place, and we fancy'd the people look'd as if they liv'd continually in the coal or lead mines. However, they are rich, and the place is very populous.

The whole county of Cardigan is so full of cattle, that 'tis said to be the nursery, or breeding-place for the whole kingdom of England, S. by Trent; but this is not a proof of its fertility, for tho' the feeding of cattle indeed requires a rich soil, the breeding them does not, the mountains and moors being as proper for that purpose as richer land.

Now we enter'd N. Wales, only I should add, that as we pass'd, we had a sight of the famous Plymlymon-Hill, out of the east side of which as I mentioned before, rises the Severn, and the Wye; and out of the west side of it, rises the Rydall

and the Ystwyth. This mountain is exceeding high, and tho'
it is hard to say which is the highest hill in Wales, yet I think
this bids fair for it; nor is the county for 20 miles round it, any
thing but a continued ridge of mountains: So that for almost
a whole week's travel, we seem'd to be conversing with the
upper regions; for we were often above the clouds, I'm sure, a
very great way, and the names of some of these hills seem'd as
barbarous to us, who spoke no Welch, as the hills themselves.

Passing these mountains, I say, we enter'd N. Wales, which
contains the counties of Montgomery, Merionith, Caernarvon,
Denbeigh, and Flint shires, and the Isle of Anglesea.

In passing Montgomery-shire, we were so tired with rocks
and mountains, that we wish'd heartily we had kept close to
the sea shore, but it not much mended the matter if we had,
as I understood afterwards: The River Severn is the only
beauty of this county, which rising I say, out of the Plymlymon
Mountain, receives instantly so many other rivers into its
bosom, that it becomes navigable before it gets out of the
county; namely, at Welch Pool, on the edge of Shropshire.
This is a good fashionable place, and has many English dwelling
in it, and some very good families; but we saw nothing farther
worth remarking.

The vales and meadows upon the bank of the Severn, are
the best of this county, I had almost said, the only good part
of it; some are of opinion, that, the very water of the Severn,
like that of Nile, impregnates the valleys, and when it over-
flows, leaves a vertue behind it, particularly to itself; and this
they say is confirm'd, because all the country is so fruitful,
wherever this river does overflow, and its waters reach. The
town, or rather as the natives call it, the city of Montgomery,
lyes not far from this river, on the outer edge of the country
next to Herefordshire. This was, it seems, a great frontier
town in the wars between the English and the Welch, and was
beautify'd and fortify'd by King Henry III; the town is now
much decay'd: It gives title to the eldest son of the ducal house
of Powis, who is call'd Lord Montgomery, and Marquis of
Powis; they have a noble seat at Troy, hard by this town on the
other side the river: But the house of Pembroke also claims the
title of Montgomery.

This county is noted for an excellent breed of Welch horses,
which, though not very large, are exceeding valuable, and much
esteem'd all over England; all the North and West part of the
county is mountainous and stony. We saw a great many old

monuments in this country, and Roman camps wherever we came, and especially if we met any person curious in such things, we found they had many Roman coins; but this was none of my enquiry, as I have said already.

Merionithshire, or Merionydshire, lyes west from Montgomery-shire; it lyes on the Irish Sea, or rather the ocean; for St. George's Chanel does not begin till further north, and it is extended on the coast, for near 35 miles in length, all still mountainous and craggy. The principal river is the Tovy, which rises among the unpassable mountains, which range along the center of this part of Wales, and which we call unpassable, for that even the people themselves call'd them so; we look'd at them indeed with astonishment, for their rugged tops, and the immense height of them: Some particular hills have particular names, but otherwise we called them all the Black Mountains, and they well deserv'd the name; some think 'tis from the unpassable mountains of this county, that we have an old saying, that the devil lives in the middle of Wales, tho' I know there is another meaning given to it; in a word, Mr. Cambden calls these parts the Alps of Wales.

There is but few large towns in all this part, nor is it very populous; indeed much of it is scarce habitable, but 'tis said, there are more sheep in it, than in all the rest of Wales. On the sea shore however, we see Harleigh-Castle, which is still a garrison, and kept for the guard of the coast, but 'tis of no great strength, but by its situation.

In the middle of these vast mountains (and forming a very large lake (viz.) near its first sources) rises the River Dee, of which I shall speak again in its proper place.

Here among innumerable summits, and rising peaks of nameless hills, we saw the famous Kader-Idricks, which some are of opinion, is the highest mountain in Britain, another call'd Rarauvaur, another call'd Mowylwynda, and still every hill we saw, we thought was higher than all that ever we saw before.

We enquired here after that strange phænomenon which was not only seen, but fatally experienced by the country round this place, namely, of a livid fire, coming off from the sea; and setting on fire, houses, barns, stacks of hay and corn, and poisoning the herbage in the fields; of which there is a full account given in the philosophical transactions: And as we had it confirm'd by the general voice of the people, I content my self with giving an account of it as follows:

It is observable, that the eclipses of the sun in Aries, have been very fatal to this place; for in the years 1542, and 1567, when the sun was eclipsed in that sign, it suffer'd very much by fire; and after the latter eclipse of the two, the fire spread so far, that about 200 houses in the town and suburbs of Caernarvon, were consum'd.

But to return to the face of things, as they appear'd to us, the mountainous country spoken of runs away N. through this county and almost the next, I mean Caernarvonshire, where Snowden Hill is a monstrous height, and according to its name, had snow on the top in the beginning of June; and perhaps had so till the next June, that is to say, all the year.

These unpassable heights were doubtless the refuges of the Britains, when they made continual war with the Saxons and Romans, and retreated on occasion of their being over power'd, into these parts; where, in short, no enemy could pursue them.

That side of the country of Carnarvon, which borders on the sea, is not so mountainous, and is both more fertile and more populous. The principal town in this part, is Carnarvon, a good town, with a castle built by Edward I. to curb and reduce the wild people of the mountains, and secure the passage into Anglesea. As this city was built by Edward I. so he kept his Court often here, and honour'd it with his presence very much; and here his eldest son and successor, tho' unhappy, (Ed. II.) was born, who was therefore call'd Edward of Caernarvon. This Edward was the first Prince of Wales; that is to say, the first of the Kings of Englands sons, who was vested with the title of Prince of Wales: And here was kept the chancery and exchequer of the Prince's of Wales, for the N. part of the principality, as it was at --- for the S. part. It is a small, but strong town, clean and well built, and considering the place, the people are very courteous and obliging to strangers. It is seated on the firth or inlet call'd Menai, parting the isle of Anglesea, or Mona, from the main land; and here is a ferry over to the island called Abermenai Ferry: And from thence a direct road to Holly Head, where we went for no purpose, but to have another view of Ireland, tho' we were disappointed, the weather being bad and stormy.

Whoever travels critically over these mountains, I mean of S. Wales, and Merionithshire, will think Stone-henge in Wiltshire, and Roll-Rich Stones in Oxfordshire no more a wonder, seeing there are so many such, and such like, in these provinces; that they are not thought strange of at all, nor is it doubted, but they were generally monuments of the dead, as also are the single stones of immense bulk any other, of which we saw so many, that we gave over remarking them; some we saw from 7, 8, to 10, and one 16 foot high, being a whole stone, but so great, that the most of the wonder is, where they were found, and how dragg'd to the place; since, besides the steep ascents to some of the hills on which they stand, it would be impossible to move some of them, now, with 50 yoke of oxen. And yet a great many of these stones are found confusedly lying one upon another on the utmost summit or top of the Glyder, or other Hills, in Merionith and Carnarvonshire; to which it is next to impossible, that all the power of art, and strength of man and beast could carry them, and the people make no diffi-culty of saying the devil set them up there.

One of these monumental stones is to be seen a little way from Harleigh-Castle: It is a large stone lying flat, supported by three other stones at 3 of the 4 angles, tho' the stone is rather oval than square, it is almost 11 foot long, the breadth unequal, but in some places its from 7 to 8 foot broad, and it may be suppos'd has been both longer and broader; 'tis in some places above 2 foot thick, but in others 'tis worn almost to an edge by time: The three stones that support it, are about 20 inches square, 'tis suppos'd there has been four, two of which that support the thickest end, are near 8 foot high, the other not above 3 foot, being suppos'd to be settled in the ground, so that the stone lyes sloping, like the roof of a barn. There is another of these to be seen in the isle of Anglesea, the flat stone is much larger and thicker than this; but we did not go to see it: There are also two circles of stones in that island, such as Stone-henge, but the stones much larger.

This is a particular kind of monument, and therefore I took notice of it, but the other are generally single stones of vast magnitude, set up on one end, column wise, which being so very large, are likely to remain to the end of time; but are generally without any inscription, or regular shape or any mark, to intimate for who, or for what they were so placed.

These mountains are indeed so like the Alps, that except the language of the people, one could hardly avoid thinking he is passing from Grenoble to Susa, or rather passing the country of the Grisons. The lakes also, which are so numerous here, make the similitude the greater, nor are the fables which the country people tell of these lakes, much unlike the stories which we meet with among the Switzers, of the famous lakes in their country; Dr. Gibson, (Mr. Cambdens continuator) tells us of

50 or 60 lakes in Carnarvonshire only, we did not count them indeed, but I believe if we had, we should have found them to be many more.

Here we met with the char fish, the same kind which we see in Lancashire, and also in the lakes of Switzerland, and no where else, that I have heard of in Europe; the Welch call it the *torgoch*.

There is nothing of note to be seen in the Isle of Anglesea but the town, and the castle of Baumaris, which was also built by King Edward I. and call'd Beau-Marsh, or the Fine Plain; for here the country is very level and plain, and the land is fruitful and pleasant. The castle was very large, as may be seen by its remains, and that it was strong; the situation will tell also, but 'tis now of no use.

As we went to Holly Head, by the S. part of the island from Newborough, and came back thro' the middle to Beaumaris, we saw the whole extent of it, and indeed, it is a much pleasanter country, than any part of N. Wales, that we had yet seen; and particularly is very fruitful for corn and cattle.

Here we cross'd the Fretum, or strait of Meneu again, and came to Bangor, at the place where King Edward I. intended to have built a great stone bridge, it wou'd indeed have been a work fit for so great and powerful a king, as K. Edward was: But the bottom being doubtful, and the sea in that place sometimes very raging and strong, the workmen thought it impracticable, and tho' as we were told, that the king was very positive in his design for a great while, yet he was prevail'd with at last to decline it.

From hence, I say, we cross'd to Bangor, a town noted for its antiquity, its being a bishops see, and an old, mean looking, and almost despicable cathedral church.

This church claims to be one of the most antient in Britain, the people say, 'tis the most antient; that St. Daniel (to whom this church was dedicated) was first bishop here, in the year 512. They allow that the pagans, perhaps of Anglesea, ruined the church, and possess'd the bishoprick after it was first built, for above 100 years; nor is there any account of it from the year 512, to 1009: After this, the bishoprick was ruined again by dilapidation, by one of its own bishops, whose name was Bulkeley, who, as the *Monasticon* says, not only sold the revenues, but even the very bells, for which sacrilege he was struck blind; but this last is a tradition only.

It is certainly at present a poor bishoprick, and has but a poor cathedral; yet the bishops are generally allow'd to hold some other good benefice *in commendam*, and the preferment seems to be a grateful introduction to the clergy, as the bishops are generally translated from hence, to a more profitable bishoprick.

From Bangor we went north, (keeping the sea on our left hand) to Conway. This is the poorest but pleasantest town in all this county for the bigness of it; it is seated on the bank of a fine river, which is not only pleasant and beautiful, but is a noble harbour for ships, had they any occasion for them there; the stream is deep and safe, and the river broad, as the Thames at Deptford: It only wants a trade suitable to so good a port, for it infinitely out does Chester or Leverpool itself.

In this passage, we went over the famous precipice call'd Penmen-muir, which indeed fame has made abundance more frightful, than it really is; for tho' the rock is indeed very high, and if any one should fall from it, it wou'd dash them in pieces, yet, on the other hand, there is no danger of their falling; and besides, there is now a wall built all the way, on the edge of the precipice, to secure them: Those who have been at the hill or pass of Enterkin in Scotland, know very well, the danger there is much greater, than what can be thought of here; as the frequent loss of lives, both of man and horse will testify.

We have but little remarkable in the road from Conway to Hollywell, but craggs and rocks all along the N. shore of Denbeigh, till we came to Denbeigh town. This is the county town, and is a large populous place, which carries something in its countenance of its neighbourhood to England, but that which was most surprizing, after such a tiresom and fatiguing journey, over the unhospitable mountains of Merioneth, and Carnarvonshire, was, that descending now from the hills, we came into a most pleasant, fruitful, populous, and delicious vale, full of villages and towns, the fields shining with corn, just ready for the reapers, the meadows green and flowery, and a fine river, with a mild and gentle stream running thro' it: Nor is it a small or casual intermission, but we had a prospect of the country open before us, for above 20 miles in length, and from 5 to 7 miles in breadth, all smiling with the same kind of complexion; which made us think our selves in England again, all on a sudden.

In this pleasant vale, turning N. from Denbeigh, and following the stream of the river, we came to S. Asaph, a small city, with a cathedral, being a bishoprick of tolerable good value, though the church is old: It is but a poor town, and ill built, tho' the country is so pleasant and rich round it. There are some old monuments in this church, but none of any note, nor could we read the Welch inscriptions.

From hence we come to Holly-well: The stories of this Well of S. Winifrid are, that the pious virgin, being ravished and murthered, this healing water sprung out of her body when buried; but this smells too much of the legend, to take up any of my time; the Romanists indeed believe it, as 'tis evident, from their thronging hither to receive the healing sanative virtue of the water, which they do not hope for as it is a medicinal water, but as it is a miraculous water, and heals them by virtue of the intercession and influence of this famous virgin, St. Winifrid; of which I believe as much as comes to my share.

Here is a fine chapel cut out of a solid rock, and was dedicated to this holy virgin; and numbers of pilgrims resort to it, with no less devotion than ignorance; under this chapel the water gushes out in a great stream, and the place where it breaks out, is form'd like a basin or cistern, in which they bathe: The water is intensely cold, and indeed there is no great miracle in that point, considering the rocks it flows from, where it is impregnated by divers minerals, the virtue of which, and not of the saint, I suppose, work the greatest part of the cures.

There is a little town near the well, which may, indeed, be said to have risen from the confluence of the people hither, for almost all the houses are either publick houses, or let into lodgings; and the priests that attend here, and are very numerous, appear in disguise: Sometimes they are physicians, sometimes surgeons, sometimes gentlemen, and sometimes patients, or any thing as occasion presents. No body takes notice of them, as to their profession, tho' they know them well enough, no not the Roman Catholicks themselves; but in private, they have their proper oratory's in certain places, whither the votaries resort; and good manners has prevail'd so far, that however the Protestants know who and who's together; no body takes notice of it, or enquires where one another goes, or has been gone.

From hence we past by Flint-Castle, a known place, but of no significance; and then in a few hours we cross'd the River Dee, and arriv'd at the city of West Chester, from whence, I shall give a farther account of my journey in my next.

I am,

SIR,

Yours, &c.

THE END OF THE SIXTH LETTER

LETTER VII

SIR,—My last from West Chester, gave you a full account of my progress thro' Wales, and my coming to Chester, at the end of that really fatiguing journey: I must confess, I that have seen the Alps, on so many occasions, have gone under so many of the most frightful passes in the country of the Grisons, and in the mountains of Tirol, never believ'd there was any thing in this island of Britain that came near, much less that exceeded those hills, in the terror of their aspect, or in the difficulty of access to them; But certainly, if they are out done any where in the world, it is here: Even Hannibal himself wou'd have found it impossible to have march'd his army over Snowden, or over the rocks of Merioneth and Montgomery Shires; no, not with all the help that fire and vinegar could have yielded, to make way for him.

The only support we had in this heavy journey, was, (1.) That we generally found their provisions very good and cheap, and very good accommodations in the inns. And (2.) That the Welsh gentlemen are very civil, hospitable, and kind; the people very obliging and conversible, and especially to strangers; but when we let them know, we travell'd merely in curiosity to view the country, and be able to speak well of them to strangers, their civility was heightened to such a degree, that nothing could be more friendly, willing to tell us every thing that belong'd to their country, and to show us every thing that we desired to see.

They value themselves much upon their antiquity: The antient race of their houses, and families, and the like; and above all, upon their antient heroes: their King Caractacus, Owen ap Tudor, Prince Lewellin, and the like noblemen and princes of British extraction; and as they believe their country to be the pleasantest and most agreeable in the world, so you cannot oblige them more, than to make them think you believe so too.

The gentlemen of Wales, indeed, justly claim a very antient descent, and have preserv'd their families entire, for many ages: They receive you well into their houses, treat you very handsomely, are very generous; and indeed, nothing is wanting within doors; and which is more than all, they have generally very good estates.

I continued at Chester for some time, except that I made two or three excursions into the neighbouring country, and particularly into that part of Shropshire, which I had not view'd as I went; as also into the north, and north west part of Cheshire.

The first trip I made, was into the Cestria Chersonesus, as I think we may properly call it, (viz.) a piece of the county, which runs out a great way into the Irish Sea, and is bounded by the two great firths, or arms of the sea, the one call'd the mouth of the Dee, and the other of two rivers, the Mersey, and the Wever; this isthmus or neck of land, is about 16 miles long, and about 6 or 7 miles over, and has not one market town in it, tho' 'tis exceeding rich and fertile; the last occasioned possibly by the neighbourhood of two such great towns, or cities rather: I mean Chester and Leverpool.

Going down from Chester, by the Rhoodee, as they call it, that is, the marshes of the River Dee, and coasting the river after it is grown broader than the marshes; the first place of any note which we come to, is Nesson, a long nase or ness of land, which running out into the sea, makes a kind of a key. This is the place where in the late war in Ireland, most of the troops embark'd, when that grand expedition begun; after which, the vessels go away to Highlake, in which as the winds may happen they ride safe in their way, as the ships from London lye in the Downs, till the wind presents for their respective voyages.

From Nesson we cross'd over that fruitful level I mentioned before, and coming to the other water, we ferry'd over to Leverpool. This town is now become so great, so populous, and so rich, that it may be call'd the Bristol of this part of England: It had formerly but one church, but upon the encrease of inhabitants, and of new buildings in so extraordinary a manner, they have built another very fine church in the north part of the town; and they talk of erecting two more.

The first thing we observ'd in this church, was a fine marble font, all of one entire stone, given to the town, or church rather, by the late Robert Heysham Esq; a citizen and very considerable merchant of London; who was many years representative for the town of Lancaster. Here is a very fine new built tower also, and in it a curious ring of eight, very good bells.

This part of the town may indeed be call'd New Leverpool, for that, they have built more than another Leverpool that way, in new streets, and fine large houses for their merchants: Besides this, they have made a great wet dock, for laying up their ships, and which they greatly wanted; for tho' the Mersey is a noble harbour, and is able to ride a thousand sail of ships at once, yet those ships that are to be laid up, or lye by the walls all the winter, or longer, as sometimes may be the case; must ride there, as in an open road, or (as the seamen call it,) be haled a shore; neither of which wou'd be practicable in a town of so much trade: And in the time of the late great storm, they suffer'd very much on that account.

This is the only work of its kind in England, except what is in the river of Thames, I mean for the merchants; nor is it many years since there was not one wet dock in England for private use, except Sir Henry Johnson's at Black Wall.

This is still an encreasing flourishing town, and if they go on in trade, as they have done for some time, 'tis probable it will in a little time be as big as the city of Dublin. The houses here are exceedingly well built, the streets strait, clean, and spacious, and they are now well supplied with water. The merchants here have a very pretty Exchange, standing upon 12 free-stone columns, but it begins to be so much too little, that 'tis thought they must remove or enlarge it. They talk already as I have said above, of building two churches more at Leverpool, and surrounding them with new streets, to the N.E. of the old town, which if they should, Leverpool will soon out do Bristol: In short, 'tis already the next town to Bristol, and in a little time may probably exceed it, both in commerce, and in numbers of people.

We went no farther this way at that time, but came back to Chester, by the same ferry as we went over.

As I am now at Chester, 'tis proper to say something of it, being a city well worth describing: Chester has four things very remarkable in it. 1. It's walls, which are very firm, beautiful, and in good repair. 2. The castle, which is also kept up, and has a garrison always in it. 3. The cathedral. 4. The River Dee, and 5. the bridge over it.

It is a very antient city, and to this day, the buildings are very old; nor do the Rows as they call them, add any thing, in my opinion, to the beauty of the city; but just the contrary, they serve to make the city look both old and ugly: These Rows are certain long galleries, up one pair of stairs, which run along the side of the streets, before all the houses, tho' joined to them, and as is pretended, they are to keep the people dry in walking along. This they do indeed effectually, but then they take away all the view of the houses from the street, nor can a stranger, that was to ride thro' Chester, see any shops in the city; besides, they make the shops themselves dark, and the way in them is dark, dirty, and uneven.

The best ornament of the city, is, that the streets are very broad and fair, and run through the whole city in strait lines, crossing in the middle of the city, as at Chichester: The walls as I have said, are in very good repair, and it is a very pleasant walk round the city, upon the walls, and within the battlements, from whence you may see the country round; and particularly on the side of the Roodee, which I mentioned before, which is a fine large low green, on the bank of the Dee. In the winter this green is often under water by the inundations of the river, and a little before I came there, they had such a terrible land flood, which flow'd 8 foot higher than usual so that it not only overflowed the said green, call'd the Roodee, but destroy'd a fine new wharf and landing-place for goods, a little below the town, bore down all the warehouses, and other buildings, which the merchants had erected for securing their goods, and carried all away goods and buildings together, to the irreparable loss of the persons concern'd: Also beyond the Roodee, one sees from the walls of Chester the county of Flint, and the mountains of Wales, a prospect best indeed, at a distance.

The castle of Chester is a good firm building, and strong, tho' not fortify'd, with many out works: There is always a good garrison kept, and here the prisoners taken at Preston, in the late time of Rebellion, were kept a great while, till compassion to their misery, mov'd the clemency of the conqueror to deliver them. They say this castle was built or at least repair'd by Hugh Lupus, the famous Earl of Chester, and brother to William the Conqueror as also was the church.

The great church here is a very magnificent building, but 'tis built of a red, sandy, ill looking stone, which takes much from the beauty of it, and which yielding to the weather, seems to crumble, and suffer by time, which much defaces the building: Here they shew'd us the monument of Henry IV. Emperor of Germany; who they say, resign'd his empire, and liv'd a recluse here, but 'tis all to be taken upon trust, for we find nothing of it in history. We saw no monument of any note, which is partly occasion'd by its remote situation, and partly by its being but a modern bishoprick; for it was formerly a part of the diocess of Litchfield, and was not made a bishop's see till the year 1541; when King Henry VIII. divided it from Litchfield; nor has there ever been above 19 bishops of this see from its foundation. The short account of it is thus. Hugh Lupus gave the old monastery dedicated to St. Werburge, to a society of monks, after which, they say, King Edgar who conquer'd all this part of Britain, and was rowed up the Dee, in his royal barge, by four kings, founded the great church; and Hugh Lupus the great, Earl of Chester, finish'd and endow'd it.

Here is a noble stone bridge over the Dee, very high and strong built, and 'tis needful it should be so, indeed; for the Dee is a most furious stream at some seasons, and brings a vast weight of water with it from the mountains of Wales. Here it was that the first army of King William, design'd for the war in Ireland, and commanded by the great Duke Schomberg, encamp'd, for a considerable time before they embark'd, ann. 1689.

Here according to the *Monasticon*, the said Hugh Lupus held his parliament for the county palatine of Chester, given him by William the Conqueror, and where he sat in as great state as the king himself. The draught of which, as it is given us from antiquity, take as follows.

There are 11 parishes in this city, and very good churches to them, and it is the largest city in all this side of England that is so remote from London. When I was formerly at this city, about the year 1690, they had no water to supply their ordinary occasions, but what was carried from the River Dee upon horses, in great leather vessels, like a pair of bakers panyers; just the very same for shape and use, as they have to this day in the streets of Constantinople, and at Belgrade, in Hungary; to carry water about the streets to sell, for the people to drink. But at my coming there this time, I found a very good water-house in the river, and the city plentifully supply'd by pipes, just as London is from the Thames; tho' some parts of Chester stands very high from the river.

Tho' this is not an antient bishoprick, 'tis an antient city, and was certainly a frontier of the Roman Empire this way; and its being so afterwards to the English Empire also, has doubtless been the reason of its being so well kept, and the castle continued in repair, when most of the other castles on the frontiers were slighted and demolished.

This county, however remote from London, is one of those which contributes most to its support, as well as to several other parts of England, and that is by its excellent cheese, which they make here in such quantities, and so exceeding good, that as I am told from very good authority, the city of London only take off 14000 ton every year; besides 8000 ton which they say goes every year down the Rivers Severn and Trent, the former to Bristol, and the latter to York; including all the towns on both these large rivers: And besides the quantity ship'd both here, and at Leverpool, to go to Ireland, and Scotland. So that the quantity of cheese made in this country, must be prodigious great. Indeed, the whole county is employ'd in it, and part of its neighbourhood too; for tho' 'tis call'd by the name of Cheshire Cheese, yet great quantities of it are made in Shropshire, Staffordshire and Lancashire, that is to say, in such parts of them as border upon Cheshire.

The soil is extraordinary good, and the grass they say, has a peculiar richness in it, which disposes the creatures to give a great quantity of milk, and that very sweet and good; and this cheese manufacture, for such it is, encreases every day, and greatly enriches all the county; raises the value of the lands, and encourages the farmers to the keeping vast stocks of cows; the very number of the cattle improving and enriching the land.

The east part of the county abounds in salt springs, from which they draw the brine, and boyl it into fine salt; and once it was a very considerable trade, which they carried on with this salt; but since the discovery of the rock salt, which they dig in great quantities, towards Warrington, the other salt is not in so much request.

I now resolv'd to direct my course east, and making the Wever and the Trent, my northern boundary in this circuit; I came forward to view the midland counties of England, I mean such as may be said to lye between the Thames and the Trent.

I had taken a little trip into the N.E. parts of Cheshire before, seen a fine old seat of the Lord Delamere's, and which is beyond it all, the fine forest, which bears the name of that noble family; intending to see the salt pits at Northwich, which are odd indeed, but not so very strange as we were made to believe; the thing is, they say, the salt spring is found to be just perpendicularly under the stream or chanel of a fresh water river, namely, the Wever, and it is so, for the spring is very deep indeed in the ground, but that very thing takes off the wonder; for as the earth under the river, is but as a gutter to carry the water, there is no difficulty that it should not penetrate through it, the soil being a strong clay. So we came away not extremely gratify'd in our curiosity.

All the way as we cross'd this part of the county, we see Beeston Castle, an antient castle, giving name to a very antient family in this county. It stands upon a very high hill, over looking the county, like as Beavoir Castle over looks the vale of that name in Leicestershire; or as Harrow on the Hill over looks Middlesex. It was formerly a very strong place, and was re-fortify'd in the late wars, Sir William Beeston being in arms at that unhappy time; but the works are now demolish'd again.

From Northwich we turn'd S. and following the stream of the river by Middle Wich, we cross'd the great London road at Nantwich, or as some write it Namptwych; these are the three salt making towns of this county; there is a fourth which is call'd Droitwych, in Worcestershire; the nature of the thing is this, they boil the brine into fine salt, which is much priz'd for the beauty of its colour, and fineness of the grain, but the salt is not so strong, as what we now make from the rock salt mentioned above, and therefore loses of its value.

Hence we turn'd a little W. to Whitchurch, in Shropshire. But before I leave Cheshire, I must note two things of it. (1.) That there is no part of England, where there are such a great number of families of gentry, and of such antient and noble extraction; Mr. Cambden is very particular in their names, and descents, but that's a work too long for this place, nor does it belong to my present design. (2.) That it is a County Palatine, and has been for so many ages, that its government is distinct from any other and very particular; it is administred by a chamberlain, a judge special, two barons of the exchequer, three sergeants at law, a sheriff, and attorney, and escheator, and all proper and useful subordinate officers; and the jurisdiction of all these offices are kept up, and preserv'd very strictly, only we are to note, that the judge special as he is call'd, tries only civil causes, not criminal, which are left to the ordinary judges of England, who go the circuits here, as in other places.

Whitchurch is a pleasant and populous town, and has a very good church, in which is the famous monument of the great Talbot, first Earl of Shrewsbury, who, perhaps, and not unworthily, was call'd in his time, the English ACHILLES. This is the Talbot so renowned in the antient wars in France, whom

no man in France dare to encounter single handed, and who
had engraven on his sword, on one side, these words, Sum
Talboti, and on the reverse, *Pro vincere inimicos meos.* His
epitaph is as follows:

ORATE PRO ANIMA PRÆNOBILIS DOMINI, DOMINI IOANNIS TALBOTT
QUONDAM COMITIS SALOPIÆ, DOMINI TALBOTT, DOMINI FVRNIVALL,
DOMINI VERDON, DOMINI STRANGE DE BLACKMERE, ET MARESCHALLI
FRANCIÆ, QUI OBIIT IN BELLO APVD BVRDEWS VII. IVLII MCCCCLIII

That is,

Pray for the soul of the right honourable Lord, Lord John Talbott,
sometime Earl of Shrewsbury, Lord Talbott, Lord Furnivall, Lord
Verdon, Lord Strange of Blackmere, and Marshall of France, who
dyed in battel, at Burdeaux, VII. of July, MCCCCLIII.

But the most to be said of this town now, is, that they have
a good market, and a great many gentry near it, whereof some
are Roman Catholicks. They tell us that this town when King
Charles I. remov'd his standard from Nottingham to Shrewsbury,
raised a whole regiment for the king: Nor has this town lost
its old loyal principle, to this time; tho' now it may run a little
another way.

From hence we went towards Wales again, and cross'd the
Dee, at Bangor Bridge; I could not satisfy myself to omit seeing
this famous town, which was once so remarkable, but was
surpriz'd when I came there, to see there was a stone-bridge
over the Dee, and indeed, a very fine one: But as for the town or
monastery, scarce any of the ruins were to be seen, and as all
the people spoke Welch, we could find no body that could give
us any intelligence. So effectually had time in so few years,
ras'd the very foundations of the place. I will not say, as some
do, that this is miraculous, and that it is the particular judgment
of God upon the place, for being the birth-place of that arch
heretick Pelagius, who from hence also began to broach his
heretical opinions, which afterwards so terribly overspread the
Church: I say I will not insist upon this: That Pelagius was a
monk of Bungor, or Banchor, is not doubted; but for the rest
I leave it where I find it.

The place is now (I say) a poor contemptible village, and has
nothing to show but a fine stone bridge over Dee, by which we
enter Denbighshire in Wales. From thence we visited Wrexham,
having heard much of a fine church there, but we were greatly
disappointed: There is indeed a very large tower steeple, if
a tower may be call'd a steeple, and 'tis finely adorn'd with

imagery; but far from fine: the work is mean, the statues seem all mean and in dejected postures, without any fancy or spirit in the workmanship, and as the stone is of a reddish crumbling kind, like the cathedral at Chester, Time has made it look gross and rough.

There are a great many antient monuments in this church, and in the church-yard also; but none of note, and almost all the inscriptions are in Welch. The church is large; but they must be much mistaken, who tell us 'tis the finest in England, no not among those which are as old as itself.

This town is large, well built and populous, and besides the church there are two large meeting-houses, in one of which we were told they preach in Welch one part of the day, and in English the other. Here is a great market for Welch flannel which the factors buy up of the poor Welch people, who manufacture it; and thence it is sent to London; and it is a very considerable manufacture indeed thro' all this part of the country, by which the poor are very profitably employ'd.

From hence we turn'd south, and passing by Wem, the title given by King James II. to the late Lord Chancellor Jefferies, we saw the house where his father, then but a private gentleman liv'd, and in but middling circumstances. Thence we came to Ellsmere, famous for a great lake or mere, which gives the town its name, and which the people pretend has in some places no bottom. This place is remarkable for good fish. From hence we came the same night to Shrewsbury.

This is indeed a beautiful, large, pleasant, populous, and rich town; full of gentry and yet full of trade too; for here too, is a great manufacture, as well of flannel, as also of white broadcloth, which enriches all the country round it.

The Severn surrounds this town, just as the Thames does the Isle of Dogs; so that it makes the form of an horse-shoe, over which there are two fine stone bridges, upon one of which is built a very noble gate, and over the arch of the gate the statue of the great Lewellin, the idol of the Welch, and their last Prince of Wales.

This is really a town of mirth and gallantry, something like Bury in Suffolk, or Durham in the north, but much bigger than either of them, or indeed than both together.

Over the market-house is kept a kind of hall for the manufactures, which are sold here weekly in very great quantities; they speak all English in the town, but on a market-day you would think you were in Wales.

Here is the greatest market, the greatest plenty of good provisions, and the cheapest that is to be met with in all the western part of England; the Severn supplies them here with excellent salmon, but 'tis also brought in great plenty from the River Dee, which is not far off, and which abounds with a very good kind, and is generally larger than that in the Severn; As an example of the cheapness of provisions, we paid here, in a publick inn, but a groat a night for hay, and six-pence a peck for oats for our horses, which is cheaper than we found it in the cheapest part of the north of England; all our other provisions were in proportion; and there is no doubt but the cheapness of provisions joined to the pleasantness and healthiness of the place, draws a great many families thither, who love to live within the compass of their estates.

Mr. Cambden calls it a city: 'Tis at this day, says he, a fine city well-inhabited: But we do not now call it a city, yet 'tis equal to many good cities in England, and superior to some. Near this place was fought the bloody battle between Henry Hotspur and Henry IV. King of England, in which the former was kill'd, and all his army overthrown, and the place is call'd Battlefield to this day.

Here are four very fine churches, whereof two St. Chad's and St. Mary's, are said to be anciently collegiate: There are abundance of ancient monuments in them all, but too many to mention here, my journey being too long, and my bounds too short to enter upon the particulars.

This town will for ever be famous for the reception it gave to King Charles the I. who, after setting up his standard at Nottingham, and finding no encouragement there, remov'd to Shrewsbury, being invited by the gentry of the town and country round, where he was receiv'd with such a general affection, and hearty zeal by all the people, that his majesty recover'd the discouragement of his first step at Nottingham, and raised and compleated a strong army in less time than could be imagin'd; insomuch that to the surprize of the Parliament, and indeed of all the world, he was in the field before them, and advanced upon them so fast, that he met them two thirds onward of his way to London, and gave them battle at Edge-hill near Banbury.

But the fate of the war turning afterward against the king, the weight of it fell heavy upon this town also, and almost ruin'd them.

But they are now fully recover'd, and it is at this time one of the most flourishing towns in England: The walls and gates are yet standing, but useless, and the old castle is gone to ruin, as is the case of almost all the old castles in England.

It should not be forgotten here, that notwithstanding the healthyness of the place, one blot lies upon the town of Shrewsbury, and which, tho' nothing can be charg'd on the inhabitants, yet it seems they are the most obliged when 'tis least spoken of; namely, that here broke out first that unaccountable plague, call'd the sweating sickness; which at first baffled all the sons of art, and spread itself through the whole kingdom of England: This happen'd in the year 1551. It afterwards spread itself into Germany, and several countries abroad; But I do not remember that it was ever in Spain or in Italy.

Here is an ancient free-school, the most considerable in this part of England; built and endow'd by Queen Elizabeth, with a very sufficient maintainance for a chief or head-master, and three under-masters or ushers. The buildings are very spacious, and particularly the library is a fine building, and has a great many books in it; but I saw nothing curious or rare among them, and no manuscripts. The school-masters have also very handsome houses to dwell in.

There was a fine school here before, erected by the townspeople, and maintain'd several years by their contribution, and some endowments also it had. But the queen being sensible of the good design of the inhabitants, took the matter into her own hands, and built the whole fabrick new from the ground, endowing it liberally out of her own royal bounty.

Here I was shew'd a very visible and remarkable appearance of the great antient road or way call'd Watling-Street, which comes from London to this town, and goes on from hence to the utmost coast of Wales; where it cross'd the Severn, there are remains of a stone bridge to be seen in the bottom of the river, when the water is low. On this road we set out now for Litchfield in our way towards London; and I would gladly have kept to this old road, if it had been possible, because I knew several remarkable places stood directly upon it. But we were oblig'd to make many excursions, and sometimes quit the street for a great way together: And first we left it to go away south to the edge of Stafford-shire, to see the old house call'd White Ladies, and the royal oak, the famous retreat of King Charles II. after the Battle of Worcester. The tree is surrounded with a palisadoe, to preserve it from the fate which threatned it from curiosity; for almost every body that came to see it for several years, carry'd away a piece of it, so that the tree was litterally in danger not to dye of age, but to be pull'd limb from limb; but the veneration of that kind is much abated, and as the palisadoes are more decay'd than the tree, the latter seems likely to stand safe without them; as for the house, there is nothing remarkable in it; but it being a house always inhabited by Roman Catholicks, it had and perhaps has still some rooms so private in it, that in those times could not have been discover'd without pulling down the whole buildings.

Entring Stafford-shire we quitted the said Street-way, a little to the left, to see Stafford the county town, and the most considerable except Litchfield in the county. In the way we were surpriz'd in a most agreeable manner, passing thro' a small but ancient town call'd Penkrige, vulgarly Pankrage, where happen'd to be a fair. We expected nothing extraordinary; but was I say surpriz'd to see the prodigious number of horses brought hither, and those not ordinary and common draught-horses, and such kinds as we generally see at country-fairs remote from London: But here were really incredible numbers of the finest and most beautiful horses that can any where be seen; being brought hither from Yorkshire, the bishoprick of Durham, and all the horse-breeding countries: We were told that there were not less than an hundred jockies and horse-kopers, as they call them there, from London, to buy horses for sale. Also an incredible number of gentlemen attended with their grooms to buy gallopers, or race-horses, for their Newmarket sport. In a word, I believe I may mark it for the greatest horse-fair in the world, for horses of value, and especially those we call saddle-horses. There are indeed greater fairs for coach-horses, and draught horses; though here were great numbers of fine large stone horses for coaches, &c. too. But for saddle-horses, for the light saddle, hunters, pads, and racers, I believe the world cannot match this fair.

We staid 3 days here to satisfy our curiosity, and indeed the sight was very agreeable, to see what vast stables of horses there were, which never were brought out or shewn in the fair. How dextrous the northern grooms and breeders are in their looking after them, and ordering them: Those fellows take such indefatigable pains with them, that they bring them out like pictures of horses, not a hair amiss in them; they lye constantly in the stables with them, and feed them by weight and measure; keep them so clean, and so fine, I mean in their bodies, as well as their outsides, that, in short, nothing can be more nice. Here were several horses sold for 150 guineas a horse; but then they were such as were famous for the breed, and known by their race, almost as well as the Arabians know the genealogy of their horses.

From hence we came in two hours easy riding to Stafford, on the River Sow; 'tis an old and indeed antient town, and gives name to the county; but we thought to have found something more worth going so much out of the way in it. The town is however neat and well built, and is lately much encreas'd; nay, as some say, grown rich by the cloathing trade, which they have fallen into but within the reach of the present age, and which has not enrich'd this town only, but Tamworth also, and all the country round.

The people of this county have been particularly famous, and more than any other county in England, for good footman-ship, and there have been, and still are among them, some of the fleetest runners in England; which I do not grant to be occasion'd by any particular temperature of the air or soil, so much as to the hardy breed of the inhabitants, especially in the moorlands or northern part of the county, and to their exercising themselves to it from their child-hood; for running foot-races seems to be the general sport or diversion of the country.

Near Stafford we saw Ingestre, where the late Walter Chetwynd, Esq; built or rather rebuilt a very fine church at his own charge, and where the late Lord Chetwynd has with a profusion of expence laid out the finest park and gardens that are in all this part of England, and which, if nothing else was to be seen this way, are very well worth a traveller's curiosity.

I am now at the utmost extent of my limits for this circuit; for Ingestre Parks reach to the very banks of the Trent, which I am not to pass; so I turn'd to the right, and intending for Litchfield, in the way we saw Beaudesert, a famous old seat, said to be built by Hugh Lupus, Earl of Chester: The name indeed intimates it to be of Norman or French original; at present it is in the honourable family of the Pagets, and the Lord Paget is also Baron of Beaudesert. The park is very fine, and its situation exceeding pleasant, but the house is antient; in the park is a famous piece of antiquity, viz. a large entrench'd camp or fortification, surrounded with a double trench, very large and deep; but the inhabitants can give no account of it, that is worth notice.

From hence 'tis about four or five miles to Litchfield, a city, and the principal, next to Chester, of all the N.W. part of England; neither indeed is there any other, but this and Coventry, in the whole road from London to Carlisle on the edge of Scotland.

Here we came into the great Lancashire and Cheshire road, or the N.W. road from London, which passing thro' this city from Warrington Bridge in Cheshire, falls into the Watling-street road, mention'd before, about three miles S.E. from the town, and crosses another antient causway or road, call'd Ickneild-street, about a mile out of the city; so that Litchfield lies as it were at the joining of all those great roads.

Litchfield is a fine, neat, well-built, and indifferent large city; there is a little lake or lough of water in the middle of it, out of which runs a small stream of water, which soon becomes a little rivulet, and save that it has but 4 or 5 miles to the Trent, would soon become a river; This lake parts Litchfield, as it were, into two cities, one is call'd the town, and the other the close; in the first is the market-place, a fine school, and a very handsome hospital well-endow'd. This part is much the largest and most populous: But the other is the fairest, has the best buildings in it, and, among the rest, the cathedral-church, one of the finest and most beautiful in England, especially for the outside, the form and figure of the building, the carv'd work'd, imagery, and the three beautiful spires; the like of which are not to be seen in one church, no not in Europe.

There are two fine causways which join the city and the close, with sluices to let the water pass, but those were cut thro' in the time of the late intestine wars in England; and the closs, which is wall'd about, and was then fortify'd for the king, was very strong, and stood out several vigorous attacks against Cromwell's men, and was not at last taken without great loss of blood on both sides, being gallantly defended to the last drop, and taken by storm.

There are in the close, besides the houses of the clergy residentiaries, a great many very well-built houses, and well inhabited too; which makes Litchfield a place of good conversation and good company, above all the towns in this county or the next, I mean Warwickshire or Darbyshire.

The description of this church would take up much time, and requires a very nice observer. The see is very antient, and was once archiepiscopal, and Eadulp the archbishop was metropolitan of all the kingdom of the Mercians and East Angles, but it did not hold it; then it suffer'd another diminution, by having the see of Chester taken away, which was once part of this of Litchfield.

They told us here a long story of St. Chad, formerly bishop of this church, and how he liv'd in a little hovel or cell in the church-yard, instead of a bishop's palace: But the bishops, since that time, have, I suppose, thought better of it, and make shift with a very fine palace in the closs, and the residentiaries live in proportion to it.

They have another legendary story also at Litchfield; namely, that a thousand poor people being instructed in the Christian faith by the care of Offa King of the Mercians, were all martyr'd here in one field by the Pagans, and that in the field where they were so murder'd, King Oswy of Northumberland caused a great church to be built; and from thence the city bears for its device, a landskip, or open field, with mangled carcasses lying dispers'd about in it, as if murder'd and left unburied: But this I take as I find it.

The church I say is indeed a most beautiful building; the west prospect of it is charming, the two spires on the corner towers being in themselves perfect beauties of architect, in the old Gothic way of building, but made still more shining and glorious by a third spire, which rising from the main tower in the body of the church, surmounts the other two, and shews itself exactly between them.

It is not easy to describe the beauty of the west end; you enter by three large doors in the porch or portico, which is as broad as the whole front; the spaces between the doors are fill'd with carv'd work and imagery, no place being void, where (by the rules of architect) any ornament could be plac'd.

Over the first cornish is a row of statues or images of all the kings which reign'd in Jerusalem from King David to the captivity; but I cannot say that they are all sufficiently distinguish'd one from another: Above there are other images, without number, whose names no account (I could meet with there) could explain.

The great window over the middle door is very large, and the pediment over it finely adorn'd, a large cross finishing the top of it; on either corner of the west front are two very fine towers, not unlike the two towers on the west end of St. Peter's Church at Westminster, only infinitely finer: Even with the battlement of the porch, and adjoining to the towers, are large pinnacles at the outer angles, and on the top of the towers are to each tower eight more, very beautiful and fine; between these pinnacles, on the top of each tower, rises a spire equal in height, in thickness, and in workmanship, but so beautiful no pen can describe them.

The imagery and carv'd work on the front, as above, has suffer'd much in the late unhappy times; and they told us the cross over the west window was frequently shot at by the rude soldiers; but that they could not shoot it down, which however they do not say was miraculous.

The inside of the church also suffer'd very much, but it has been very well repaired since the Restoration, as well by the famous Bishop Hacket, as by the bounty of several noble and generous benefactors.

The *Monasticon* makes mention of a shrine given here for the holy St. Chad, or St. Cedda, which cost 200000l. but I conceive that to smell as much of the legend, as the miracles of St. Chad himself; since such a gift at that time must be equal to two millions of our money.

They tell us the main spire of this church is, from the ground, 385 foot, and the two spires at the angles at the west end each 260.

From Litchfield we came to Tamworth, a fine pleasant trading town, eminent for good ale and good company, of the middling sort; from whence we came into the great road again at Coleshill in Warwickshire.

This is a small but very handsome market-town; it chiefly, if not wholly belongs to the Lord Digby, who is lord of the mannor, if not real owner of almost all the houses in the town, and as that noble person is at present a little on the wrong side as to the government, not having taken the oaths to King George, so the whole town are so eminently that way too, that they told me there was but one family of Whiggs, as they call'd them, in the whole town, and they hoped to drive them out of the place too very quickly.

The late incumbent of this parish quitted his living, which is very considerable, because he would not take the oaths, and his successor was the famous ——— who, when I was there, was newly proscrib'd by proclamation, and the reward of 1000l. order'd to whoever should apprehend him; so their instructors being such, 'tis no wonder the people have follow'd their leader.

From Coles-hill we came to Coventry, the sister city to Litchfield, and join'd in the title of the see, which was for some little time seated here, but afterwards return'd to Litchfield.

It was a very unhappy time when I first came to this city;

for their heats and animosities for election of members to serve in Parliament, were carry'd to such a hight, that all manner of method being laid aside, the inhabitants (in short) enraged at one another, met, and fought a pitch'd battle in the middle of the street, where they did not take up the breadth of the street, as two rabbles of people would generally do; in which case no more could engage, but so many as the breadth of the street would admit in the front; but, on the contrary, the two parties meeting in the street, one party kept to one side of the way, and one side to the other, the kennel in the middle only parting them, and so marching as if they intended to pass by one another, 'till the front of one party was come opposite to the reer of the other, and then suddenly facing to one another, and making a long front, where their flanks were before, upon a shout given, as the signal on both sides, they fell on with such fury with clubs and staves, that in an instant the kennel was cover'd with them, not with slain, but with such as were knock'd down on both sides, and, in a word, they fought with such obstinacy that 'tis scarce credible.

Nor were these the scum and rabble of the town, but in short the burgesses and chief inhabitants, nay even magistrates, aldermen, and the like.

Nor was this one skirmish a decision of the quarrel, but it held for several weeks, and they had many such fights; nor is the matter much better among them to this day, only that the occasion does not happen so often.

Coventry is a large and populous city, and drives a very great trade; the manufacture of tammies is their chief employ, and next to that weaving of ribbons of the meanest kind, chiefly black. The buildings are very old, and in some places much decay'd; the city may be taken for the very picture of the city of London, on the south side of Cheapside before the Great Fire; the timber-built houses, projecting forwards and towards one another, till in the narrow streets they were ready to touch one another at the top.

The tale of the Lady Godiva, who rode naked thro' the High Street of the city to purchase her beloved city of Coventry exemption from taxes, is held for so certain a truth, that they will not have it question'd upon any account whatever; and the picture of the poor fellow that peep'd out of window to see her, is still kept up, looking out of a garret in the High Street of the city: But Mr. Cambden says positively no body look'd at her at all.

There are eleven churches in this city; but three of them are particular ornaments to it, having fine high spires, after the manner of those at Litchfield, but nothing like them for the beauty of the building. Here is no cathedral, as some have falsly said, neither is the great church, so call'd, either collegiate or conventual.

It was indeed a monastry or priory, and, as has been said, the bishop's see was remov'd from Chester hither, but no cathedral was built, for the change was not continued, and the see was soon remov'd to Litchfield, where it continues to this day.

Yet this city contended a great while for it indeed, but could not carry it. In King Henry 8th's time, the priory being dissolv'd, the church which they would have call'd a cathedral, was reduc'd to a private parish-church, and continues so to this day; 'tis an archdeaconry indeed, and the bishop is stiled Bishop of Litchfield and Coventry.

From Coventry we could by no means pass the town of Warwick, the distance too being but about six miles, and a very pleasant way on the banks of the River Avon: 'Tis famous for being the residence of the great Guy Earl of Warwick, known now only by fame, which also has said so much more than the truth of him, that even what was true is become a kind of romance, and the real history of his actions is quite lost to the world.

That there was such a man, no body (I find) makes a question, any more than they do that half of what is said of him is fable and fiction; but be that as it will, they show us here his castle, his helmet, his sword, and tell abundance of things of him, which have some appearance of history, tho' not much authority to support them; so I leave that part to the curious searchers into antiquity, who may consult Mr. Cambden, Rous, Dugdale, and other antiquaries on that subject, who tell us the castle was built before our Saviour's time, and has been a place of great consideration ever since.

As to the town of Warwick, it is really a fine town, pleasantly situated on the bank of the Avon, over which there is a large and stately bridge, the Avon being now grown a pretty large river, Warwick was ever esteem'd a handsome, well-built town, and there were several good houses in it, but the face of it is now quite alter'd; for having been almost wholly reduc'd to a heap of rubbish, by a terrible fire about two and twenty years ago, it is now rebuilt in so noble and so beautiful a manner, that few towns in England make so fine an appearance. The new church also is a fine building, but all the old monuments, which were very many, are entirely defac'd, and lost by the fire: However the memory and even the figure of 'em are eminently preserv'd by Mr. Dugdale, in his *Antiquities* of this county, to which I refer.

The castle is a fine building, beautiful both by situation and its decoration; it stands on a solid rock of free-stone, from whose bowels it may be said to be built, as likewise is the whole town; the terrass of the castle, like that of Windsor, overlooks a beautiful country, and sees the Avon running at the foot of the precipice, at above 50 foot perpendicular hight: the building is old, but several times repair'd and beautify'd by its several owners, and 'tis now a very agreeable place both within and without: the apartments are very nicely contrived, and the communication of the remotest parts of the building, one with another, are so well preserved by galleries, and by the great hall, which is very magnificent, that one finds no irregularity in the whole place, notwithstanding its ancient plan, as it was a castle not a palace, and built for strength rather than pleasure.

The possession of this castle is now in the family of Grevil Lord Brook, but the honour and possession is separated, and has been for some time; the ancient family of Beauchamp, or Bello Campo, E. of Warwick, held it for many ages, from whom 'tis now descended to the Earls of Holland, who are Earls of Holland and also of Warwick. But this by the way.

Here we saw the antient cell or hermitage, where they say the famous Guy Earl of Warwick ended his days in a private retreat for his devotion, and is from him call'd Guy Clift, by others Gibclift; 'tis now, as Mr. Cambden gives an account, which Mr. Dugdale also confirms, the pleasant seat of an antient Norman family of the name of De Beau-foe, whose posterity remain there, and in several other parts of the county, retaining the latter part of their sirname, but without the former to this day. Mr. Dugdale gives the monuments of them, and it appears they removed hither, on account of some marriage, from Seyton in Rutlandshire, where they were lords of the mannor, and patrons of the church, and where several of the name also still remain.

Being at Warwick, I took a short circuit thro' the S.E. part of the county, resolving after viewing a little the places of note, that lay something out of my intended rout, to come back to the same place.

Three miles from Warwick we pass'd over the Foss Way,

which goes on to Leicester; then we came by Southam to Daventry, a considerable market town, but which subsists chiefly by the great concourse of travellers on the old Watling-street way, which lies near it; and the road being turned by modern usage, lies now thro' the town itself, then runs on to Dunsmore Heath, where it crosses the Foss, and one branch goes on to Coventry, the other joins the Foss, and goes on to a place call'd High-Cross, where it falls into the old Watling-street again, and both meet again near Litchfield.

It is a most pleasant curiosity to observe the course of these old famous highways; the Icknild Way, the Watling-street, and the Foss, in which one sees so lively a representation of the antient British, Roman and Saxon governments, that one cannot help reallizing those times to the imagination; and tho' I avoid meddling with antiquity as much as possible in this work, yet in this case a circuit or tour thro' England would be very imperfect, if I should take no notice of these ways, seeing in tracing them we necessarily come to the principal towns, either that are or have been in every county.

From Daventry we cross'd the country to Northampton, the handsomest and best built town in all this part of England; but here, as at Warwick, the beauty of it is owing to its own disasters, for it was so effectually and suddenly burnt down, that very few houses were left standing, and this, tho' the fire began in the day-time; the flame also spread itself with such fury, and run on with such terrible speed, that they tell us a townsman being at Queen's Cross upon a hill, on the south side of the town, about two miles off, saw the fire at one end of the town then newly begun, and that before he could get to the town it was burning at the remotest end, opposite to that there he first saw it; 'tis now finely rebuilt with brick and stone, and the streets made spacious and wide.

The great new church, the town-hall, the jayl, and all their public buildings, are the finest in any country town in England, being all new built: But he took very little notice of North-ampton, or rather had never seen it, who told us of a cathedral, a chapter-house and a cloyster.

The great inn at the George, the corner of the High Street, looks more like a palace than an inn, and cost above 2000*l*. building; and so generous was the owner, that, as we were told, when he had built it, he gave it to the poor of the town.

This is counted the center of all the horse-markets and horse-fairs in England, there being here no less than four fairs in a year: Here they buy horses of all sorts, as well for the saddle as for the coach and cart, but chiefly for the two latter.

Near this town is the ancient royal house of Holmby, which was formerly in great esteem, and by its situation is capable of being made a royal palace indeed. But the melancholy reflection of the imprisonment of King Charles the First in this house, and his being violently taken hence again by the mutinous rebels, has cast a kind of odium upon the place, so that it has been, as it were, forsaken and uninhabited. The house and estate has been lately purchas'd by the Dutchess of Marlborough; but we do not see that the house is like to be built or repair'd, as was at first discours'd; on the contrary it goes daily to decay.

The Earl of Sunderland's house at Althorp, on the other hand, has within these few years changed its face to the other extreme, and had the late earl liv'd to make some new apartments, which, as we were told, were design'd as two large wings to the buildings, it would have been one of the most magnificent palaces in Europe. The gardens are exquisitely fine, and add, if it be possible, to the natural beauty of the situation.

From hence we went north to Harborough, and in the way, in the midst of the deep dismal roads, the dirtyest and worst in all that part of the country, we saw Boughton, the noble seat of the Duke of Mountague, a house built at the cost and by the fancy of the late duke, very much after the model of the Palace of Versailles; the treble wings projecting and expanded, forming a court or space wider and wider, in proper stades, answerable to the wings, the body of the house closing the whole view.

The pavillions are also after the manner of Versailles; the house itself is very large and magnificent, but the situation facing so beautiful a park adds to the glory of it; the park is wall'd round with brick, and so finely planted with trees, and in such an excellent order, as I saw nothing more beautiful, no not in Italy itself, except that the walks of trees were not orange and limon, and citron, as it is in Naples, and the Abruzzo, and other southern parts of Italy.

Here they shew'd us a petrifying spring, and told us so many stories of its turning every thing that was laid in it into stone, that we began to discredit the tale as fabulous; but I have been assur'd, that the water of this spring does really petrify, and that in such a manner as deserves the observation of the curious.

From hence we went on to Harborough intending to go forward to Leicester; but curiosity turn'd us west a little to see an old town call'd Lutterworth, famous for being the birth-place of honest John Wickliff, the first preacher of the Reformation in England, whose disciples were afterwards called Lollards; when we came there we saw nothing worth notice, nor did the people, as I could find, so much as know in general, that this great man was born amongst them.

Being thus got a little out of our way, we went on with it, and turning into the great Watling-street way, at High Cross, where the Foss crosses it, and which I suppose occasioned the name, we kept on the street way to Non-Eaton, a manufacturing town on the River Anker, and then to Atherstone, a town famous for a great cheese fair on the 8th of September; from whence the great cheese factors carry the vast quantities of cheese they buy to Sturbridge Fair, which begins about the same time, but holds much longer; and here 'tis sold again for the supply of the counties of Essex, Suffolk, and Norfolk.

From Atherston we turn'd N. to see Bosworth-Field, famous for the great battle which put an end to the usurpation of Richard III. and to the long and bloody contention between the red rose and the white, or the two royal houses of York and Lancaster, which, as fame tells us, had cost the lives of eleven princes, three and twenty earls and dukes, three thousand noblemen, knights, and gentlemen, and two hundred thousand of the common people: They shew'd us the spot of ground where the battle was fought, and at the town they shew'd us several pieces of swords, heads of lances, barbs of arrows, pieces of pole-axes, and such like instruments of death, which they said were found by the country people in the several grounds near the place of battle, as they had occasion to dig, or trench, or plough up the ground.

Having satisfy'd our curiosity in these points, we turn'd east towards Leicester. The E. of Stamford has a good old hunting seat on this side of the country, call'd Bradgate, and a fine park at Grooby; but they were too much out of our way, so we came on through a fine forest to Leicester.

Leicester is an ancient large and populous town, containing about five parishes, 'tis the capital of the county of Leicester, and stands on the River Soar, which rises not far from that High Cross I mention'd before: They have a considerable manufacture carry'd on here, and in several of the market towns round for weaving of stockings by frames; and one would scarce think it possible so small an article of trade could employ such multitudes of people as it does; for the whole county seems to be employ'd in it: as also Nottingham and Darby, of which hereafter.

Warwickshire and Northamptonshire are not so full of antiquities, large towns, and gentlemens seats, but this county of Leicester is as empty. The whole county seems to be taken up in country business, such as the manufacture above, but particularly in breeding and feeding cattle; the largest sheep and horses in England are found here, and hence it comes to pass too, that they are in consequence a vast magazine of wool for the rest of the nation; even most of the gentlemen are grasiers, and in some places the grasiers are so rich, that they grow gentlemen: 'tis not an uncommon thing for grasiers here to rent farms from 500*l.* to two thousand pounds a year rent.

The sheep bred in this county and Lincolnshire, which joins to it, are, without comparison, the largest, and bear not only the greatest weight of flesh on their bones, but also the greatest fleeces of wool on their backs of any sheep of England: nor is the fineness of the wool abated for the quantity; but as 'tis the longest staple, (so the clothiers call it) so 'tis the finest wool in the whole island, some few places excepted, such as Lemster in Herefordshire, the South Downs in Sussex, and such little places, where the quantity is small and insignificant, compar'd to this part of the country; for the sheep-breeding country reaches from the River Anker on the border of Warwickshire to the Humber at the farthest end of Lincolnshire, which is near a hundred miles in length, and from the bank of Trent in Lincoln and Leicestershire, to the bank of Ouse bordering Bucks, Bedford, Cambridge, and Huntingdonshires, above sixty miles in breadth.

These are the funds of sheep which furnish the city of London with their large mutton in so incredible a quantity: There are indeed a few sheep of a large breed, which are brought up from Rumney Marsh, and the adjoining low grounds in Kent and Sussex, but they are but few, and indeed scarce worth naming, compar'd to the vast quantity, which are produced in these counties.

The horses produced here, or rather fed here, are the largest in England, being generally the great black coach horses and dray horses, of which so great a number are continually brought up to London, that one would think so little a spot as this of Leicestershire could not be able to supply them: Nor indeed are they all bred in this county, the adjoining counties of Northampton and Bedford having of late come into the same business; but the chief supply is from this county, from whence the other counties rather buy them and feed them up, as jockeys and chapmen, than breed them up from their beginning.

In the south west part of the country rise four considerable second rate rivers, which run every one a directly contrary course in a most remarkable manner.

1. The Avon, which runs by Rugby, and goes away to Warwick; SOUTH WEST.

2. The Soar, which runs by Leicester, and goes away to the Trent; NORTH EAST.

3. The Anker, which runs by Nun-Eaton, and goes away to Tamworth; NORTH WEST.

4. The Welland, which runs by Harborough, and goes away to Stamford; SOUTH WEST.

I should not pass over this just remark of the town, or, as Mr. Cambden calls it, city of Leicester, namely, that as it was formerly a very strong and well fortify'd town, being situated to great advantage for strength, the river compassing it half about, so it was again fortify'd in the late unhappy wars, and being garrison'd by the Parliament forces, was assaulted by the Royalists, and being obstinately defended, was taken sword in hand, with a great slaughter, and not without the loss also of several of the inhabitants, who too rashly concern'd themselves in opposing the conquerors. They preserve here a most remarkable piece of antiquity, being a piece of mosaick work at the bottom of a cellar; 'tis the story of Actæon, and his being kill'd by his own hounds, wrought as a pavement in a most exquisite manner; the stones are small, and of only two colours, white and brown, or chesnut, and very small.

The great Henry Duke of Lancaster, and the earl his father lye both bury'd in this town, in the hospital church, without the south gate, which church and hospital also the said duke was the founder of; but there is no monument to be found that shews the particular place of their interment.

The Foss Way leads us from hence through the eastern and north east part of the county, and particularly through the vale of Belvoir, or, as it is commonly call'd, of Bever, to Newark in Nottinghamshire: In all this long tract we pass a rich and fertile country, fruitful fields, and the noble River Trent, for twenty miles together, often in our view; the towns of Mount Sorrel, Loughborough, Melton Mowbray, and Waltham in the Would, that is to say, on the Downs; all these are market towns, but of no great note.

Belvoir Castle is indeed a noble situation, tho' on a very high precipice; 'tis the antient seat of the Dukes of Rutland, a family risen by just degrees to an immense state both of honour and wealth. I shall mention the house again in my return out of Lincolnshire.

At Newark one can hardly see without regret the ruins of that famous castle, which maintain'd itself through the whole Civil War in England, and keeping a strong garrison there for the king to the last, cut off the greatest pass into the north that is in the whole kingdom; nor was it ever taken, 'till the king, press'd by the calamity of his affairs, put himself into the hands of the Scots army, which lay before it, and then commanded the governor to deliver it up, after which it was demolish'd, that the great road might lye open and free; and it remains in rubbish to this day. Newark is a very handsome well-built town, the market place a noble square, and the church is large and spacious, with a curious spire, which, were not Grantham so near, might pass for the finest and highest in all this part of England: The Trent divides itself here, and makes an island, and the bridges lead just to the foot of the castle wall; so that while this place was in the hands of any party, there was no travelling but by their leave; But all the travelling into the north at that time was by Nottingham Bridge, of which by itself.

From Newark, still keeping the Foss Way, which lies as strait as a line can mark it out, we went on to Lincoln, having a view of the great church call'd the minster all the way before us, the River Trent on the left, and the downs call'd Lincoln Heath on the right.

Lincoln is an antient, ragged, decay'd, and still decaying city; it is so full of the ruins of monasteries and religious houses, that, in short, the very barns, stables, out-houses, and, as they shew'd me, some of the very hog-styes, were built church-fashion; that is to say, with stone walls and arch'd windows and doors. There are here 13 churches, but the meanest to look on that are any where to be seen; the cathedral indeed and the ruins of the old castle are very venerable pieces of antiquity.

The situation of the city is very particular; one part is on the flat and in a bottom, so that the Wittham, a little river that runs through the town, flows sometimes into the street, the other part lies upon the top of a high hill, where the cathedral stands, and the very steepest part of the ascent of the hill is the best part of the city for trade and business.

Nothing is more troublesome than the communication of the

upper and lower town, the street is so steep and so strait, the coaches and horses are oblig'd to fetch a compass another way, as well on one hand as on the other.

The River Wittham, which as I said runs thro' the city, is arch'd over, so that you see nothing of it as you go thro' the main street; but it makes a large lake on the west side, and has a canal, by which it has a communication with the Trent, by which means the navigation of the Trent is made useful for trade to the city; this canal is called the Foss-dike.

There are some very good buildings, and a great deal of very good company, in the upper city, and several families of gentlemen have houses there, besides those of the prebendaries and other clergy belonging to the cathedral.

This cathedral is in itself a very noble structure, and is counted very fine, though I thought it not equal to some that I have already describ'd, particularly not to that at Litchfield: Its situation indeed is infinitely more to advantage, than any cathedral in England, for it is seen far and wide; it stands upon an exceeding high hill, and is seen into five or six counties.

The building in general is very noble, and the church itself is very large; it has a double cross, one in the nave or center on which the great tower stands, and one at the east end of the choir, under which are several antient monuments; the length of the church is near 500 foot, the breadth 126; so that it is much larger than that at Litchfield; but the spires on the towers at the angles of the west end are mean, small, and low, and not to be nam'd with those at Litchfield: The tower also is very plain, and has only four very ill-proportion'd spires, or rather pinnacles, at the four corners small and very mean.

As the church is very large, so the revenue of the bishoprick is large also, and was formerly immensely great, as may be seen by the *Monasticon*, where there is an astonishing account of the wealth of the place.

The church, as it is the seat of the bishoprick, is not antient, the see being remov'd, since the Norman Conquest, from Dorchester, a little town in Oxfordshire, on the River Thames, not far from Tame, of which I have spoken in its place; but the city is antient, and the ruins of it tell us as much; it was certainly a flourishing city in the time of the Romans, and continued so after the fall of their empire.

Mr. Cambden says King Vortimer, that valiant Britain, dy'd here, and was bury'd in the church of the great monastery; but we see nothing of his remains in the cathedral, for that was not built 'till several ages after.

The city was a large and flourishing place at the time of the Norman Conquest, tho' neither the castle or the great church were then built; there were then three and fifty parish churches in it, of which I think only thirteen remain; the chief extent of the city then was from the foot of the hill south, and from the lake or lough which is call'd Swanpool east; and by the Domesday Book they tell us it must be one of the greatest cities in England, whence perhaps that old English proverbial line:

> Lincoln was, London is, and York shall be.

It is certain William the Conqueror built the castle, and, as 'tis said, to curb the potent citizens; and the ruins show that it was a most magnificent work, well fortify'd, and capable of receiving a numerous garrison.

The bishoprick of Lincoln at that time contain'd all that now is contain'd in the dioceses of Ely, Peterborough, and Oxford, besides what is now the diocess of Lincoln: and 'tis still the largest diocess, tho' not of the greatest revenue, in England; containing the several counties of Lincoln, Leicester, Huntingdon, Bedford, Bucks, and part of Hertford; and in them 1255 parishes, whereof 577 are impropriations; and there are in this bounds six arch-deacons, viz. Lincoln, Leicester, Bedford, Buckingham, Stow, and Huntington. This see, tho' of no longer date than since the conquest, has produced to the Church and State

> Three Saints,
> One Cardinal, (namely Wolsey)
> Six Lord Chancellors,
> One Lord Treasurer,
> One Lord Privy Seal,
> Four Chancellors of Oxford,
> Two ditto, of Cambridge.

Here was the famous battle fought between the friends of the Empress Maud, mother to Henry II. and King Stephen, in which that magnanimous prince was overthrown and taken prisoner.

But all this relates to times past, and is an excursion, which I shall attone for by making no more. Such is the present state of Lincoln, that it is an old dying, decay'd, dirty city; and except that part, which, as above, lies between the castle and the church, on the top of the hill, it is scarce tolerable to call it a city.

Yet it stands in a most rich, pleasant, and agreeable country; for on the north, and again on the south east, the noble plain, call'd Lincoln Heath, extends itself, like the plains about Salisbury, for above fifty miles; namely, from Sleeford and Ancaster south to the bank of the Humber north, tho' not with a breadth equal to the vast stretch'd out length; for the plain is hardly any where above three or four miles broad.

On the west side of this plain, the Trent waters a pleasant and rich valley, running from Newark to Gainsborough, a town of good trade, as well foreign as home trade, thence to Burton, and so into the Humber.

As the middle of the country is all hilly, and the west side low, so the east side is the richest, most fruitful, and best cultivated of any county in England, so far from London; one part is all fen or marsh grounds, and extends itself south to the Isle of Ely, and here it is that so vast a quantity of sheep are fed, as makes this county and that of Leicester an inexhaustible fountain of wool for all the manufacturing counties in England.

There are abundance of very good towns too in this part, especially on the sea coast, as Grimsby, in the utmost point of the county north east, facing the Humber and the ocean, and almost opposite to Hull: a little farther within Humber is Barton, a town noted for nothing that I know of, but an ill-favoured dangerous passage, or ferry, over the Humber to Hull; where in an open boat, in which we had about fifteen horses, and ten or twelve cows, mingled with about seventeen or eighteen passengers, call'd Christians; we were about four hours toss'd about on the Humber, before we could get into the harbour at Hull; whether I was sea-sick or not, is not worth notice, but that we were all sick of the passage, any one may suppose, and particularly I was so uneasy at it, that I chose to go round by York, rather than return to Barton, at least for that time.

Grimsby is a good town, but I think 'tis but an indifferent road for shipping; and in the great storm, (ann. 1703.) it was proved to be so, for almost all the ships that lay in Grimsby road were driven from their anchors, and many of them lost.

Here within land we see Brigg upon the River Ankam, Castor, Louth, Horncastle, Bolingbroke, Spilsby, Wainfleet, and Boston: As these are all, except the last, inland towns, they afford little remarkable, only to intimate that all this country is employ'd in husbandry, in breeding and feeding innumerable droves and flocks of black cattle and sheep: Indeed I should not have said black cattle. I should have call'd them red cattle; for it was remarkable, that almost all their cows for 50 miles together are red, or py'd red and white, and consequently all the cattle raised there, are the same; what they feed which are brought from other counties, (for the fens feed infinite numbers which they buy from other places); that (I say) is another case.

The Fen Country begins about Wainfleet, which is within twenty miles of Grimsby, and extends itself to the Isle of Ely south, and to the grounds opposite to Lynn Regis in Norfolk east.

This part is indeed very properly call'd Holland, for 'tis a flat, level, and often drowned country, like Holland itself; here the very ditches are navigable, and the people pass from town to town in boats, as in Holland: Here we had the uncouth musick of the bittern, a bird formerly counted ominous and presaging, and who, as fame tells us, (but as I believe no body knows) thrusts its bill into a reed, and then gives the dull, heavy groan or sound, like a sigh, which it does so loud, that with a deep base, like the sound of a gun at a great distance, 'tis heard two or three miles, (say the people) but perhaps not quite so far.

Here we first saw Boston, a handsome well-built sea port town, at the mouth of the River Wittham. The tower of this church is, without question, the largest and highest in England; and, as it stands in a country, which (they say) has no bottom, nothing is more strange, than that they should find a foundation for so noble and lofty a structure; it had no ornament, spire, or pinnacle on the top, but it is so very high, that few spires in England, can match it, and is not only beautiful by land, but is very useful at sea to guide pilots into that port, and even into the mouth of the River Ouse; for in clear weather 'tis seen quite out at sea to the entrance of those channels, which they call Lynn Deeps, and Boston Deeps, which are as difficult places as most upon the whole eastern shore of Britain.

The town of Boston is a large, populous, and well-built town, full of good merchants, and has a good share of foreign trade, as well as Lynn. Here is held one of those annual fairs, which preserve the antient title of a Mart, whereof I remember only four in England of any considerable note, viz. Lynn, Gainsborough, Beverly, and Boston.

The country round this place is all fenn and marsh grounds, the land very rich, and which feeds prodigious numbers of large sheep, and also oxen of the largest size, the overplus and best of which goes all to London market; and from this part, as also from the downs or heath above-mentioned, comes the greatest part of the wool, known, as a distinction for its credit, because of its fineness, by the name of Lincolnshire Wool; which is sent in great quantities into Norfolk and Suffolk, for the manufacturers of those counties, and indeed to several other of the most trading counties in England.

These fens are indeed very considerable for their extent, for they reach in length in some places fifty miles, and in breadth above thirty: and as they are so level that there is no interruption to the sight, any building of extraordinary hight is seen a long way; for example, Boston steeple is seen upon Lincoln Heath near thirty miles, Peterborough and Ely minsters are seen almost throughout the whole level, so are the spires of Lynn, Whittlesea, and Crowland, seen at a very great distance, which adds a beauty to the country.

From Boston we came on through the fen country to Spalding, which is another sea port in the level, but standing far within the land on the River Welland. Here was nothing very remarkable to be seen as to antiquity, but the ruins of an old famous monastry, of which the *Monasticon* gives a particular description. There is a bridge over the Welland, and vessels of about fifty or sixty ton may come up to the town, and that is sufficient for the trade of Spalding, which is chiefly in corn and coal.

We must not pass by Crowland, another place of great religious antiquity, here being once a famous monastry, the remains of which are still to be seen: The monks of Crowland were eminent in history, and a great many stories are told of the devils of Crowland also, and what conversation they had with the monks, which tales are more out of date now, than they were formerly; for they tell us, that in antient times those things were as certainly believ'd for truths, as if they had been done before their faces.

There is one thing here that is curious indeed, and very remarkable, and which is not to be seen in any other place in Britain, if it be in Europe; namely, a triangular bridge: The case is this; The River Welland and another river, or rather branch from the River Nyne, join together just at Crowland, and the bridge being fixed at the very point where they join, stands upon a center in the middle of the united waters, and then parting into two bridges, lands you one to the right upon Thorney, and one to the left upon Holland; and yet they tell us there is a whirlpool, or bottomless pit, in the middle too; but that part I see no reason to give credit to.

The town of Spalding is not large, but pretty well built and well inhabited; but for the healthyness or pleasantness of it, I have no more to say than this, that I was very glad when I got out of it, and out of the rest of the fen country; for 'tis a horrid air for a stranger to breathe in.

The history of the draining those fens, by a set of gentlemen call'd the Adventurers, the several laws for securing and preserving the banks, and dividing the lands; how they were by the extraordinary conflux of waters from all the inland counties of England frequently overflow'd, and sometimes lay under water most part of the year; how all the water in this part of England, which does not run into the Thames, the Trent, or the Severn, falls together into these low grounds, and empty themselves into the sea by those drains, as thro' a sink; and how by the skill of these Adventurers, and, at a prodigious expence, they have cut new channels, and even whole rivers, with particular drains from one river to another, to carry off the great flux of waters, when floods or freshes come down either on one side or on the other; and how notwithstanding all that hands could do, or art contrive, yet sometimes the waters do still prevail, the banks break, and whole levels are overflow'd together; all this, tho' it would be very useful and agreeable to have it fully and geographically describ'd, yet it would take up so much room, and be so tedious here, where you are expecting a summary description of things, rather than the history and reasons of them, that I cannot think of entering any farther into it.

I have only to add, that these fens of Lincolnshire are of the same kind with, and contiguous to those already mentioned in the Isle of Ely, in the counties of Cambridge and Huntingdon, and that here as well as there, we see innumerable numbers of cattle, which are fed up to an extraordinary size by the richness of the soil.

Here are also an infinite number of wild fowl, such as duck and mallard, teal and widgeon, brand geese, wild geese, &c. and for the taking of the four first kinds, here are a great number of decoys or duckoys, call them which you please, from all which the vast number of fowls they take are sent up to London; the quantity indeed is incredible, and the accounts which the country people give of the numbers they sometimes take, are such, that one scarce dares to report it from them. But this I can say, of my certain knowledge, that some of these decoys are of so great an extent, and take such great quantities of fowl, that they are let for great sums of money by the year, viz. from 100l. to 3, 4, and 500l. a year rent.

The art of taking the fowls, and especially of breeding up a set of creatures, call'd decoy ducks, to entice and then betray their fellow-ducks into the several decoys, is very admirable indeed, and deserves a description; tho' 'tis not very easy to describe it, take it in as few words as I can.

The decoy ducks are first naturalised to the place, for they are hatch'd and bred up in the decoy ponds: There are in the ponds certain places where they are constantly fed, and where being made tame, they are used to come even to the decoy man's hand for their food.

When they fly abroad, or, as might be said, are sent abroad, they go none knows where; but 'tis believ'd by some they fly quite over the seas in Holland and Germany; There they meet with others of their acquaintance, that is to say, of their own kind, where sorting with them, and observing how poorly they live, how all the rivers are frozen up, and the lands cover'd with snow, and that they are almost starv'd, they fail not to let them know, (in language that they make one another understand) that in England, from whence they came, the case is quite alter'd; that the English ducks live much better than they do in those cold climates; that they have open lakes, and sea shores full of food, the tides flowing freely into every creek; that they have also within the land, large lakes, refreshing springs of water, open ponds, covered and secured from human eyes, with large rows of grown trees and impenetrable groves; that the lands are full of food, the stubbles yielding constant supplies of corn, left by the negligent husbandmen, as it were on purpose for their use, that 'tis not once in a wild duck's age, that they have any long frosts or deep snows, and that when they have, yet the sea is never frozen, or the shores void of food; and that if they will please but to go with them into England, they shall share with them in all these good things.

By these representations, made in their own duck language, (or by whatever other arts which we know not) they draw together a vast number of the fowls, and, in a word, kidnap them from their own country; for being once brought out of their knowledge, they follow the decoys, as a dog follows the huntsman; and 'tis frequent to see these subtle creatures return with a vast flight of fowls with them, or at their heels, as we may say, after the said decoy ducks have been absent several weeks together.

When they have brought them over, the first thing they do is to settle with them in the decoy ponds, to which they (the decoy ducks) belong: Here they chatter and gabble to them, in their own language, as if they were telling them, that these are the ponds they told them of, and here they should soon see how well they should live, how secure and how safe a retreat they had here.

When the decoy-men perceive they are come, and that they are gathering and encreasing, they fail not to go secretly to the pond's side, I say secretly, and under the cover which they have made with reeds, so that they cannot be seen, where they throw over the reeds handfuls of corn, in shallow places, such where the decoy ducks are usually fed, and where they are sure to come for it, and to bring their new guests with them for their entertainment.

This they do for two or three days together, and no harm follows, 'till throwing in this bait one time in an open wide place, another time in another open wide place, the third time it is thrown in a narrower place; that is to say, where the trees, which hang over the water and the banks, stand nearer, and then in another yet narrower, where the said trees are overhead like an arbour, though at a good hight from the water.

Here the boughs are so artfully managed, that a large net is spread near the tops of the trees among the branches, and fasten'd to hoops which reach from side to side: This is so high and so wide, and the room is so much below, and the water so open, that the fowls do not perceive the net above them at all.

Here the decoy-man keeping unseen, behind the hedges of reeds, which are made perfectly close, goes forward, throwing corn over the reeds into the water; the decoy ducks greedily fall upon it, and calling their foreign guests, seem to tell them, that now they may find their words good, and how well the ducks live in England; so inviting or rather wheedling them forward, 'till by degrees they are all gotten under the arch or sweep of the net, which is on the trees, and which by degrees, imperceptibly to them, declines lower and lower, and also narrower and narrower, 'till at the farther end it comes to a point like a purse; though this farther end is quite out of sight, and perhaps two or three hundred yards from the first entrance

When the whole quantity are thus greedily following the leading ducks or decoys, and feeding plentifully as they go; and the decoy-man sees they are all within the arch of the net, and so far within as not to be able to escape, on a sudden a dog, which 'till then he keeps close by him, and who is perfectly taught his business, rushes from behind the reeds, and jumps into the water, swimming directly after the ducks, and (terribly to them) barking as he swims.

Immediately the ducks (frighted to the last degree) rise upon the wing to make their escape, but to their great surprize, are beaten down again by the arched net, which is over their heads: Being then forced into the water, they necessarily swim forward, for fear of that terrible creature the dog; and thus they crowd on, 'till by degrees the net growing lower and narrower, as is said, they are hurried to the very farther end, where another decoy-man stands ready to receive them, and who takes them out alive with his hands.

As for the traytors, that drew the poor ducks into this snare, they are taught to rise but a little way, and so not reaching to the net, they fly back to the ponds, and make their escape; or else, being used to the decoy-man, they go to him fearless, and are taken out as the rest; but instead of being kill'd with them, are strok'd, made much of, and put into a little pond just by him, and fed and made much of for their services.

There are many particulars in the managing and draining these levels, throwing off the water by mills and engines, and cultivating the grounds in an unusual manner, which would be very useful to be describ'd; but the needful brevity of this work will not admit of it: yet something may be touch'd at.

1. That here are some wonderful engines for throwing up water, and such as are not to be seen any where else, whereof one in particular threw up, (as they assur'd us) twelve hundred ton of water in half an hour, and goes by wind-sails, 12 wings or sails to a mill: This I saw the model of, but I must own I did not see it perform.

2. Here are the greatest improvements by planting of hemp, that, I think, is to be seen in England; particularly on the Norfolk and Cambridge side of the Fens, as about Wisbech, Well, and several other places, where we saw many hundred acres of ground bearing great crops of hemp.

3. Here is a particular trade carry'd on with London, which is no where else practis'd in the whole kingdom, that I have met with, or heard of, (viz.) For carrying fish alive by land-carriage; this they do by carrying great buts fill'd with water

in waggons, as the carriers draw other goods: The buts have a little square flap, instead of a bung, about ten, twelve, or fourteen inches square, which, being open'd, gives air to the fish, and every night, when they come to the inn, they draw off the water, and let more fresh and sweet water run into them again. In these carriages they chiefly carry tench and pike, pearch and eels, but especially tench and pike, of which here are some of the largest in England.

Whittlesea and Ramsey meres are two lakes, made by the River Nyne or Nene, which runs through them; the first is between five and six miles long, and three or four miles broad, and is indeed full of excellent fish for this trade.

From the Fenns, longing to be deliver'd from fogs and stagnate air, and the water of the colour of brew'd ale, like the rivers of the Peak, we first set foot on dry land, as I call'd it, at Peterborough.

This is a little city, and indeed 'tis the least in England; for Bath, or Wells, or Ely, or Carlisle, which are all call'd cities, are yet much bigger; yet Peterborough is no contemptible place neither; there are some good houses in it, and the streets are fair and well-built; but the glory of Peterborough is the cathedral, which is truly fine and beautiful; the building appears to be more modern, than the story of the raising this pile implies, and it wants only a fine tower steeple, and a spire on the top of it, as St. Paul's at London had, or as Salisbury still has; I say, it wants this only to make it the finest cathedral in Britain, except St. Paul's, which is quite new, and the church of St. Peter at York.

In this church was bury'd the body of the unhappy Mary Queen of Scots, mother to King James the First, who was beheaded not far off in Fotheringay Castle in the same county; but her body was afterwards remov'd by King James the First, her son, into Westminster Abbey, where a monument is erected for her, in King Henry the VIIth's chappel; tho' some do not stick to tell us, that tho' the monument was erected, the body was never remov'd.

Here also lies interred another unhappy queen, namely, the Lady Katherine of Spain, the divorc'd wife of King Henry VIII. and mother to Queen Mary: who reigned immediately after King Edward VI. Her monument is not very magnificent, but 'tis far from mean. Here is an old decay'd monument of

Bishop Wulfer, the founder of the church; but this church has so often been burnt and demolish'd, since that time, that 'tis doubtful when they shew it you, whether it be authentick or not.

The chappel here, call'd St. Mary's, is a very curious building, tho' now not in use; the choir has been often repair'd and beautify'd, and is now very fine; but the west end, or great gate, is a prodigy for its beauty and variety: 'Tis remarkable, that as this church, when a monastry, was famous for its great revenues, so now, as reduced, 'tis one of the poorest bishopricks in England, if not the meanest.

Coming to this little city landed us in Northamptonshire; but as great part of Lincolnshire, which is a vastly extended large county, remain'd yet unseen, we were oblig'd to turn north from Peterborough, and take a view of the fens again, though we kept them at some distance too. Here we pass'd the Welland at Market Deeping, an old, ill-built and dirty town; then we went thro' Bourn to Folkingham, near which we saw two pieces of decay'd magnificence; one was the old demolish'd monastry of Sempringham, the seat of the Gilbertine nuns, so famous for austerity, and the severest rules, that any other religious order have yielded to, and the other was the antient house of the Lord Clinton, Queen Elizabeth's admiral, where that great and noble person once liv'd in the utmost splendor and magnificence; the house, tho' in its full decay, shows what it has been, and the plaister of the cielings and walls in some rooms is so fine, so firm, and so entire, that they break it off in large flakes, and it will bear writing on it with a pencil or steel pen, like the leaves of a table book. This sort of plaister I have not seen anywhere so very fine, except in the palace of Nonesuch in Surrey, near Epsom, before it was demolish'd by the Lord Berkeley.

From hence we cross'd part of the great heath mentioned before, and came into the high road again at Ankaster, a small but antient Roman village, and full of remnants of antiquity: This town gives now the title of duke to the ancient family of Lindsey, now Dukes of Ankaster, formerly only Earls of Lindsey, and hereditary Lords Chamberlains of England.

This place and Panton, a village near it, would afford great subject of discourse, if antiquity was my present province, for here are found abundance of Roman coins, urns, and other remains of antiquity, as also in several parts here about; and Mr. Cambden puts it out of doubt, that at this town of Ankaster there was a station or colony settled of Romans, which afterwards swell'd up into a city, but is now sunk again out of knowledge.

From hence we came to Grantham, famous for a very fine church and spire steeple, so finely built, and so very high, that I do not know many higher and finer built in Britain. The vulgar opinion, that this steeple stands leaning, is certainly a vulgar error: I had no instrument indeed to judge it by, but, according to the strictest observation, I could not perceive it, or anything like it, and am much of opinion with that excellent poet:

'Tis hight makes Grantham steeple stand awry.

This is a neat, pleasant, well-built and populous town, has a good market, and the inhabitants are said to have a very good trade, and are generally rich. There is also a very good free-school here. This town lying on the great northern road is famous, as well as Stamford, for abundance of very good inns, some of them fit to entertain persons of the greatest quality and their retinues, and it is a great advantage to the place.

From a hill, about a mile beyond this town north west, being on the great York road, we had a prospect again into the Vale of Bever, or Belvoir, which I mentioned before; and which spreads itself here into 3 counties, to wit, Lincoln, Leicester, and Rutlandshires: also here we had a distant view of Bever, or Bellevoir Castle, which 'tis supposed took its name from the situation, from whence there is so fine a prospect, or Bellevoir over the country; so that you see from the hill into six counties, namely, into Lincoln, Nottingham, Darby, Leicester, Rutland, and Northampton Shires. The castle or palace (for such it now is) of Bevoir, is now the seat of the noble family of Mannors, Dukes of Rutland, who have also a very noble estate, equal to the demesnes of some sovereign princes, and extending itself into Nottingham and Darbyshire far and wide, and in which estate they have an immense subterranean treasure, never to be exhausted; I mean the lead mines and coal-pits, of which I shall say more in its place.

Turning southward from hence we enter'd Rutlandshire, remarkable for being the least county in England, having but two market towns in it, viz. Okeham and Uppingham, but famous for abundance of fine seats of the gentlemen, and some of the first rank, as particularly the Earls of Gainsborough and Nottingham; the latter has at a very great expence, and some years labour, rebuilt the ancient seat of Burleigh on the Hill, near Okeham, and on the edge of the vale of Cathross. This house would indeed require a volume of itself, to describe the pleasant situation, and magnificent structure, the fine gardens, the perfectly well-finish'd apartments, the curious paintings, and well-stor'd library: all these merit a particular view, and consequently an exact description; but it is not the work of a few pages, and it would be to lessen the fame of this palace, to say any thing by way of abstract, where every part calls for a full account: at present, all I can say of it is, there may be some extraordinary palaces in England, where there are so many fine ones, I say there may be some that excell in this or that particular, but I do not know a house in Britain, which excels all the rest in so many particulars, or that goes so near to excelling them all in every thing. Take something of it in the following lines, part of a poem, written wholly upon the subject, by an anonymous author.

ON THE EARL OF NOTTINGHAM'S HOUSE AT BURLEIGH ON THE HILL, IN RUTLANDSHIRE

Hail, happy fabrick! whose majestick view
First sees the sun, and bids him last adieu;
Seated in majesty, your eye commands
A royal prospect of the richest lands,
Whose better part, by your own lord possess'd,
May well be nam'd the crown of all the rest:
The under-lying vale shews with delight
A thousand beauties, at one charming sight;
No pencil's art can such a landskip feign,
And Nature's self scarce yields the like again:
Few situations may with this compare,
A fertile soil and a salubrious air.

Triumphant structure! while you thus aspire
From the dead ruin of rebellious fire;
Methinks I see the genius of the place
Advance its head, and, with a smiling face,
Say, Kings have on this spot made their abodes,
'Tis fitted now to entertain the GODS.

From hence we came to Stamford; the town is placed in a kind of an angle of the county of Lincoln, just upon the edge of three counties, viz. Lincoln, Northampton, and Rutland: this town boasts greatly too of its antiquity, and indeed it has evident marks of its having been a very great place in former days.

History tells us it was burnt by the Danes above 1500 years ago, being then a flourishing city: Tradition tells us, it was once a university, and that the schools were first erected by Bladud

King of the Britains; the same whose figure stands up at the King's Bath in the city of Bath, and who liv'd 300 years before our Saviour's time: But the famous camps and military ways, which still appear at and near this town, are a more visible testimony of its having been a very ancient town, and that it was considerable in the Romans time.

It is at this time a very fair, well-built, considerable and wealthy town, consisting of six parishes, including that of St. Martin in Stamford-Baron; that is to say, in that part of the town which stands over the river, which, tho' it is not a part of the town, critically speaking, being not in the liberty, and in another county, yet 'tis all called Stamford, and is rated with it in the taxes, and the like.

This town is the property, as it may be called, of the Earles of Excester; for the author of the *Survey of Stamford*, page 15, says, "William Cecil, Baron Burleigh, and afterwards Earl of Excester, obtain'd the fee farm of Queen Elizabeth for himself, in whose posterity it yet remains."

The government of this town is not, it seems, as most towns of such note are, by a mayor and aldermen, but by an alderman, who is chief magistrate, and twelve comburgesses, and twenty four capital burgesses, which, abating their worships titles, is, to me, much the same thing as a mayor, aldermen, and common council.

They boast in this town of very great privileges, especially to their alderman, who is their chief magistrate, and his comburgesses; such as being freed from the sheriffs jurisdiction, and from being empannel'd on juries out of the town; to have the return of all writs, to be freed from all lords lieutenants, and from their musters, and for having the militia of the town commanded by their own officers, the alderman being the king's Lord Lieutenant, and immediately under his Majesty's command, and to be (within the liberties and jurisdiction of the town) esteem'd the second man in the kingdom; and the grant of those privileges concludes thus; *Ut ab antiquo usu fuerunt,* as of antient time they had been accustomed: So that this Charter, which was granted by Edward IV. ann. 1461. seems to be only a confirmation of former privileges, not a grant of new ones.

In the church of St. Martin in Stamford-Baron, that is on this side the bridge, at the upper end of the choir, is a very noble monument of William Cecil Lord Burleigh, who lies bury'd there in a large vault just under it; and opposite to it, on the north side, is a more antient (but handsome) monument, tho' not so magnificent as the former, being in memory of Richard Cecil, Esq; and Jane his wife, the father and mother of the said famous Lord Burleigh; also a more modern monument for the great earl who re-edify'd the house, being the last earl but one, and father of the present earl; and for his countess, a sister of the present Duke of Devonshire: This is a finish'd piece, 'tis all of the finest marble, and, they told us, it was made at Florence, and sent over: The said earl dy'd on his travels at Paris.

There is a very fine stone bridge over the River Welland of five arches, and the town-hall is in the upper part of the gate, upon or at the end of the bridge, which is a very handsome building. There are two constant weekly markets here, viz. on Mondays and Fridays, but the last is the chief market: They have also three fairs, viz. St. Simon and Jude, St. James's, and Green-goose Fair, and a great Midlent mart; but the latter is not now so considerable, as it is reported to have formerly been.

But the beauty of Stamford is the neighbourhood of the noble palace of the Earl of Excester, call'd Burleigh House, built by the famous Sir William Cecil, Lord Burleigh, and Lord High Treasurer to Queen Elizabeth, the same whose monument I just now mentioned, being in St. Martin's Church at Stamford-Baron, just without the park.

This house, built all of free-stone, looks more like a town than a house, at which avenue soever you come to it; the towers and the pinnacles so high, and placed at such a distance from one another, look like so many distant parish-churches in a great town, and a large spire cover'd with lead, over the great clock in the center, looks like the cathedral, or chief church of the town.

The house stands on an eminence, which rises from the north entrance of the park, coming from Stamford: On the other side, viz. south and west, the country lies on a level with the house, and is a fine plain, with posts and other marks for horse-races; As the entrance looks towards the flat low grounds of Lincolnshire, it gives the house a most extraordinary prospect into the Fens, so that you may see from thence twenty or near thirty miles, without any thing to intercept the sight.

As you mount the hill, you come to a fine esplanade, before the great gate or first entrance of the house, where there is a small but very handsome semi-circle, taken in with an iron balustrade, and from this, rising a few steps, you enter a most noble hall, but made infinitely more noble by the invaluable paintings, with which it is so fill'd, that there is not room to place any thing between them.

The late Earl of Excester, father of his present lordship, had a great genius for painting and architecture, and a superior judgment in both, as every part of this noble structure will testify; for he chang'd the whole face of the building; he pull'd down great part of the front next the garden, and turn'd the old Gothic windows into those spacious sashes which are now seen there; and tho' the founder or first builder, who had an exquisite fancy also, (as the manner of buildings then was) had so well ordered the situation and avenues of the whole fabrick, that nothing was wanting of that kind, and had also contriv'd the house itself in a most magnificent manner; the rooms spacious, well directed, the cielings lofty, and the decorations just, yet the late earl found room for alterations, infinitely to the advantage of the whole; as particularly, a noble stair case, a whole set of fine apartments, with rooms of state, fitting for the entertainment of a prince, especially those on the garden side; tho' at present a little out of repair again.

As this admirable genius, the late earl, lov'd paintings, so he had infinite advantage in procuring them; for he not only travell'd three times into Italy, and stay'd every time a considerable while at Florence, but he was so entertain'd at the Court of Tuscany, and had, by his most princely deportment and excellent accomplishments, so far obtain'd upon the great duke, that he might be said indeed to love him, and his highness shew'd the earl many ways that esteem; and more particularly, in assisting him to purchase many excellent pieces at reasonable prices; and not only so, but his highness presented him with several pieces of great value.

Among the rest, there is, in the great hall, his lordship's picture, on horseback, done by the great duke's principal painter, at his highness's charge, and given to his lordship, as a mark of the great duke's special favour: There is also a fine piece of Seneca bleeding to death in the warm bath, and dictating his last morals to his scholars; the passions are in so lively a manner described in the scholars, their eager attention, their generous regard to their master, their vigilant catching at his words, and some of them taking minutes, that it is indeed admirable and inexpressible. I have been told, that the King of France offer'd the earl 6000 pistoles for it.

It would be endless to give a detail of the fine pieces his lordship brought from Italy, all originals, and by the best masters; 'tis enough to say, they infinitely exceed all that can be seen in England, and are of more value than the house itself, and all the park belonging to it.

His lordship had indeed infinite advantage, join'd to his very good judgment, besides what I have mention'd, at the Court of the grand duke, for the furnishing himself with extraordinary paintings, having made his three journeys into Italy by several routs, and stopt at several Courts of princes; and his collection would doubtless have been still enlarg'd, had he liv'd to finish a fourth tour, which he was taking; but he was surpriz'd with a sudden and violent distemper, and dy'd at Paris (as we were told) of a dysentrie.

Besides the pictures, which, as above, were brought from abroad, the house itself, at least the new apartments may be said to be one entire picture. The stair-case, the cielings of all the fine lodgings, the chapel, the hall, the late earl's closet, are all finely painted by VARRIO, of whose work I need say no more than this, that the earl kept him twelve years in his family, wholly employ'd in painting those cielings and staircases, &c. and allow'd him a coach and horses, and equipage, a table, and servants, and a very considerable pension.

N.B. The character this gentleman left behind him at this town, is, that he deserv'd it all for his paintings; but for nothing else; his scandalous life, and his unpaid debts, it seems, causing him to be but very meanly spoken of in the town of Stamford.

I might dwell a long while upon this subject, and could do it with great pleasure, Burleigh House being well worth a full and compleat description; but this work will not admit of enlargements.

By the park wall, or, as some think, through the park, adjoining to Burleigh House, pass'd an old Roman highway, beginning at Castor, a little village near Peterborough; but which was anciently a Roman station, or colony, call'd Durobrevum; this way is still to be seen, and is now call'd The 40 Foot Way, passing from Gunworth Ferry (and Peterborough) to Stamford: This was, as the antiquaries are of opinion, the great road into the north, which is since turn'd from Stilton in Huntingdonshire to Wandsworth or Wandsford, where there is a very good bridge over the River Nyne; which coming down from Northampton, as I have observ'd already, passes thence by Peterborough, and so into the Fen country: But if I may straggle a little into antiquity, (which I have studiously avoided) I am of opinion, neither this or Wandsford was the ancient northern road in use by the Romans; for 'tis evident, that the great Roman causway is still seen on the left hand of that road, and passing the Nyne at a place call'd Water Neuton, went directly to Stamford, and pass'd the Welland, just above that town, not in the place where the bridge stands now; and this Roman way is still to be seen, both on the south and the north side of the Welland, stretching itself on to Brig Casterton, a little town upon the River Guash, about three miles beyond Stamford; which was, as all writers agree, another Roman station, and was call'd Guasennæ by the antients, from whence the river is supposed also to take its name; whence it went on to Panton, another very considerable colony, and so to Newark, where it cross'd the Foss.

This Forty Foot Way then must be a cross road from Castor, and by that from the Fen Country, so leading into the great highway at Stamford: as likewise another cross road went out of the said great road at Panton, above-named, to Ankaster, where was a Roman cohort plac'd, and thence join'd the Foss again at Lincoln.

Near this little village of Castor lives the Lord FitzWilliams, of an ancient family, tho' an Irish title, and his lordship has lately built a very fine stone bridge over the River Nyne, near Gunworth, where formerly was the ferry.

I was very much applauding this generous action of my lord's, knowing the inconvenience of the passage there before, especially if the waters of the Nyne were but a little swell'd, and I thought it a piece of publick charity; but my applause was much abated, when coming to pass the bridge (being in a coach) we could not be allow'd to go over it, without paying 2s. 6d. of which I shall only say this, That I think 'tis the only half crown toll that is in Britain, at least that ever I met with.

As we pass by Burleigh Park wall, on the great road, we see on the west side, not above a mile from it, another house, built by the same Lord Burleigh, and which might pass for a very noble seat, were not Burleigh by. This is call'd Wathorp, and stands just on the Great Roman Way, mention'd above; this is the house of which the old earl said he built it to remove to, and to be out of the dust, while Burleigh House was a sweeping. This saying is indeed father'd upon the noble founder, but I must acknowledge, I think it too haughty an expression to come from so wise and great a man.

At Overton, now call'd Cherry Orton, a village near Gunworth Ferry, is an old mansion house, formerly belonging to a very antient and almost forgotten race, or family of great men, call'd Lovetoft, which I nam'd for a particular reason. The estate is now in the heirs of the late Duke of Newcastle, and the house lies neglected. On the other side of the river is a fine new-built house, all of free stone, possess'd by Sir Francis St. John, Bart. which affords a very beautiful prospect to travellers, as they pass from the hill beyond Stilton to Wansford Bridge. This Wansford has obtain'd an idle addition to its name, from a story so firmly believ'd by the country people, that they will hardly allow any room for contradiction; namely, That a great flood coming hastily down the River Nyne, in hay-making-time, a country fellow, having taken up his lodging on a cock of hay in the meadow, was driven down the stream in the night, while he was fast asleep; and the hay swimming, and the fellow sleeping, they drove together towards Wisbech in the Fens, whence he was fairly going on to the sea; when being wakened, he was seen and taken up by some fishermen, almost in the open sea; and being ask'd, who he was? he told them his name; and where he liv'd? he answer'd, at Wansford in England: from this story the town is called Wansford in England; and we see at the great inn, by the south end of the bridge, the sign of a man floating on a cock of hay, and over him written, Wansford in England.

Coming south from hence we pass'd Stilton, a town famous for cheese, which is call'd our English Parmesan, and is brought to table with the mites, or maggots round it, so thick, that they bring a spoon with them for you to eat the mites with, as you do the cheese.

Hence we came through Sautrey Lane, a deep descent between two hills, in which is Stangate Hole, famous for being the most noted robbing-place in all this part of the country. Hence we pass'd to Huntington, the county town, otherwise not consider-able; it is full of very good inns, is a strong pass upon the Ouse, and in the late times of rebellion it was esteemed so by both parties.

Here are the most beautiful meadows on the banks of the River Ouse, that I think are to be seen in any part of England; and to see them in the summer season, cover'd with such in-numerable stocks of cattle and sheep, is one of the most agree-able sights of its kind in the world.

This town has nothing remarkable in it; 'tis a long continued street, pretty well built, has three parish churches, and a pretty good market-place; but the bridge, or bridges rather, and causway over the Ouse is a very great ornament to the place.

On the west side of this town, and in view of the plain lower side of the county, is a noble, tho' ancient seat, of the Earl of Sandwich; the gardens very fine and well kept; the situation seems a little obscur'd by the town of Huntington. In the same plain we saw Bugden, a small village, in which is remarkable a very pleasant, tho' ancient house or palace, of the Bishops of Lincoln: The house and garden surrounded by a very large and deep moat of water; the house is old, but pleasant, the chappel very pretty, 'tho' small; there is an organ painted against the wall, but in a seeming organ-loft, and so properly placed and well painted, that we at first believed it really to be an organ.

Hinchingbrook, another house belonging to a noble family, well known by the same title, shews itself at a small distance from Huntington; and a little way south stands that most nobly situated and pleasant seat of the Duke of Manchester, called Kimbolton, or Kimbolton Castle, where no pains or cost has been spar'd to make the most beautiful situation still more beautiful, and to help nature with art.

Hence we went a little north to see Oundle, being told that the famous drum was to be heard just at that time in the well; but when we came there, they shew'd us indeed the well and the town, but as for the drum, they could only tell us they heard of it, and that it did drum; but we could meet with no person of sufficient credit, that would say seriously they had heard it: so we came away dissatisfy'd.

This town of Oundle is pleasantly seated on the River Nyne, of which I have so often spoken. There are indeed a range of eminent towns upon this river; (viz.) Northampton, Wellingborough, Thrapston, Oundle, Fotheringay, Wandsford, and Peterborough; at all which, except Peterborough, there are very good stone bridges over the river.

Here again there is a most beautiful range of meadows, and perhaps they are not to be equall'd in England for length; they continue uninterrupted for above thirty miles in length, from Peterborough to Northampton, and, in some places, are near two miles in breadth, the land rich, the grass fine and good, and the cattle, which are always feeding on them, hay-time excepted, numberless.

From Oundle we cross'd the county of Northampton into

Bedfordshire, and particularly to the town of Bedford, the chief town of the county; for this county has no city in it, tho' even this town is larger and more populous, than several cities in England, having five parish-churches, and a great many, and those wealthy and thriving inhabitants. This is one of the seven counties, which they say lie together, and have not one city among them; namely, Huntington, Bedford, Bucks, Berks, Hertford, Essex, and Suffolk.

But here I must do a piece of justice to the usage of England in denominating of cities, namely, that it is not here as in France, and Flanders, and Holland, where almost all their towns of note are call'd cities, and where the gentry chiefly live in those cities, and the clergy also; I mean the religious houses, of which there are great numbers sometimes in one city, which are enough to make a city, where antient there was none before.

But as we have no authority, but antient usage and custom, for the distinguishing places by the names of towns and cities, so since that ancient usage or authority had the titles of places, 'tis observable some places, formerly of note, are considerably decay'd, and scarce preserve the face of their ancient greatness; as Lincoln, Old Sarum, Carlisle, Verulam, and others; and several towns which in those times scarce deserv'd the name of cities, are now, by the encrease of commerce and numbers of inhabitants, become greater, more populous and wealthy, than others, which are call'd cities.

Nor is this all, but several towns, which Mr. Cambden tells us, were call'd cities in his time, are now sunk from the dignity, and are only call'd towns, and yet still retain a greatness, wealth, and populousness, superior to many cities, such as Colchester, Ipswich, Shrewsbury, Cambridge, Stamford, Leicester, and others, which are without all comparison greater now than Wells, Peterborough, Ely, or Carlisle, and yet have lost the title of cities, which the other retain.

Thus we have at this time the towns of Froom, Taunton, Tiverton, Plymouth, Portsmouth, and others in the west, and the towns of Liverpool, Manchester, Leeds, Sheffield, Birmingham, Hull, and several others in the north, that are much larger, richer, and more populous, than Rochester, Peterborough, Carlisle, Bath, and even than York itself, and yet these retain but the name of towns, nay even of villages, in some of which the chiefest magistrate is but a constable, as in Manchester, for example.

It is remarkable of Bedfordshire, that tho' a great part of the county lies on the north side of the Ouse; that is to say, the two whole hundreds of Stodden and Barford; yet there is not one market town in all that side of the Ouse, but Bedford only.

Another thing is scarce to be equall'd in the whole isle of Britain; namely, that tho' the Ouse, by a long and winding course, cuts through the county, and by its long reachings, so as to make above seventy miles between Oulney and St. Neots, tho' not above twenty by land, yet in all that course it receives but one river into it, namely the little River Ivel, which falls into the Ouse a little above Temsford.

Bedford, as I have said, is a large, populous, and thriving town, and a pleasant well-built place; it has five parish churches, a very fine stone bridge over the Ouse, and the High Street, (especially) is a very handsome fair street, and very well-built; and tho' the town is not upon any of the great roads in England, yet it is full of very good inns, and many of them; and in particular we found very good entertainment here.

Here is the best market for all sorts of provisions, that is to be seen at any country town in all these parts of England; and this occasions, that tho' it is so far from London, yet the higglers or carriers buy great quantities of provisions here for London markets; also here is a very good trade down the river to Lynn.

Here is also a great corn market, and great quantities of corn are bought here, and carry'd down by barges and other boats to Lynn, where it is again shipp'd, and carry'd by sea to Holland: The soil hereabouts is exceeding rich and fertile, and particularly produces great quantities of the best wheat in England, which is carry'd by waggons from hence, and from the north part of the county twenty miles beyond this, to the markets of Hitchin and Hertford, and bought again there, and ground and carry'd in the meal (still by land) to London.

Indeed the whole product of this county is corn, that is to say, wheat and malt for London; for here are very few manufactures, except that of straw-hats and bone-lace, of which by itself: There are but ten market towns in the whole county, and yet 'tis not a small county neither: The towns are,

Bedford,	Ampthill,	Potton,
Biggleswood,	Shefford,	Tuddington,
Leighton,	Luton,	Wooburn.
Dunstable,		

The last of these was almost demolish'd by a terrible fire, which happen'd here just before my writing this account; but as this town has the good luck to belong to a noble family, particularly eminent for being good landlords; that is to say, bountiful and munificent to their poor tenants, I mean the ducal house of Bedford; there is no doubt but that the trustees, tho' his grace the present duke is in his minority, will preserve that good character to the family, and re-edify the town, which is almost all their own.

The duke's house, call'd Wooburn Abbey, is just by the town, a good old house, but very ancient, spacious and convenient rather than fine, but exceedingly pleasant by its situation; and for the great quantity of beach woods which surround the parks and cover the hills, and also for great woods of oak too, as rich and valuable, as they are great and magnificent: The very situation of this house to promise itself another Burleigh or Chatsworth, whenever an heir comes to enjoy the vast estate of this family, who has a genius for building; But at present, as above, the heir is an infant.

Ampthill is grac'd like Wooburn; for tho' in itself, like the other, it is not a considerable town, and has no particular manufacture to enrich it, yet by the neighbourhood of that great and noble family of Bruce Earls of Ailesbury, the very town is made both rich and honourable: It is however the misfortune of this noble family, that the present earl lives abroad, being a Roman; but the next heirs are in view of recovering the grandeur of that ancient family. The old venerable seat of the family is near the town, and is a noble and magnificent palace, tho' not wholly re-built, as is the fortune of many of the seats of our nobility of this age.

From hence, thro' the whole south part of this county, as far as the border of Buckinghamshire and Hertfordshire, the people are taken up with the manufacture of bone-lace, in which they are wonderfully encreas'd and improv'd within these few years past.

Also the manufactures of straw-work, especially straw hats, spreads itself from Hertfordshire into this county, and is wonderfully encreased within a few years past.

Having thus viewed this county in all its most considerable towns, we came from Dunstable to St. Albans, and so into London, all which has been spoken of before; I therefore break off this circuit here, and subscribe,

SIR,

Your most obedient Servant.

THE END OF THE SEVENTH LETTER

APPENDIX TO THE SECOND VOLUME

THE same reasons which occasioned an Appendix to the last volume hold good still, and will hold, if ten volumes of the same kind were to be written; seeing no man can take so strict a view of England, but something will occur, which the nicest observer could not possibly see, or the most busy enquirer be inform'd of at one journey; and, which is still more, some things will be undertaken and begun in the smallest intervals of time, which were not heard of before; for example:

On a more exact enquiry into the particular state of the city of Bristol, I find it necessary to mention first, That there are but seventeen parishes in the city, tho' there are nineteen churches, including the cathedral and the church of St. Mark: There are, besides those churches, seven meeting-houses, two Presbyterian, one Independent, two Quakers, one Baptist; also one or two other meetings not to be nam'd.

As to the Exchange design'd to be built, and for which an Act of Parliament actually pass'd, ann. 1723, it was at first intended to be built where the Tolsey now is; but so many buildings both publick and private and one church, namely Christ Church, at the corner of Vine-street, standing so near, as that they would crowd the place too much, the first measures were chang'd, and now the intended place is the meal market, between Vine-street and St. Mary Port, being on the north side of the Tolsey; but the citizens do not seem so hasty to build, as they were to get the Act of Parliament pass'd to give them power to do it.

There are no less than fifteen glass-houses in Bristol, which is more than are in the city of London: They have indeed a very great expence of glass bottles, by sending them fill'd with beer, cyder, and wine to the West Indies, much more than goes from London; also great numbers of bottles, even such as is almost incredible, are now used for sending the waters of St. Vincent's Rock away, which are now carry'd, not all over England only, but, we may say, all over the world.

The ground is now so rais'd in Queen's Square, (that which

was formerly call'd the Mead) that the highest tide does not flow over it, and all the sides of the square are now fully built and inhabited, except one house only.

There is in the great church of Ratcliff, or Redcliff, a very antient monument for one Mr. William Cannings, burgess and merchant of Bristol, who besides repairing or new buiding part of Ratcliff great church, gave to the vicar and church-wardens, and major part of the inhabitants of the parish, in trust for the poor, 340*l*. This was in the year 1474. 17th of Edw. IV. *N.B.* Such a sum at that time was equal to eight times that money in these days.

On one part of the monument is a Latin inscription, in an odd way of writing, and full of abbreviations; and, on the other side, in English, the following account of this worthy citizen, and of the regard paid to him at that time.

Mr. William Cannings, the richest merchant of the town of Bristow; afterwards chosen five times Mayor of the town, for the good of the common wealth of the same: He was in Order of Priest-hood, and afterwards Dean of Westburgh; and dy'd the 7th of November, 1474: Which said William did build within the said town of Westburgh a college with his canons and said William did maintain, by the space of 8 years, 8 hundred handy crafts men, besides carpenters and masons, every day 100 men. —— Besides King Edward the 4th had of the said William 3000 marks for his peace, in 2470 tuns of shipping. These are the names of the shipping with their burthen.

	Tons.		Tons.
The *Mary Canning*,	400	The *Mary Batt*,	220
The *Mary Redcliff*,	500	The little *Nicholas*,	140
The *Mary* and *John*,	900	The *Margaret*,	200
The Galliot,	50	The *Katherine Boston*,	22
The *Katherine*,	140	A ship in Ireland,	100

No age nor time can wear out well-won fame,
    The stones themselves a stately work doth show;
From senseless stones we ground may mens good name,
    And noble minds by virtuous deeds we know.
A lanthorn clear sets forth a candle-light:
A worthy act declares a worthy wight.
The buildings rare that here you may behold:
To shrine his bones deserves a tomb of gold:
The famous fabrick, that he here hath done,
Shines in his sphere, as glorious as the sun:
What needs more words? the future world he sought
And set the pomp and pride of this at naught;
Heaven was his aim! let Heaven be his station,
That leaves such works for others imitation.

Also here is the following inscription on the monument of Sir William Penn, Bart. the father of the great William Penn, one of the heads of the Quakers, who was a native of the city of Bristol: as follows.

To the just memory of Sir William Penn, Knt. and sometime general; borne at Bristol, in 1621, son of Capt. Giles Penn, several years consul for the English in the Mediterranean: Descended from the Penns of Penn Lodge in the county of Wilts, and the Penns of Penn near Wickham in the county of Bucks; and, by his mother, from the Gilberts in the county of Somerset, originally from Yorkshire; addicted from his youth to maritime affairs: He was made captain at the years of 21, Rear-Admiral of Ireland at 23, Vice-Admiral of Ireland at 25, Admiral to the Streights at 29, Vice-Admiral of England at 31, and General of the first Dutch Wars at 32; whence retiring, in anno 1655, he was chosen Parliament man for the town of Weymouth 1660, made Commissioner of the Admiralty and Navy, Governour of the towns and forts of Kingsaile, Vice-Admiral of Munster, and a member of the Provincial Councell; and, in anno 1664, was chosen Great Captain Commander under his Royal Highness, in that signal and most prudently successful fight against the Dutch Fleet. Thus he took leave of the sea, his old element, but continued still his other employs 'till 1669, at what time, thro' bodily Infirmities (contracted by the care and fatigue of the publick affairs) he withdrew, prepar'd, and made for his end, and with a gentle and even gale, in much peace, arriv'd and anchor'd in his last and best port, at Wanstead in the county of Essex, on the 16th of September, 1670, being then but 49 and 4 months old. To whose name and merit his surviving lady hath erected this remembrance.

In travelling this latter part of this second tour, it has not been taken notice of, though it very well deserves mention; That the soil of all the midland part of England, even from sea to sea, is of a deep stiff clay, or marly kind, and it carries a breadth of near 50 miles at least, in some places much more; nor is it possible to go from London to any part of Britain, north, without crossing this clayey dirty part. For example;

1. Suppose we take the great northern post road from London to York, and so into Scotland; you have tolerable good ways and hard ground, 'till you reach Royston about 32, and to Kneesworth, a mile farther: But from thence you enter upon the clays, which beginning at the famous Arrington-Lanes, and going on to Caxton, Huntington, Stilton, Stamford, Grantham, Newark, Tuxford (call'd for its deepness Tuxford in the Clays) holds on 'till we come almost to Bautree, which is the first town in Yorkshire, and there the country is hard and sound, being part of Sherwood Forest.

2. Suppose you take the other northern road, namely, by St. Albans, Dunstable, Hockley, Newport Pagnel, Northampton, Leicester, and Nottingham, or Darby: On this road, after you are pass'd Dunstable, which, as in the other way, is about 30 miles, you enter the deep clays, which are so surprisingly soft, that it is perfectly frightful to travellers, and it has been the wonder of foreigners, how, considering the great numbers of carriages which are continually passing with heavy loads, those ways have been made practicable; indeed the great number of horses every year kill'd by the excess of labour in those heavy ways, has been such a charge to the country, that new building of causeways, as the Romans did of old, seems to me to be a much easier expence: From Hockley to Northampton, thence to Harborough, and Leicester, and thence to the very bank of Trent these terrible clays continue; at Nottingham you are pass'd them, and the forest of Sherwood yields a hard and pleasant road for 30 miles together.

3. Take the same road as it leads to Coventry, and from thence to West Chester, the deep clays reach through all the towns of Brickhill, Fenny and Stony Stratford, Towcester, Daventry, Hill Morton, or Dunchurch, Coventry, Coleshill, and even to Birmingham, for very near 80 miles.

4. If we take the road to Worcester, it is the same through the vale of Aylesbury to Buckingham, and westward to Banbury, Keynton, and the vale of Evesham, where the clays reach, with some intermissions, even to the bank of Severn, as they do more northernly quite to West Chester.

The reason of my taking notice of this badness of the roads, through all the midland counties, is this; that as these are counties which drive a very great trade with the city of London, and with one another, perhaps the greatest of any counties in England; and that, by consequence, the carriage is exceeding great, and also that all the land carriage of the northern counties necessarily goes through these counties, so the roads had been plow'd so deep, and materials have been in some places so difficult to be had for repair of the roads, that all the surveyors rates have been able to do nothing; nay, the very whole country has not been able to repair them; that is to say, it was a burthen too great for the poor farmers; for in England it is the tenant, not the landlord, that pays the surveyors of the highways.

This necessarily brought the country to bring these things

before the Parliament; and the consequence has been, that turnpikes or toll-bars have been set up on the several great roads of England, beginning at London, and proceeding thro' almost all those dirty deep roads, in the midland counties especially; at which turn-pikes all carriages, droves of cattle, and travellers on horseback, are oblig'd to pay an easy toll; that is to say, a horse a penny, a coach three pence, a cart four pence, at some six pence to eight pence, a waggon six pence, in some a shilling, and the like; cattle pay by the score, or by the head, in some places more, in some less; but in no place is it thought a burthen that ever I met with, the benefit of a good road abundantly making amends for that little charge the travellers are put to at the turn-pikes.

Several of these turn-pikes and tolls had been set up of late years, and great progress had been made in mending the most difficult ways, and that with such success as well deserves a place in this account: And this is one reason for taking notice of it in this manner; for as the memory of the Romans, which is so justly famous, is preserv'd in nothing more visible to common observation, than in the remains of those noble caus-ways and highways, which they made through all parts of the kingdom, and which were found so needful, even then, when there was not the five hundredth part of the commerce and carriage that is now: How much more valuable must these new works be, tho' nothing to compare with those of the Romans, for the firmness and duration of their work?

The causways and roads, or streetways of the Romans, were perfect solid buildings, the foundations were laid so deep, and the materials so good, however far they were oblig'd to fetch them, that if they had been vaulted and arch'd, they could not have been more solid: I have seen the bottom of them dug up in several places, where I have observ'd flint-stones, chalk-stones, hard gravel, solid hard clay, and several other sorts of earth, laid in layers, like the veins of oar in a mine; a laying of clay of a solid binding quality, then flint-stones, then chalk, then upon the chalk rough ballast or gravel, 'till the whole work has been rais'd six or eight foot from the bottom; then it has been cover'd with a crown or rising ridge in the middle, gently sloping to the sides, that the rain might run off every way, and not soak into the work: This I have seen as fair and firm, after having stood, as we may conclude, at least 12 or 1600 years, as if it had been made but the year before.

And that I may not be charg'd with going beyond the most

exact truth, I refer the curious to make their observations upon that causeway, call'd the Fosse, which is now remaining, and to be seen between Cirencester and Marshfield in Wiltshire, on the road to the Bath, or between the same Cirencester and Birdlip Hill in Gloucestershire, on the road to Gloucester; but more particularly, between Castleford Bridge, near Pontefract in Yorkshire, upon the River Aire, and the town of Aberford, in the road to Tadcaster and York.

In several parts of this causeway, the country being hard, and the way good on either side, travellers have not made much use of the causeway, it being very high, and perhaps exposing them too much to the wind and weather, but have rather chosen to go on either side, so that the causeway in some places, lies as flat and smooth on the top, as if it had never been made use of at all; and perhaps it has not, there being not so much as the mark of a wheel upon it, or of a horse foot for a good way together, for which I refer to the curious traveller that goes that way.

This very causeway have I seen cut into, so as to discover the very materials with which it was built; and in some parts of the same causeway, farther north, where the great road has taken some other way, I have seen the old causeway dug down to carry the materials away, and mend the road which was then in use.

It is true the Romans being lords of the world, had the command of the people, their persons and their work, their cattle, and their carriages; even their armies were employ'd in these noble undertakings; and if the materials they wanted, were to fetch 20, nay 30 to 40 miles off, if they wanted them, they would have them, and the works were great and magnificent like themselves: Witness the numberless encampments, lines, castles and fortifications, which we see the remains of to this day.

But now the case is alter'd, labour is dear, wages high, no man works for bread and water now; our labourers do not work in the road, and drink in the brook; so that as rich as we are, it would exhaust the whole nation to build the edifices, the causeways, the aqueducts, lines, castles, fortifications, and other publick works, which the Romans built with very little expence.

But to return to this new method of repairing the highways at the expence of the turn-pikes; that is to say, by the product of funds rais'd at those turn-pikes; it must be acknowledg'd they are very great things, and very great things are done by them; and 'tis well worth recording, for the honour of the present age, that this work has been begun, and is in an extraordinary manner carry'd on, and perhaps may, in a great measure be compleated within our memory. I shall give some examples here of those which have been brought to perfection already, and of others which are now carrying on.

First, that great county of Essex, of which our first tour gives an ample account. The great road from London, thro' this whole county towards Ipswich and Harwich, is the most worn with waggons, carts, and carriages; and with infinite droves of black cattle, hogs, and sheep, of any road (that leads thro' no larger an extent of country) in England: The length of it from Stratford-bridge by Bow, to Streetford-bridge over the Stour, on the side of Suffolk, is 50 miles, and to Harwich above 65 miles.

These roads were formerly deep, in time of floods dangerous, and at other times, in winter, scarce passable; they are now so firm, so safe, so easy to travellers, and carriages as well as cattle, that no road in England can yet be said to equal them; this was first done by the help of a turnpike, set up by Act of Parliament, about the year 1697, at a village near Ingerstone. Since that, another turnpike, set up at the corner of the Dog Row, near Mile-end; with an additional one at Rumford, which is called a branch, and paying at one, passes the person thro' both: This I say, being set up since the other, compleats the whole, and we are told, that as the first expires in a year or two, this last will be sufficient for the whole, which will be a great ease to the country: The first toll near Ingerstone, being the highest rated public toll in England; for they take 8d. for every cart, 6d. for every coach, and 12d. for every waggon; and in proportion for droves of cattle: For single horsemen indeed, it is the same as others pay, viz. 1d. per horse, and we are told, while this is doing, that the gentlemen of the county, design to petition the Parliament, to have the Commissioners of the last Act, whose turnpike, as above, is at Mile-end and Rumford, empowered to place other turnpikes, on the other most considerable roads, and so to undertake, and repair all the roads in the whole county, I mean all the considerable roads.

But to come back to the counties which I am now speaking of, some very good attempts have been made of this kind on the northern roads, thro' those deep ways I mention'd, in the high post road; for example.

That an Act of Parliament was obtained about 30 years since, for repairing the road between Ware and Royston, and a turn-pike was erected for it at Wade's-mill, a village so called, about a mile and half beyond Ware: This proved so effectual, that the road there, which was before scarce passable, is now built up in a high, firm causeway; the most like those mentioned above, of the Romans, of any of these new undertakings. And, though this road is continually work'd upon, by the vast number of carriages, bringing malt and barly to Ware, for whose sake indeed, it was obtained; yet, with small repairs it is maintain'd, and the toll is reduced from a penny, to a half-penny, for the ease of the country, and so in proportion.

Beyond this, two grants have been obtained; one for repair of those wretched places, call'd Arrington Lanes, and all the road beyond Royston, to Caxton and Huntington; and another, for repairing the road from Stukely to Stilton, including the place called Stangate-Hole, and so on, towards Wansford and Santry Lane and Peterborough; by which these roads, which were before intollerable, are now much mended, but I cannot say, they are yet come up to the perfection of that road from London to Colchester.

One great difficulty indeed here, is, that the country is so universally made up of a deep, stiff clay; that 'tis hard to find any materials to repair the ways with, that may be depended upon. In some places they have a red sandy kind of a slate or stone, which they lay with timber and green faggots, and puts them to a very great expence; but this stone does not bind like chalk and gravel, or endure like flint and pebbles, but wears into clay from whence it proceeds; and this is the reason why they cannot expect those roads can reach up, however chargeable the repairs are to the goodness of the roads in Essex.

We see also a turnpike set up at a village very justly called Foul Mire near Cambridge, for the repair of the particular roads to the university, but those works are not yet brought to any perfection.

There is another road, which is a branch of the northern road, and is properly called the coach road, and which comes into the other near Stangate Hole; and this indeed is a most frightful way, if we take it from Hatfield, or rather the park corners of Hatfield House, and from thence to Stevenage, to Baldock, to Biggleswade, and Bugden. Here is that famous lane call'd Baldock Lane, famous for being so unpassable, that the coaches and travellers were oblig'd to break out of the way even by force, which the people of the country not able to prevent, at length placed gates, and laid their lands open, setting men at the gates to take a voluntary toll, which travellers always chose to pay, rather than plunge into sloughs and holes, which no horse could wade through.

This terrible road is now under cure by the same methods, and probably may in time be brought to be firm and solid, the chalk and stones being not so far to fetch here, as in some of those other places I have just now mention'd.

But the repair of the roads in this county, namely Bedford-shire, is not so easy a work, as in some other parts of England. The drifts of cattle, which come this way out of Lincolnshire and the fens of the Isle of Ely, of which I have spoken already, are so great, and so constantly coming up to London markets, that it is much more difficult to make the ways good, where they are continually treading by the feet of the large heavy bullocks, of which the numbers that come this way are scarce to be reckon'd up, and which make deep impressions, where the ground is not very firm, and often work through in the winter what the commissioners have mended in the summer.

But leaving these undertakings to speak for themselves when finish'd; for they can neither be justly prais'd or censur'd before; it ought to be observ'd, that there is another road branching out from this deep way at Stevenage, and goes thence to Hitchin, to Shefford, and Bedford. Hitchin is a large market town, and particularly eminent for its being a great corn market for wheat and malt, but especially the first, which is bought here for London market. The road to Hitchin, and thence to Bedford, tho' not a great thorough-fare for travellers, yet is a very useful high-way for the multitude of carriages, which bring wheat from Bedford to that market, and from the country round it, even as far as Northamptonshire, and the edge of Leicestershire; and many times the country people are not able to bring their corn for the meer badness of the ways.

This road, I hear, will be likewise repair'd, by virtue of a turn-pike to be plac'd near Hitchin on this side, and at the two bridges over the Ouse, namely Barford Bridge and Bedford Bridge, on the other side; as also at Temsford, where they drive through the river without the help of a bridge.

But to leave what may be, I return to what is. The next turn-pikes are on the great north west road, or, as I have distinguish'd it already, the Watling-street Way; which, to describe it once for all, begins at Islington near London, and leads to Shrewsbury, West Chester, and Hollyhead in Wales; with other branches breaking out from it to the north, leading to Nottingham, Darby, Burton on the Trent, and Warrington, and from them all, farther north, into the north west parts of Great Britain; for they are the grand passes into Yorkshire, Darbyshire, and Lancashire, and thro' them to Westmoreland, Cumberland, Durham, and Northumberland; of all which I shall give a farther account in my next letters.

Upon this great road there are wonderful improvements made and making, which no traveller can miss the observation of, especially if he knew the condition these ways were formerly in; nor can my account of these counties be perfect, without taking notice of it; for certainly no publick edifice, almshouse, hospital, or nobleman's palace, can be of equal value to the country with this, no nor more an honour and ornament to it.

The first attempt upon this road was at Brickhill in Buckinghamshire, and the turn-pike was set up on the hill, near the town call'd Little Brickhill, by vertue of which, they repair'd the road from thence to Stony Stratford, for about ten miles, and with very good success; for that road was broad, and capable of giving room for such a work; and tho' materials were hard to come at, and far to fetch, yet we soon found a large firm causway, or highway, and of a full breadth, reaching from Fenny Stratford to Stony Stratford, which is six miles, and where the way was exceeding bad before.

This encourag'd the country to set about the work in good earnest; and we now see the most dismal piece of ground for travelling, that ever was in England, handsomly repair'd; namely, from the top of the chalky hill beyond Dunstable down into Hockley Lane, and thro' Hockley, justly called Hockley in the Hole, to Newport Pagnall, being a bye branch of the great road, and leading to Northampton, and was call'd the coach road; but such a road for coaches, as worse was hardly ever seen.

The next (to come southward) was the road from St. Albans to South Mims, a village beyond Barnet: Soon after this road parts from the great coach road to the north, which I mention'd before, beginning at Hatfield.

This road, from Mims to St. Albans, is so well mended, the work so well done, and the materials so good, so plentifully furnish'd, and so faithfully apply'd, that, in short, if possible, it out-does the Essex road mention'd before; for here the bottom is not only repair'd, but the narrow places are widen'd, hills levell'd, bottoms raised, and the ascents and descents made easy, to the inexpressible ease and advantage of travellers, and especially of the carriers, who draw heavy goods and hard loads, who find the benefit in the health and strength of their cattle.

From hence, to come still more towards London, another undertaking reaches from the foot of Barnet Hill, call'd formerly the Blockhouse, to Whetstone, and so over the great heath, call'd Finchley Common, to Highgate Hill, and up the hill to the gatehouse at Highgate, where they had their turn-pike; as also at the Blockhouse; and this work is also admirably well perform'd, and thro' a piece of ground, which was very full of sloughs and deep places before.

But from Highgate to London still requir'd help; the road branch'd into two, at the top of Highgate Hill, or just at the gatehouse there; one came to London by Islington, and there branch'd again into two, one coming by the north end of Islington, and another on the back of the town, and entring the town at the south west end near the Angel Inn, there dividing again, one branch entred London at Goswell-street and Aldersgate street; and this was the principal road for waggons and pack-horses: The other going directly to St. John-street and into Smithfield; and this way was the chief road for cattle to Smithfield Market.

The other road parting off at Highgate, came down the hill by the late Sir William Ashurst's house, of which I made mention in its place, and thence passing through Kentish Town, entred London by two ways: one by Grays Inn Lane, and the other by Clerkenwell.

All these roads were to the last extremity run to ruin, and grew worse and worse so evidently, that it was next to impossible, the country should be able to repair them: Upon which an Act of Parliament was obtain'd for a turnpike, which is now erected at Islington aforesaid, as also all the other branches by the Kentish Town way, and others; so that by this new toll, all these roads are now likely to be made good, which were before almost a scandal to the city of London.

Another turnpike, and which was erected before this, was on the great north road, beginning at Shoreditch, and extending to Enfield Street, in the way to Ware; though this road is exceedingly throng'd, and raises great sums, yet I cannot say, that the road itself seems to be so evidently improv'd, and so effectually repair'd, as the others last mention'd, notwithstanding no materials are wanting; even on the very verge of the road itself, whether it be, that the number of carriages, which come this way, and which are indeed greater than in any other road about London, is the occasion, or whether the persons concern'd do not so faithfully, or so skilfully perform, I will not undertake to determine.

After so many encouraging examples on this great Watling-street road, as I have mention'd above, they have now begun the like on the same way farther down, and particularly from Stony Stratford to Daventry and Dunchurch, and so on to Coventry and Coles-hill; all those parts of it are at this time repairing, and they promise themselves that in a few years those roads will be compleatly sound and firm, as Watling-street was in its most antient and flourishing state; but this must be mention'd, like any publick edifice, which is now building, and perhaps may require some time to finish.

I come next to mention other works of the same kind in remoter places, also more westerly, but within the compass of this midland circuit; as particularly the road from Birdlip Hill to Gloucester, formerly a terrible place for poor carriers and travellers out of Wales, &c. But now repair'd very well.

Likewise the road from Sandy Lane Hill in Wiltshire to the Bath, which began to be repair'd by the direction of her late Majesty Queen Anne.

Also another piece of bad road near Beaconsfield in Oxford-shire.

By the same happy example, turnpikes are erected at the west end of the town, for repairing that horrid road, formerly also a part of the Watling-street Way, from St. Giles's Church to Paddington, and thence to Edgworth, obtain'd first by the interest and motion of his grace the Duke of Chandos.

On the other side of the river is another turnpike erected, or rather two turnpikes, one at the north end of the town of Newington, call'd Newington Buts, which has two or three colateral branches, viz. one at Vaux-Hall, at the bridge near the Spring Garden corner, and another at Croydon, besides smaller toll-bars on the bye-lanes. This undertaking has been very well prosecuted, and the great Sussex road, which was formerly unsufferably bad, is now become admirably good; and this is done at so great an expence, that they told me at Strettham, that one mile between the two next bridges south of that town, cost a thousand pounds repairing, including one of the bridges, and yet it must be acknowledg'd, that the materials are very near hand, and very good all the way to Croydon.

The other turnpike on that side is placed near New Cross on the road into Kent, a little before the road to Lusum parts from the road to Deptford Bridge; so that all the road to Lee and Eltham, the road to Bromley and Tunbridge, as well as the great road to Rochester and Canterbury, are taken in there; and this undertaking, they tell us, is likewise very well perform'd.

So that upon the whole, this custom prevailing, 'tis more than probable, that our posterity may see the roads all over England restor'd in their time to such a perfection, that travelling and carriage of goods will be much more easy both to man and horse, than ever it was since the Romans lost this island.

Nor will the charge be burthensome to any body; as for trade, it will be encourag'd by it every way; for carriage of all kind of heavy goods will be much easier, the waggoners will either perform in less time, or draw heavier loads, or the same load with fewer horses; the pack-horses will carry heavier burthens, or travel farther in a day, and so perform their journey in less time; all which till tend to lessen the rate of carriage, and so bring goods cheaper to market.

The fat cattle will drive lighter, and come to market with less toil, and consequently both go farther in one day, and not waste their flesh, and heat and spoil themselves, in wallowing thro' the mud and sloughs, as is now the case.

The sheep will be able to travel in the winter, and the city not be oblig'd to give great prizes to the butchers for mutton, because it cannot be brought up out of Leicestershire and Lincolnshire, the sheep not being able to travel: the graziers and breeders will not be oblig'd to sell their stocks of weathers cheap in October to the farmers within 20 miles of London, because after that they cannot bring them up; but the ways being always light and sound, the grasiers will keep their stocks themselves, and bring them up to market, as they see cause, as well in winter as in summer.

Another benefit of these new measures for repairing the roads by turnpikes, is the opening of drains and water-courses, and building bridges, especially over the smaller waters, which are oftentimes the most dangerous to travellers on hasty rains, and always most injurious to the roads, by lying in holes and puddles, to the great spoiling the bottom, and making constant sloughs, sometimes able to bury both man and horse; 'tis very remarkable that the overseers of these works take effectual care to have bridges built in such places, and currents made or opened for the waters to pass, by which abundance of labour is sav'd in constantly tending the waters on such occasions; but of this also we shall say more presently.

To give an eminent instance of it, we refer the curious to take the road from Blackman-street in Southwark, to Croydon, for an example, where, if we are not mistaken, he will find eleven bridges wholly new-built in ten miles length, by which the whole road is laid dry, sound, and hard, which was before a most uncomfortable road to travel.

This improving of the roads is an infinite improvement to the towns near London, in the convenience of coming to them, which makes the citizens flock out in greater numbers than ever to take lodgings and country-houses, which many, whose business call'd them often to London, could not do, because of the labour of riding forward and backward, when the roads were but a little dirty, and this is seen in the difference in the rents of houses in those villages upon such repair'd roads, from the rents of the like dwellings and lodgings in other towns of equal distance, where they want those helps, and particularly the encrease of the number of buildings in those towns, as above.

This probably has not been the least reason why such tolls are erected now on every side of London, or soon will be, and I doubt not but in time it will be the like all over England.

There are indeed some very deep roads in many places of England, and that south by Trent too, where no such provision is yet made for repair of the roads, as particularly in and through the vale of Aylesbury, and to Buckingham, and beyond it into Oxfordshire; also beyond Northampton to Harborough and Leicester; also in Lincolnshire, beyond what we nam'd to be from Huntington to Stilton, the road from Stamford to Grantham, Newark, and Tuxford, in the clays, all which remain very deep, and in some seasons dangerous.

Likewise the roads in Sussex, and that in particular which was formerly a Roman work, call'd Stony-street or Stone-street: Mr. Cambden mentions it as going from Leatherhead to Darking, and thro' Darking church-yard, then cross a terrible deep country, call'd the Homeward, and so to Petworth and Arundel: But we see nothing of it now; and the country indeed remains in the utmost distress for want of good roads: So also all over the Wild of Kent and Sussex it is the same, where the corn is cheap at the barn, because it cannot be carry'd out; and dear at the market, because it cannot be brought in.

But the specimens above, will, we doubt not, prompt the country gentlemen in time to go through with it all over England;

and 'tis to give a clear view of this important case, that we have given this account of them.

The benefit of these turnpikes appears now to be so great, and the people in all places begin to be so sensible of it, that it is incredible what effect it has already had upon trade in the countries where it is more compleatly finish'd; even the carriage of goods is abated in some places, 6*d*. per hundred weight, in some places 12*d*. per hundred, which is abundantly more advantage to commerce, than the charge paid amounts to, and yet at the same time the expence is paid by the carriers too, who make the abatement; so that the benefit in abating the rate of carriage is wholly and simply the tradesmens, not the carriers.

Yet the advantage is evident to the carriers also another way; for, as was observ'd before, they can bring more weight with the same number of horses, nor are their horses so hard work'd and fatigued with their labour as they were before; in which one particular 'tis acknowledg'd by the carriers, they perform their work with more ease, and the masters are at less expence.

The advantage to all other kinds of travelling I omit here; such as the safety and ease to gentlemen travelling up to London on all occasions, whether to the term, or to Parliament, to Court, or on any other necessary occasion, which is not a small part of the benefit of these new methods.

Also the riding post, as well for the ordinary carrying of the mails, or for the gentlemen riding post, when their occasions require speed; I say, the riding post is made extreamly easy, safe, and pleasant, by this alteration of the roads.

I mention so often the safety of travelling on this occasion, because, as I observ'd before, the commissioners for these repairs of the highways have order'd, and do daily order, abundance of bridges to be repair'd and enlarg'd, and new ones built, where they find occasion, which not only serve to carry the water off, where it otherwise often spreads, and lies as it were, damm'd up upon the road, and spoils the way; but where it rises sometimes by sudden rains to a dangerous height; for it is to be observ'd, that there is more hazard, and more lives lost, in passing, or attempting to pass little brooks and streams, which are swell'd by sudden showers of rain, and where passengers expect no stoppage, than in passing great rivers, where the danger is known, and therefore more carefully avoided.

In many of these places the commissioners have built large and substantial bridges for the benefit of travelling, as is said already, and in other places have built sluices to stop, and open'd channels to carry off the water, where they used to swell into the highway: We have two of these sluices near London, in the road thro' Tottenham High-Cross and Edmonton, by which the waters in those places, which have sometimes been dangerous, are now carry'd off, and the road clear'd; and as for bridges I have been told, that the several commissioners, in the respective districts where they are concern'd, have already built above three hundred new ones, where there were none before, or where the former were small and insufficient to carry the traveller safe over the waters; many of these are within a few miles of London, especially, for example, on the great road from London to Edgeworth, from London to Enfield, from London to St. Albans, and, as before, from London to Croydon, where they are very plain to be seen, and to which I refer.

And for farther confirmation of what I have advanc'd above, namely, that we may expect, according to this good beginning, that the roads in most parts of England will in a few years be fully repair'd, and restor'd to the same good condition, (or perhaps a better, than) they were in during the Roman government, we may take notice, that there are no less than twelve Bills, or Petitions for Bills, depending before the Parliament, at this time sitting, for the repair of the roads, in several remote parts of England, or for the lengthening the time allow'd in former Acts; some of which, besides those hereafter mentioned, give us hopes, that the grants, when obtain'd, will be very well manag'd, and the country people greatly encourag'd by them in their commerce; for there is no doubt to be made, but that the inland trade of England has been greatly obstructed by the exceeding badness of the roads.

A particular example of this, I have mention'd already, viz. the bringing of fat cattle, especially sheep to London in the winter, from the remoter counties of Leicester and Lincoln, where they are bred; by which the country grasiers are oblig'd to sell their stocks off, at the latter end of the summer, namely September and October, when they sell cheap, and the butchers and farmers near London engross them, and keeping them 'till December and January, sell them, tho' not an ounce fatter than before, for an advanc'd price, to the citizens of London; whereas were the roads made good and passable, the city would be serv'd with mutton almost as cheap in the winter as in the summer, or the profit of the advance would be to the graziers of Leicester and Lincolnshires, who were the original breeders.

This is evidenc'd to a demonstration in the counties of Essex and Suffolk, from whence they already bring their fat cattle, and particularly their mutton in droves, from sixty, seventy, or eighty miles, without fatiguing, harrassing, or sinking the flesh of the creatures, even in the depth of winter.

I might give examples of other branches of inland commerce, which would be quite alter'd for the better, by this restoring the goodness of the roads, and particularly that of carrying cheese, a species of provision so considerable, that nothing, except that of live cattle, can exceed it.

This is chiefly made in the three north west counties of England, viz. Cheshire, Gloucester, and Warwickshires, and the parts adjacent, from whence the nation is very meanly supply'd, by reason of the exceeding distance of the country where the cheese is made, from those counties where it is chiefly expended.

The Cheshire men indeed carry great quantities about by long sea, as they call it, to London; a terrible long, and some-times dangerous, voyage, being thro' the Irish Channel, round all Wales, cross the Bristol Channel, round the Land's End of Cornwall, and up the English Channel to the mouth of the Thames, and so up to London; or else by land to Burton upon Trent, and so down that river to Gainesborough and Hull, and so by sea to London.

Again, the Gloucestershire men carry all by land-carriage to Lechlade and Cricklade on the Thames, and so carry it down the river to London.

But the Warwickshire men have no water-carriage at all, or at least not 'till they have carry'd it a long way by land to Oxford; but as their quantity is exceeding great, and they supply not only the city of London, but also the counties of Essex, Suffolk, Norfolk, Cambridge, Huntingdon, Hertford, Bedford, and Northampton, the gross of their carriage is by meer dead draught, and they carry it either to London by land, which is full an hundred miles, and so the London cheese-mongers supply the said counties of Essex, Suffolk, and Norfolk, besides Kent, and Sussex, and Surrey by sea and river naviga-tion: or the Warwickshire men carry it by land once a year to Sturbridge Fair, whence the shop-keepers of all the inland country above-named, come to buy it; in all which cases land-carriage being long, and the ways bad, makes it very dear to the poor, who are the consumers.

But were the ways from Warwickshire made good, as I have shewn they are already in Essex, and some other places; this carriage would be perform'd for little more than half the price that it now is, and the poor would have their provisions much cheaper.

I could enlarge here upon the convenience that would follow such a restoring the ways, for the carrying of fish from the sea coasts to the inner parts of the kingdom, where, by reason of the badness of the ways, they cannot now carry them sweet; This would greatly encrease the consumption of fish in its season, which now for that very reason, is but small, and would employ an innumerable number of horses and men, as well as encrease the shipping by that consumption.

By this carriage of fish, I do not only mean the carrying herrings and mackerell to London, as is practis'd on the coast of Sussex and Kent in particular, and bringing salmon from the remote rivers of Severn and Trent; but the carrying of herrings, mackerell, and sprats in their season, and whitings and flat fish at other times, from the coasts of Yarmouth, Swole, Ipswich, Colchester, Malden, &c. and supplying all the inland counties with them sweet and good, which 'tis plain they might do, were the roads made good, even as far as Northampton, and Coventry, and farther too.

I might give examples where the herrings, which are not the best fish to keep neither, are, even as it is, carry'd to those towns, and up to Warwick, Birmingham, Tamworth and Stafford, and tho' they frequently stink before they come thither, yet the people are so eager of them, that they buy them, and give dear for them too; whereas were the roads good, they would come in less time, by at least two days in six, and ten-fold the quantity, nay, some say, an hundred times the quantity, be consum'd.

These, and many others, are the advantages to our inland commerce, which we may have room to hope for upon the general repair of the roads, and which I shall have great occasion to speak of again in my northern circuit, which is yet to come.

THE AUTHOR'S PREFACE TO THE THIRD VOLUME

THE TOUR is now finish'd; and you have the account contracted into as narrow a compass, as, considering the extent of ground pass'd over, with the number of cities, populous towns, and a country infinitely rich, populous and prosperous, to be described, could be reasonably expected.

As I mentioned in the last volume, every new view of Great Britain would require a new description; the improvements that encrease, the new buildings erected, the old buildings taken down: New discoveries in metals, mines, minerals; new undertakings in trade; inventions, engines, manufactures, in a nation, pushing and improving as we are: These things open new scenes every day, and make England especially shew a new and differing face in many places, on every occasion of surveying it.

Since our last volume, we have to add to the description of the parts in and about London, a large variety both of publick and private buildings; as a new East-India House building in the city, and a South-Sea Company-House finished, both lofty and magnificent. Mr. Guy's Hospital in Southwark, the noblest foundation of the age for one private charity, finished and filled at the foot of above an hundred thousand pounds gift, if common fame may be believed: The additions to Bethlehem Hospital, and several new steeples and churches; Sir Gregory Page's house, or rather palace, upon Black-Heath, erected and finished, one of the most beautiful seats belonging to a private gentleman, that not England only, but that all Europe can produce.

Add to this the cookery, as they properly enough call it, of the South-Sea Company for their Greenland trade, their whale-fishing, and boiling their blubber, &c. being the largest magazine of all sorts of materials for the shipping, fishing, &c. that is belonging to any private branch of commerce. Then there is a little city of buildings, streets and squares, added to those mentioned before, at the west end of Hanover and Cavendish

Square, with the repair of two terrible fires at Wapping and Ratcliff.

And, to close all: There is the erecting a new stone bridge over the Thames at Putney and Fulham, for which an Act of Parliament was obtained last sessions, and preparations are now actually making to set about it, which is like to be a very stately and magnificent work.

If all these additions are to be found in the small interval between the publishing the second volume and this of the third, and that in so narrow a compass, what may not every subsequent year produce? and what encouragement is here for new and more accurate surveys of this country? which, whoever travels over it, will always furnish new materials, and a variety both profitable and delightful.

The fine house built by the Right Honourable Sir Robert Walpole, in the north part of the county of Norfolk, is, as I am told, now also finished, at least the outside work and figure of the building is; so it is a mistake that must be acknowledged in form, (however not the author's) when, in our last, the inscription fixed on the foundation-stone of the building, was said to be ordered for the frize; the necessary absence of the author, (who was then on a journey for preparing this volume) may answer for a fault owing to the corrector of the press, and which, had the author seen it, could not have pass'd his notice. But the triumph one impertinent has made upon the occasion, is fully check'd by this more than needful concession. It is a happy testimony of the care and caution used by the author of this work, in every part of it, when such earnest endeavours are used to expose it, and so little found, to lay hold of. Any mistake that can be found, and, in a friendly manner, hinted, we shall receive with thankfulness, and amend chearfully; But a cavil, evidently malicious, of an author without a name, lest an answer should be given, will be treated as it deserves, with the contempt of silence.

INTRODUCTION TO THE THIRD VOLUME

SIR,—I have now finished my account of the several circuits which I took the last year, compleating the southern parts of the isle of Britain; my last brought me to the banks of the River Trent, and from thence back to London, where I first set out.

I have yet the largest, tho' not the most populous, part of Britain to give you an account of; nor is it less capable of satisfying the most curious traveller: Though, as in some places things may stand more remote from one another, and there may, perhaps, be more waste ground to go over; yet 'tis certain a traveller spends no waste hours, if his genius will be satisfied with just observations. The wildest part of the country is full of variety, the most mountainous places have their rarities to oblige the curious, and give constant employ to the enquiries of a diligent observer, making the passing over them more pleasant than the traveller cou'd expect, or than the reader perhaps at first sight will think possible.

The people in these northern climes will encrease the variety; their customs and genius differing so much from others, will add to our entertainment; the one part of them being, till now, a distinct nation, the inhabitants thereof will necessarily come in as a part of what we are to describe: Scotland [1] is neither so considerable, that we should compliment her at the expence of England; or so inconsiderable, that we should think it below us to do her justice; I shall take the middle of both extremes.

I shall be tempted very often to make excursions here on account of the history and antiquities of persons and places both private and publick. For the northern parts of Britain, especially of England, as they were long the seat of war between the several nations; such as the Britains, Scots, Picts, Romans, Saxons, and Danes, so there are innumerable remains of antiquity left behind them, and those more visible in those parts, and less defac'd by time, and other accidents than in any other part of the island.

He that travels through such a country, if he sees and knows the meaning of those monuments of antiquity, and has due

[1] Defoe's Tour through Scotland is omitted in this edition.

memoirs of the historical part still in his head, must be inexcusable if he takes up his own time, or his reader's pateince, in
observing trifles, and recording things of no signification.

I knew two gentlemen who travelled over the greatest part
of England in several journies together; the result of their
observations were very different indeed; one of them took some
minutes of things for his own satisfaction, but not much; but
the other, as he said, took an exact journal; the case was thus:

He that took minutes only, those minutes were very critical,
and upon some very significant things; but for the rest his
memory was so good, and he took so good notice of every thing
worth observing, that he wrote a very good and useful account
of his whole journey after his return; that account I have seen,
and had the advantage to look it over again upon this occasion,
and by it to correct and enlarge some of my own observations;
it being as impossible any one man could see or observe every
thing worth seeing in England, as it is to know every face he
meets in a croud.

The other gentleman's papers, which I called an exact journal,
contained the following very significant heads:

I. The day of the month when he set out.
II. The names of the towns where they din'd every day, and
where they lodg'd at night.
III. The signs of the inns where they din'd and lodg'd, with
the memorandums of which had good claret, which not.
IV. The day of the month when he return'd.

The moral of this brief story, which I insist that I know to be
true, is very much to my purpose. The difference between these
two gentlemen in their traveliing, and in their remarks upon
their journey, is a good emblem of the differing genius in readers,
as well as authors, and may be a guide to both in the work now
before us.

I have endeavoured that these letters shall not be a journal of
trifles; if it is on that account too grave for some people, I hope
it will not for others; I have study'd the advancement and
encrease of knowledge for those that read, and shall be as glad
to make them wise, as to make them merry; yet I hope they
will not find the story so ill told, or so dull as to tyre them too
soon, or so barren as to put them to sleep over it.

The north part of Great Britain, I mean Scotland, is a country
which will afford a great variety to the observation, and to the

pen of an itinerate; a kingdom so famous in the world for great
and gallant men, as well states-men as soldiers, but especially
the last, can never leave us barren of subject, or empty of
somewhat to say of her.

The Union has seemed to secure her peace, and to encrease
her commerce: But I cannot say she has raised her figure in
the world at all since that time, I mean as a body; She was
before considered as a nation, now she appears no more but as
a province, or at best a dominion; she has not lost her name as
a place; but as a state, she may be said to have lost it, and that
she is now no more than a part of Great Britain in common
with other parts of it, of which England it self is also no more.
I might enlarge here upon the honour it is to Scotland to be a
part of the British Empire, and to be incorporated with so
powerful a people under the crown of so great a monarch; their
being united in name as one, Britain, and their enjoying all the
privileges of, and in common with, a nation who have the greatest
privileges, and enjoy the most liberty of any people in the world.
But I should be told, and perhaps justly too, that this was talking
like an Englishman, rather than like a Briton; that I was gone
from my declared impartiality, and that the Scots would perhaps
talk a different stile when I came among them. Nor is it my
business to enquire which nation have the better end of the staff
in the late coalition, or how the articles on which it is established,
are performed on one side or other.

My business is rather to give a true and impartial description
of the place; a view of the country, its present state as to
fertility, commerce, manufacture, and product; with the
manners and usages of the people, as I have done in England;
and to this I shall confine my self as strictly as the nature of a
journey thro' the country requires.

I shall, in doing this, come indeed of course to make frequent
mention of the various turns and revolutions which have
happened in those northern parts; for Scotland has changed its
masters, and its forms of government, as often as other nations;
and, in doing this, it will necessarily occur to speak of the Union,
which is the last, and like to be the last revolution of affairs in
Scotland for, we hope, many ages. But I shall enter no farther
into this, than is concerned in the difference between the face
of things there now, and what was there before the said Union,
and which the Union has been the occasion or cause of; as
particularly the division and government of the countries, and
towns, and people in particular places; the communication of

privileges, influence of government, and enlarging of the liberty of trade.

This will also bring on the needful account of alterations and improvements, in those counties, which, by reason of the long and cruel wars between the two nations in former reigns, lay waste and unimproved, thinly inhabited, and the people not only poor because of the continual incursions of the troops on either side; but barbarous and ravenous themselves, as being inured to rapine, and living upon the spoil of one another for several ages; all which is now at an end, and those counties called the marches or borders, are now as well peopled and cultivated as other counties, or in a fair way to be so.

This alteration affords abundance of useful observations, and 'tis hop'd they shall be fruitfully improved in this work; and as it is a subject which none have yet meddled with, so we believe it will not be the less acceptable for its novelty, if tolerably well handled, as we hope it shall be.

Those few cavils which have been raised at the former parts of this work; for it is with great satisfaction I can say they are but few, are far from discouraging me in this hardest and most difficult part of the undertaking; I believe it is impossible for any man to observe so narrowly upon Great Britain, as to omit nothing, or to mistake in nothing; the great Mr. Cambden has committed many mistakes, which his reverend continuator has corrected; and there are yet many more which that learned and reverend author has not seen; and both together have omitted many things very well worth observing; yet their works are justly valued, their labours and endeavours commendable and profitable to the world; and no man lessens the author for not seeing every thing, or knowing critically every thing, tho' worth knowing, which persons inhabiting those places may be respectively informed of.

If our endeavour has been, as it really has, to give a full and just representation of persons and things wherever we came, I think the end is as fully pursued as any author can undertake to do; and for cavils and querulous criticisms, or for unavoidable omitting of what did not occur to observation, they are not worth notice; what real mistakes we have yet discovered in the last volume, are touch'd at in the Preface; and if we had met with more, they should have been mentioned faithfully; for no wise man will be ashamed to amend a mistake; but 'tis a satisfaction enough to tempt one's vanity to be able to say how few they are.

LETTER VIII

Sir,—As I am to begin this circuit from the River Trent, and to confine my observations to that part of Britain which the Scots and Northumberlanders, and others on that side, call North by Trent, it seems necessary (at least it cannot be improper) to give some description of the river it self, and especially the course which it runs, by which, adding a little river call'd the Weaver, and a branch of it call'd the Dane in Staffordshire and Cheshire, the whole island of Britain is, as it were, divided into two parts.

The River Trent is rated by ancient writers as the third river in England, the two greater being the Thames and the Severn: It is also one of the six principal rivers which running across the island from the west to the east, all begin with the letter *T*; namely, the Thames, Trent, Tees, Tine, Tweed, and Tay.

The Trent is not the largest river of the six; yet it may be said to run the longest course of any of them, and rises nearer to the west verge of the island than any of the other; also it is the largest, and of the longest course of any river in England, which does not empty its waters immediately into the sea; for the Trent runs into the Humber, and so its waters lose their name before they reach to the ocean.

It rises in the hills or highlands of Staffordshire, called the Moorlands, receiving, from the edge of Cheshire, and towards Lancashire, a great many (some say thirty, and that thence it had its name) little rivulets into it, very near its head, all which may claim a share in being the originals of the Trent; thus it soon becomes one large river, and comes down from the hills with a violent current into the flat country; where, being encreased by several other little rivers, it carries a deeper channel, and a stiller current; and having given its name to Trentham, a small market town in the same county, it goes on to Stone, a considerable town on the great road to West-Chester.

The original of its name is very uncertain, as is the case in most other rivers of England; that it takes the name of Trent, as above, because of its receiving thirty rivers into it, or because there are thirty several sorts of fish in it, or that, like the Tibiscus in Hungary, it is three parts water, and two parts fish; all these the learned and judicious Mr. Cambden rejects, as I do for the same reason, namely, because they have no authority for the suggestion.

One branch of the Trent rises within a quarter of a mile of the Dane, (viz.) from a moor adjoining to, or part of a little ridge of hills called Molecop Hill, near Congleton, and is within twenty two miles of the Irish Sea, or that arm or inlet of the sea which the Mersee makes from Frodsham to Liverpool and Hyle-lake; and as the Dane runs into the Weaver, and both into that arm of the sea, and the Trent into the Humber, which opens into the great German Ocean, those rivers may be said to cut the island across in the middle.

It is true, the northern part is much larger than the southern, now Scotland is united; otherwise the country south by Trent, including Wales, is by far the largest: But it must be allowed still, that the country south by Trent is the richest by far, and most populous; occasioned chiefly by the city of London, and the commerce of the Thames; as for the cities of Bristol, Exceter, and Norwich, which are large and very populous, and in some things drive a prodigious trade, as well in merchandise as manufacture, we shall find them matched, if not out-done, by the growing towns of Liverpool, Hull, Leeds, Newcastle, and Manchester, and the cities of Edinburgh and Glasgow, as shall be shown in its place.

The Trent runs a course of near two hundred miles, through the four counties of Stafford, Derby, Nottingham, and Lincoln; it receives, besides lesser waters, the larger rivers of the Sowe from the west side of the county, and from the town of Stafford; the Tame from Birmingham and Tamworth; the Soar from Leicester; and the Dove and Derwent, two furiously rapid streams, from the Peak of Derby; the Idle, a gentle navigable stream from Rhetford and Nottinghamshire; with part of the Wittham, called the Fossdike from Lincoln, also navigable; and the greatest of them all, the Don, from Doncaster, Rothram, and Sheffield, after a long and rapid course through the moors called Stanecross on the edge of Derby, and the West-Riding of Yorkshire.

The Trent is navigable by ships of good burthen as high as Gainsbrough, which is near 40 miles from the Humber by the river. The barges without the help of locks or stops go as high as Nottingham, and farther by the help of art, to Burton upon Trent in Staffordshire. The stream is full, the channel deep and safe, and the tide flows up a great way between Gainsborough and Newark. This, and the navigation lately, reaching up to Burton and up the Derwent to Derby, is a great support to, and encrease of the trade of those counties which border upon it; especially for the cheese trade from Cheshire and Warwickshire, which have otherwise no navigation but about from West Chester to London; whereas by this river it is brought by water to Hull, and from thence to all the south and north coasts on the east side of Britain; 'tis calculated that there is about four thousand ton of Cheshire cheese only, brought down the Trent every year from those parts of England to Gainsborough and Hull; and especially in time of the late war, when the seas on the other side of England were too dangerous to bring it by long-sea.

Thus much for the River Trent; The towns standing upon it, and especially on the north shore or bank are but few, at least of note: Beginning at the mouth of it, and going up the stream, all the towns, such as Burton, Stockwith, Gainsborough, and Newark, are on the south bank, and consequently have been spoken to already. The only towns of any note that are to be found on the north bank of Trent, are Nottingham, and the other Burton, of which I shall speak in their order; at present, as I took a different circuit in my riding, I must do so in my account of it also, or else if my pen does not follow my foot, I shall wander rather than travel, at least in my paper, whatever I did on my horse.

The counti s north by Trent are few; but most of them large; I mean on the side of England, (viz.) York, which I shall call three counties, as it is divided into three Ridings, and are large counties too; and Lancashire, which is very large, Derbyshire and Nottinghamshire, which are the most southerly, are but small; I shall begin there, and take them together.

As I am travelling now cross the island, and begin at the mouth of Trent, the first town of note that I meet with is Nottingham, the capital of that shire, and is the most considerable in all that part of England. The county is small, but, like the Peak, 'tis full of wonders; and indeed there are abundance of remarkables in it: (1.) 'Tis remarkable for the soil, which on the south part is the richest and the most fruitful; and on the north part the most wild and waste, and next to barren of any part of England within many miles of it. (2.) For the fine seats of noblemen and gentlemen, not a few; such as the Dukes of Shrewsbury, Kingston, Rutland, Newcastle, and several others. But as I purpose to begin at the south entrance, I mean at the town of Nottingham, I shall speak a little of that before I describe the country about it.

Nottingham is one of the most pleasant and beautiful towns in England. The situation makes it so, tho' the additions to it were not to be nam'd. It is seated on the side of a hill overlooking a fine range of meadows about a mile broad, a little rivulet running on the north side of the meadows, almost close to the town; and the noble River Trent parallel with both on the further or south side of the meadows: Over the Trent there is a stately stone-bridge of nineteen arches, and the river being there join'd into one united stream, is very large and deep; having, as is said, but lately received the addition of the Dove, the Derwent, the Irwash, and the Soar, three of them very great rivers of themselves, and all coming into the Trent since its passing by Burton in Staffordshire mentioned before.

The town of Nottingham is situated upon the steep ascent of a sandy rock; which is consequently remarkable, for that it is so soft that they easily work into it for making vaults and cellars, and yet so firm as to support the roofs of those cellars two or three under one another; the stairs into which, are all cut out of the solid, tho' crumbling rock; and we must not fail to have it be remember'd that the bountiful inhabitants generally keep these cellars well stock'd with excellent ALE; nor are they uncommunicative in bestowing it among their friends, as some in our company experienc'd to a degree not fit to be made matter of history.

They tell us there, speaking of the antiquity of Nottingham, that the hill where it was built, was called the Dolorous Hill, or the Golgotha of ancient time; because of a great slaughter of the Britains there by King Humber, a northern monarch; the same who, being afterwards drowned in the passage of the sea between Hull and Barton, gave name to that arm of the sea which is now called the Humber, and which receives the Trent, and almost all the great rivers of Yorkshire into it.

They also tell us, those caves and cellars, mentioned above, served the people for a retreat in those days, from the pursuit of their enemies, and that from thence the town took its first name, which was Snottengaham, which signifies hollow vaults in a rock, *Speluncarum Domum*, or, as Mr. Cambden observes, the British word was *Tui ogo bauc*; that is, the same as the Latin, and meant a house of dens, or secret caves to hide in; but this is remote.

Besides the scituation of Nottingham towards the river; it is most pleasantly seated to the land side; that is to say, to the side of the forest on the north of the town. And here they have (1.) a most pleasant plain to accommodate the gentlemen who assemble once a year (at least) for the manly noble diversion of racings, and chiefly horse-races; 'tis a most glorious show they have here when the running season begins; for here is such an assembly of gentlemen of quality, that not Bansted Down, or New Market Heath, produces better company, better horses, or shews the horse and master's skill better.

At the west end of the town there is a very steep hill, and the south side of it a cliff, which descends in a precipice towards the river; on this hill stood an old castle, but when, we know not; so that if we may plead its antiquity, 'tis only because we have no account of its beginning; the oldest thing that we read of it is, that there was a tower here which the Danes obstinately defended against King Alfred, and his brother Æthelred.

This castle, or some other building in the room of it, remained till the time of the late wars; 'tis evident it was standing in the reign of Queen Elizabeth; Mr. Cambden says, William the Norman built it; and, as he says, it was done to awe the English; it was so strong that nothing could ever reduce it but famine; after this it was repair'd and beautified, or rather rebuilt, by Edward IV. who added fine apartments to it, which Richard III. his brother, enlarged.

It was so strong, it seems, that it had not been subject to the ordinary fate of other fortify'd places; namely, to be often taken and retaken; for it was never storm'd, that is to say, never taken sword in hand; once it was indeed taken by surprize in the barons wars by Robert Earl Ferrers, who also plundered the town, (city 'twas then call'd.)

The stories that people tell us here, of one of the Davids, King of Scotland, kept prisoner in it, I believe little of, any more than I do that of Roger Mortimore Earl of March, and his being hid in a vault under ground in this castle, whence being discovered, he was taken, brought to justice, and hang'd for treason; yet the place where they say he was taken, is shewed still to strangers, and is call'd Mortimer's Hole, to this day.

It is true, that here are such places; Mr. Cambden also gives an account that in the first court of the castle there is a way down by a great many steps to a vault under ground, where there are chambers cut out of the stone, and the people offer'd to carry us down the same; but we did not like the aspect of it, so we ventur'd rather to take their words.

Whoever built this great castle (for the dispute lies only between William the Conqueror and William de Peverell, his bastard son) I say, whoever built it, we know not; but we know who pull'd it down; namely, the government, upon the Restoration, because it had been forfeited, and held out against the Royalists: After the Restoration Cavendish, late Marquis of Newcastle, entirely bought it of King Charles II. or of the Duke of Buckingham, to whom he would have sold it; and, having bought it, went to work immediately with it, in order to pull it quite down; for it lay, as it were, waste to him, and useless. In the year 1674 he clear'd the old foundations, a small part excepted, and founded the noble structure which we see now standing; and which, thro' several successions, has revolved to the present branch of the house of Pelham, now Duke of Newcastle; who has beautified if not enlarged the building, and has laid out a plan of the finest gardens that are to be seen in all that part of England; but they are not yet finish'd; they take up, as they tell us, threescore acres of ground in the design, and would, no doubt, be exquisitely fine; but it requires an immense sum to go on with it.

In the great church of St. Mary's in Nottingham, we see the monument of the Plumtree's, an honourable family, who built the hospital at the bridge end; also the family of Holles Lord Houghton, Earl of Clare, and afterwards Duke of Newcastle, lye buried here. But the learned Dr. Thornton, in his antiquities of this county, having copied all the epitaphs and inscriptions in the churches of this town; if I should repeat them, it would look as if I wanted matter to fill up; just the contrary of which is my case to an extreme.

The beauties of Nottingham, next to its situation, are the castle, the market-place, and the gardens of Count Tallard; who, in his confinement here as prisoner of war taken by the Duke of Marlborough at the great Battle of Blenheim, amused himself with making a small, but beautiful parterre, after the French fashion. But it does not gain by English keeping.

There was once a handsome town-house here for the sessions or assises, and other publick business; but it was very old, and was either so weak, or so ill looked after, that, being over-crowded upon occasion of the assises last year, it cracked, and frighted the people, and that not without cause. As it happened, no body was hurt, nor did the building fall directly down. But it must be said, (I think) that Providence had more care of the judges, and their needful attendants, than the townsmen had, whose business it was to have been well assured of the place, before they suffered a throng of people to come into it; and therefore we cannot deny, but it was a seasonable justice in the court to amerce or fine the town, as they did; as well for the omission, as for the repair of the place. We are told now that they are collecting money, not for the repair of the old house, but for erecting a new one, which will add to the beauty of the town.

The Trent is navigable here for vessels or barges of great burthen, by which all their heavy and bulky goods are brought from the Humber, and even from Hull; such as iron, block-tin, salt, hops, grocery, dyers wares, wine, oyl, tar, hemp, flax, &c. and the same vessels carry down lead, coal, wood, corn; as also cheese in great quantities, from Warwickshire and Staffordshire. By which the commerce of these counties is greatly increased, as I have mentioned already.

When I said the bridge over Trent had nineteen arches, I might as well have said the bridge was a mile long; for the Trent being, at the last time I was there, swelled over its ordinary bound, the river reached quite up to the town; yet a high causeway, with arches at proper distances, carried us dry over the whole breadth of the meadows, which, I think, is at least a mile; and it may be justly called a bridge, on several accounts, as another at Swarston is called, which is full a mile in length.

Nottingham, notwithstanding the navigation of the Trent, is not esteemed a town of very great trade, other than is usual to inland towns; the chief manufacture carried on here is frame-work knitting for stockings, the same as at Leicester, and some glass, and earthen ware-houses; the latter much increased since the increase of tea-drinking; for the making fine stone-mugs, tea-pots, cups, &c. the glass-houses, I think, are of late rather decayed.

As there is a fine market-place, so is there a very good market, with a vast plenty of provisions, and those of the best sort, few towns in England exceeding it; to say nothing of their ale, as having reserved it to a place by it self.

As they brew a very good liquor here, so they make the best malt, and the most of it of any town in this part of England, which they drive a great trade for, sending it by land-carriage to Derby, through all the Peak as far as Manchester, and to other towns in Lancashire, Cheshire, and even into Yorkshire itself; to which end all the lower lands of this county, and especially on the banks of Trent, yield prodigious crops of barley.

The government of Nottingham is in the mayor, two sheriffs, six aldermen, coroners and chamberlains, twenty four common-council, whereof six are called juniors; the rest of course, I suppose, may pass for seniors.

I might enter into a long description of all the modern buildings erected lately in Nottingham, which are considerable, and of some just now going forward. But I have a large building in the whole to overlook; and I must not dwell too long upon the threshold.

The forest of Sherwood is an addition to Nottingham for the pleasure of hunting, and there are also some fine parks and noble houses in it, as Welbeck, the late Duke of Newcastle's, and Thoresby, the present noble seat of the Pierrepont's, Dukes of Kingston, which lies at the farthest edge of the forest. But this forest does not add to the fruitfulness of the county, for 'tis now, as it were, given up to waste; even the woods which formerly made it so famous for thieves, are wasted; and if there was such a man as Robin Hood, a famous out-law and deer-stealer, that so many years harboured here, he would hardly find shelter for one week, if he was now to have been there: Nor is there any store of deer, compared to the quantity which in former times they tell us there usually was.

From Nottingham, a little mile west on the road to Derby, we saw Woollaton Hall, the noblest antient-built palace in this county, the mansion of the antient family of Willoughby, now Lord Middleton, created baron in the late Queen Anne's time. The house, the gardens, the great hall, the monuments of the family in the church of Woollaton, and the pedigree of that noble family, are well worth a stranger's view.

The park, walled in with a new brick-wall, is much finer than the great park adjoining to the castle of Nottingham, being much better planted with timber; whereas that at Nottingham was all cut down, and sequestred in the late wars.

This house, all of stone, was built by Sir Francis Willoughby, second son of the honourable —— Willoughby Esq; slain in the 4th of Edward VI. in the rebellion or tumult at Norwich, anno 1546, and Dame Anne, daughter of the Marquis of Dorchester; the first and eldest son, Sir Thomas Willoughby, dying unmarried. The stately fabrick shews the genius, as well as the wealth, of the founder; the hall, at the first entrance, is so high that a man on horseback might exercise a pike in it. The figure of building, as an artist said of it to me, was rather antick than antient; the architect is noble, and the order of building regular, except the four pavilions of the Dorick order on the top, which they alledge is inexcusable in architecture. Some, who excuse the design, will have it to be, that the upper building is an attick, and set on to grace the other. But I must be allowed to differ from that opinion too.

However it be, take it all together, the building is far beyond any thing in this part of England, of equal antiquity, Belvoir, or Bevoir Castle excepted, and even not that for excellence of workmanship.

One of the ancestors of this noble family, Sir Richard Willoughby, was judge of the Court of King's Bench for almost thirty years; from the third year of King Edward III. to his thirty third year; in which time he greatly advanced the honour and estate of his family.

Another branch was less fortunate, though not less famous, namely, Sir Hugh Willoughby, the famous navigator and searcher out of new discoveries; who, after many extraordinary adventures in the reign of Queen Elizabeth, went at last in search of the north east passages of Nova Zembla; and having beaten up and down among the ice a long time, was at length driven into a small fuell or inlet of the sea, near the Mer Blanch, or White Sea; and being out of his knowledge, was there found the next spring frozen to death with all his ship's company, every one of them.

The monuments of this antient and wealthy family, for many years past, are still to be seen at Wollaton Church. Some of them are very magnificent; and others of them being very antient, are solemn even in their very ruins.

> For monuments of men, like men, decay.

Having thus passed the Rubicon (Trent) and set my face northward, I scarce knew which way to set forward, in a country too so full of wonders, and on so great a journey, and yet to leave nothing behind me to call on as I came back, at least not to lead me out of my way in my return. But then considering that I call this work, a Tour, and the parts of it, Letters; I think, that tho' I shall go a great length forward, and shall endeavour to take things with me as I go; yet I may take a review of some parts as I came back, and so may be allowed to pick up any fragments I may have left behind in my going out.

I resolved indeed first for the Peak, which lay on my left-hand north east; but, as I say, to leave as little behind me as possible, I was obliged to make a little excursion into the forest, where, in my way, I had the diversion of seeing the annual meeting of the gentry at the horse-races near Nottingham. I could give a long and agreeable account of the sport it self, how it brought into my thoughts the Olympick Games among the Greeks; and the Circus Maximus at Rome; where the racers made a great noise, and the victors made great boasts and triumphs: But where they chiefly drove in chariots, not much unlikes our chaises, and where nothing of the speed, or of skill in horsemanship could be shown, as is in our races.

It is true, in those races the young Roman and Grecian gentlemen rod, or rather drove themselves; whereas in our races the horses, not the riders, make the show; and they are generally ridden by grooms and boys, chiefly for lightness; sometimes indeed the gentlemen ride themselves, as I have often seen the Duke of Monmouth, natural son to King Charles II. ride his own horses at a match, and win it too, though he was a large man, and must weigh heavy.

But the illustrious company at the Nottingham races was, in my opinion, the glory of the day; for there we saw, besides eleven or twelve noblemen, an infinite throng of gentlemen from all the countries round, nay, even out of Scotland it self; the appearance, in my opinion, greater, as it was really more numerous, than ever I saw at Newmarket, except when the king have been there in ceremony; for I cannot but say, that in King Charles II.'s time, when his majesty used to be frequently at Newmarket, I have known the assembly there have been with far less company than this at Nottingham; and, if I might go back to one of these Nottingham meetings, when the Mareschal Duke de Tallard was there, I should say, that no occasions at Newmarket, in my memory, ever came up to it, except the first time that King William was there after the Peace of Ryswick.

Nor is the appearance of the ladies to be omitted, as fine and without comparison more bright and gay, tho' they might a little fall short in number of the many thousands of nobility and gentry of the other sex; in short, the train of coaches filled with the beauties of the north was not to be described; except we were to speak of the garden of the Tulleries at Paris, or the Prado at Mexico, where they tell us there are 4000 coaches with six horses each, every evening taking the air.

From hence I was going on to see Rugford Abbey, the fine seat of the late Marquis of Hallifax, but was called aside to take a view of the most famous piece of church history in this part of the whole island, I mean the collegiate church of Southwell.

Paulinus, Archbishop of York, was (so antient record supplies the tale) the founder of this church, having preached to the people of the country round, and baptized them in the River Trent; the antient words imports Christianized them, by dipping them in the River Trent. Whether our Antipedo-Baptists will take any advantage of the word, I know not; but I cannot see any doubt but that antiently baptism was performed in the water; whether it was performed there by immersion, putting the person into the water, or pouring the water upon him, we know not; neither do I see any extraordinary, much less any essential difference in it, be it one way or the other; but that is not my business, especially not here: The reason of naming it, is to give you the pious occasion which made the good bishop build this church, namely, that having converted a whole province, or part of one at least, he was desirous they should not want a place of worship to serve God in.

The thing which makes this foundation the more remarkable, is, that though it was surrendered into the king's hands, with all the rest of the religious foundations, in the reign of King Henry VIII. yet it was restored whole as it was before, in the 35th of the same reign.

But because I love to speak not from my self in cases where good authorities are to be had, and that in a cursory view of a place, such as that of a journey must be, the outsides or appearances of things only are to be seen, or such farther knowledge as may be obtained by report of inhabitants; for I copy nothing from books, but where I quote the books, and refer to them; I say, for this reason I give you an account of this venerable pile, its foundation and present constitution, from a reverend and very good friend, and one of the present prebendaries the place, and whose authority I do, and the reader may depend upon, as follows, (viz.)

AN ACCOUNT OF THE TOWN AND CHURCH OF SOUTHWELL

Southwell, in the county of Nottingham, is about nine miles
north east from Nottingham, four miles west from Newark, eight
south east from Mansfield, and about two south west from the
River Trent. The soil of it rich clay and marle; the air very good,
and well watered; the River Greet runs by it. It is a market town,
and the market day Saturday; it is remarkable for no sort of
manufacture.

There is in it but one church, which is both parochial and collegiate; which, I think, is the case of no other in England, except
Rippon in Yorkshire.

The parish consists of Southwell, and the hamlets of Eastrope,
which joins to Southwell on the east; Westrope, about a quarter
of a mile west of Southwell; and Normanton, about a mile north;
it contains about 350 families. There is a parish-vicar so called,
who is generally one of the vicars choral, whose business it is to
visit the sick, bury the dead, etc. the preaching part being performed by the prebendaries. This vicarage was lately augmented
by Queen Anne's Bounty, which benefit fell to it by lot.

The collegiate church consists of 16 prebendaries or canons,
6 vicars choral, an organist, 6 singing-men, 6 choristers, a register
to the chapter, a treasurer; an auditor, a verger, etc. The prebends
are all in the gift of the Archbishop of York. All the rest of the
members disposed of by the chapter.

The foundation of this church is doubtless very antient. It is
generally supposed to be founded by Paulinus, the first Archbishop
of York, about the year 630.

The church was, by the several members thereof, viz. the archbishop, the prebendaries, vicars choral, chantry priests, and by the
chapter, surrendered to the king, 32 Henry VIII. as appears by
the records in Chancery; and was actually in the king's possession,
until by Act of Parliament, anno 35 Henry VIII. it was refounded,
and restored to its antient privilege, and incorporated by the name
of the Chapter of the Collegiate Church of the Blessed Mary the
Virgin of Southwell.

Afterward, by the statute for the dissolution of chantries, anno
primo Edward VI. it was conceived, that the said church was
again dissolved. But the members of the church did not quit their
possession till the 4th and 5th of Philip and Mary, when ——
Griffin, the Attorney General, exhibited an Information of Intrusion
against the Chapter, pleading the Crown's title to their lands, by
virtue of the Act of Edward VI. But upon full hearing it was
adjudged that the Chapter was not adjudged within the said
statute; and therefore the Bill was dismissed; and the Chapter
continued to enjoy their rights and privileges.

Queen Elizabeth confirmed the same, and gave statutes to the
said church, with this preamble: Eliz. Dei Grat. Regina, &c. Dilectis
subditis nostris, Capitulo, cæterisq; Ministris Ecclesiæ nostræ Colleg.
Beatæ Mariæ Virginis de Southwell per Illustrissimum Patrem
nostrum Hen. VIII. nuper Regem Ang. fundatæ. Notwithstanding
this, in King James's reign, the same plea was revived against the

church, by the then Attorney General, and met with the same success; that is, was dismissed. And King James, in the second year of his reign, by Letters Patent under the Great Seal, confirmed and established the said church in perpetuity, according to the refoundation and restitution thereof by King Henry VIII.

There is no dean of this church; but the residentiary for the time being has the government of it; and one of the prebendaries, by the statutes, is obliged to be resident, which at present is by agreement and by consent of the archbishop, performed by every one in their turns, and each prebendary keeps residence a quarter of a year.

Most of the prebendaries, I think twelve of them, have prebendal houses in the town of Southwell. But those being let out on lease, they now keep residence in a house built for that purpose about 30 years ago, in the east end of the college of the vicars; which house is ready furnished, and kept in repair at the charge of the chapter.

The prebendaries preach in their turn every Sunday morning, and on such festivals, &c. as preaching is required. In the afternoon on Sundays there is a lecture usually preached by the residentiary for the time being.

The Chapter of Southwell have a peculiar jurisdiction, and there are 28 parishes subject to it; to most of which they have the right of presentation; besides some others in Lincolnshire and Yorkshire. This jurisdiction is exercised by a commissary or vicar-general, chosen by the Chapter out of their body, who holds visitations, &c. twice a year. And besides these, there are two synods yearly, to which all the clergy of the county of Nottingham pay their attendance. And a certain number of the prebendaries, and others of the considerable clergy, are appointed commissioners, by a commission granted by the Archbishop of York to preside at the synods.

There are many privileges belonging to this church; one of which is, That every parish and hamlet in the county pay certain small pensions yearly to the church, called Pentecostal Offerings.

There are houses for the vicars choral adjoining to the residence house, built about a square; with a gate locked up every night, and the key kept by the residentiary. There are but five of the vicars have houses allotted them in the college. The other vicar, being parish vicar also has a vicarage house in the town. There are prayers twice every day at the usual hours, and likewise at six or seven in the morning, from Ashwednesday to St. Matthew's Day.

The civil government of the jurisdiction of Southwell, is distinct from the county at large. It is called the Soke of Southwell cum Scrooby, which is another town in this county. There are about 20 towns subject to this jurisdiction.

The *Custos Rotulorum*, and the Justices of the Peace, are nominated by the Archbishop of York, and constituted by a commission under the Great Seal of England; who hold their session both at Southwell and Scrooby, and perform all other justiciary acts distinct from the county. There is no *Custos Rotulorum* yet appointed in the room of Lord Lexington, who died about two years ago; but a new commission is expected as soon as the archbishop is confirmed.

The Names of the present Prebendaries and
Prebends, are,

The Reverend

Mr. Geo. Mompesson.	Oxton 1 Pars.
Mr. Tho. Sabourne.	North Muskam.
Mr. John Pigot.	Beckingham.
Mr. Edward Clark.	Dunham.
Mr. Benjamin Carter.	Sacrista.
Mr. Stephen Cooper.	Normanton.
Mr. Samuel Berdmore.	Oxton 2 Pars.
Mr. Thomas Sharp.	Norwell Overall.
Mr. Robert Ayde.	Woodborough.
Mr. John Lloyd.	South Muskam.
Mr. Robert Marsden.	Norwell Palishall.
Mr. John Abson.	Eaton.
Mr. Humphrey Bralesford.	Norwell 3 Pars.
Mr. Ri. Wood, Present resid.	North Severton.
Mr. Henry Cook.	Rampton.
Mr. Edward Parker.	Halloughton.

The Present Vicars.

Mr. Benjamin Cooper.	An Organist.
Mr. John Barnard.	Six Singing-Men.
Mr. Charles Benson.	Six choristers, besides six more
Mr. Samuel Bird.	boys who attend as proba-
Mr. Joseph Ellis.	tioners.
Mr. William Hodgson.	

The present Register and Auditor }	Mr. Jos. Clay.
The Treasurer ——	Mr. George Cooper.
The Virger	

The fabrick of the church is at present in good and decent order.
It is a strong building of the Gothick order, very plain. I remember
to have met with this passage in some of our old writings; That
when the dispute was about the dissolution of the church, I think
in King James's reign; among other things, it was urged by the
Chapter, that the church of Southwell was a plain fabrick, free from
all superstitious ornaments; that there were no painted figures in
the glass-work, nor images, nor so much as a nitch capable of
placing an image in; which I think is true. And from hence too it
has been conjectur'd concerning the antiquity of this church, that
it was probably built, before image-worship was practised or
thought of in the Christian Church.

This church was a great part of it burnt down in the year 1711,
by lightning; of which I find this memorandum in one of our
books, viz. "On Monday the 5th of November, 1711. about ten
a-clock at night, the top of the ball on one of the south spires of
this collegiate church of Southwell was fired by lightning; which,
backed by a furious wind that drove it almost directly on the body
of the church, in a few hours burnt down the spire and roof, melted

down the bells, and spared nothing that was combustible, except the other spire, till it came to the quire, where, after it had consumed the organs, it was by singular providence stopt and extinguish'd."

This is a pretty exact account; to which I must add, that the damage was computed at near 4000*l.* which great misfortune was happily repaired by the industry of the Chapter, joined with the help of the then Archbishop of York, Dr. Sharp; who not only contributed largely themselves, but by their solicitations obtained a brief, which, with the liberal contributions of several of the nobility and gentry, and the inhabitants of Southwell and its neighbourhood, enabled them to repair the church, and to put it in as good order as it was before the fire.

Among the benefactors ought particularly to be remembered with gratitude the last Dutchess Dowager of Newcastle, who, at the intercession of the archbishop, kindly seconded by her chaplain Dr. Brailsford, now Dean of Wells,

	l.
Gave	500
Dr. Sharp, Archbishop	200
The late Duke of Leeds	200
The Earl of Thanet	50
The late Duke of Rutland	60
Bartholomew Burton, Esq;	30
Sir William Daws, late Archbishop	100

The church is built in form of a cross; a great tower in the middle, in which are eight bells, and two spires at the west end. There is a handsome chapter-house on the north side of the quire.

The length of the church from east to west is 306 feet, of which the choir is — feet; the length of the cross isle from north to south is 121 feet; the breadth of the church 59 feet.

On a pillar at the entrance into the choir, is this inscription:

Sint Reges Nutritii tui & Reginæ Nutrices,
Ecclesiam hanc Collegiatam & Parochialem
Fundavit Antiquitas.
Refundavit Illustrissimus Henricus Rex Octavus,
Edwardo Lee Archiepiscopo Eborac. intercedente.
Sancivit Serenissima Elizabetha Regina,
Edvino Sands Eborum Archiepiscopo mediante.
Stabilivit Præpotentissimus Monarcha Jac. Rex,
Henrico Howard Comite Northamp. aliisque
Supplicantibus.
Sint sicut Oreb & Zeb, Zeba & Salmana
Qui dicunt Hæreditate possideamus
Sanctuarium Dei.

There are no very remarkable monuments in this church, only one of Archbishop Sands, which is within the communion rails, and is a fair tomb of alabaster, with his effigies lying on it at full length. ——Round the verge of it is this inscription:

Edvinus Sandes Sacræ Theologiæ Doctor, postquam Vigorniensem Episcopatum Annos X, totidemque tribus demptis Londinensem gessisset Eboracensis sui Archiepiscopatus Anno XII° Vitæ autem LXIX°. obiit Julii X. A.D. 1588.

At the head of the tomb is this inscription:

Cujus hic Reconditum Cadaver jacet, genere non humilis vixit, Dignitate locoque magnus, exemplo major; duplici functus Episcopatu, Archi-Episcopali tandem Amplitudine Illustris. Honores hosce mercatus grandi Pretio, Meritis Virtutibusque Homo hominum a Malitia & Vindicta Innocentissimus; Magnanimus, Apertus, & tantum Nescius adulari; Summe Liberalis atque Misericors: Hospitalissime optimus, Facilis, & in sola Vitia superbus. Scilicet haud minora, quam locutus est, vixit & fuit. In Evangelii prædicand. Laboribus ad extremum usque Halitum mira-biliter assiduus; a sermonibus ejus nunquam non melior discederes. Facundus nolebat esse & videbatur; ignavos, sedulatitis suæ Conscius, oderat. Bonas literas auxit pro Facultatibus; Ecclesiæ Patrimonium, velut rem Deo consecratum decuit, intactum defendit; gratia, qua floruit, apud Illustrissimam mortalium Elizabetham, effecit, ne hanc, in qua jacet, Ecclesiam ti jacentem cerneres. Venerande Præsul! Utrius memorandum Fortunæ exemplar! Qui tanta cum gesseris, multa his majora, animo ad omnia semper impavido, perpessus es; Carceres, Exilia, amplissimarum Facultatum amissiones; quodque omnium difficillime Innocens perferre animus consuevit, immanes Calumnias; & si re una votis tuis memor, quod Christo Testimonium etiam sanguine non præbueris; attamen, qui in prosperis tantos fluctus, & post Aronum tot adversa, tandem quietis sempternæ Portum, fessus Mundi, Deique sitiens, reperisti, Æturnum lætare; vice sanguinis sunt sudores tui; abi lector, nec ista scias, tantum ut sciveris, sed ut imiteris.

At the feet under the coat of arms:

Verbum Dei manet in Æternum.

Round the border of another stone in the south isle of the choir.

Hic jacet Robertus Serlby, Generosus, quondam Famulus Willielmi Booth Archiepiscopo Eborac. Qui obiit 24° die Mensis Augusti, A.D. 1480, cujus animæ propitietur Deus. Amen.

On a stone fixed in the wainscot under one of the prebendal stalls in the choir, is this inscription, very antient, but without a date.

Hic jacet Wilhelmus Talbot, miser & indignus sacerdos, expectans Resurrectionem in signo Thau—— I suppose it means a *Tau* to denote a cross.

On the south-side of the church in the churchyard,

Me Pede quando teris, Homo qui Mortem mediteris
Sic contritus eris, & pro me quæro, preceris,

without name or date.

Here was formerly a palace belonging to the Archbishop of York, which stood on the south side of the church, the ruins of which still remain; by which it appears to have been a large and stately palace. It was demolished in the time of the Rebellion against King Charles I. and the church, I have heard, hardly escaped the fury of those times; but was indebted to the good offices of one Edward Cludd, Esq; one of the Parliament side, who lived at Norwood, in the parish of Southwell, in a house belonging to the archbishop, where he lived in good esteem for some time after the Restoration; and left this estate at Norwood, which he held by lease of the archbishop, to his nephew Mr. Bartholomew Fillingham, who was a considerable officer in the Exchequer, and from whom

Bartholomew Burton, Esq; who was his nephew and heir, inherited it, with the bulk of all the rest of his estate and who now enjoys it by a lease of three lives, granted by the late Archbishop Sir William Dawes. Here were no less than three parks belonging to the archbishop, which tho' disparked, still retain the name; one of which is Norwood Park, in which is a good house, which has been very much enlarged and beautified by the said Mr. Burton, who lives in it some part of the year.

There is a free-school adjoining to the church, under the care of the Chapter; where the choristers are taught gratis; and other boys belonging to the town. The master is chosen by the Chapter; and is to be approved by the Archbishop of York.

There are also two fellowships and two scholarships in St. John's College in Cambridge, founded by Dr. Keton, Canon of Salisbury, in the 22d year of King Henry VIII. to be chosen by the master and fellows of the said college, out of such who have been choristers of the church of Southwell, if any such able person for learning and manners, can be found in Southwell, or in the university of Cambridge; and for want of such, then out of any scholars abiding in Cambridge; which said fellowships are to be thirteen shillings and four-pence each better than any other fellowship of the college.

Hence crossing the forest I came to Mansfield, a market town, but without any remarkables. In my way I visited the noble seat of the Duke of Kingston at Thoresby, of the Duke of Newcastle at Welbeck, and the Marquis of Hallifax at Rufford, of Rugeford Abbey, all very noble seats, tho' antient, and that at Welbeck especially, beautify'd with large additions, fine apartments, and good gardens; but particularly the park, well stocked with large timber, and the finest kind, as well as the largest quantity of deer that are any where to be seen; for the late duke's delight being chiefly on horseback and in the chace, it is not to be wondered if he rather made his parks fine than his gardens, and his stables than his mansion-house; yet the house is noble, large, and magnificent.

Hard by Welbeck is Wirksop Mannor, the antient and stately seat of the noble family of Talbot, descended by a long line of ancestors from another family illustrious, though not enobled (of Lovetot's). This house, (tho' in its antient figure) is outdone by none of the best and greatest in the county, except Wollaton Hall, already mentioned; and that though it is, as it were, deserted of its noble patrons; the family of Shrewsbury being in the person of the last duke, removed from this side of the country to another fine seat in the west, already mentioned.

From hence leaving Nottinghamshire, the west part abounding with lead and coal, I cross'd over that fury of a river called the Derwent, and came to Derby, the capital of the county.

This is a fine, beautiful, and pleasant town; it has more families of gentlemen in it than is usual in towns so remote, and therefore here is a great deal of good and some gay company: Perhaps the rather, because the Peak being so near, and taking up the larger part of the county, and being so inhospitable, so rugged and so wild a place, the gentry choose to reside at Derby, rather than upon their estates, as they do in other places.

It must be allowed, that the twelve miles between Nottingham and this town, keeping the mid-way between the Trent on the left, and the mountains on the right, are as agreeable with respect to the situation, the soil, and the well planting of the country, as any spot of ground, at least that I have seen of that length, in England.

The town of Derby is situated on the west bank of the Derwent, over which it has a very fine bridge, well built, but antient, and a chapel upon the bridge, now converted into a dwelling-house. Here is a curiosity in trade worth observing, as being the only one of its kind in England, namely, a throwing or throwster's mill, which performs by a wheel turn'd by the water; and though it cannot perform the doubling part of a throwster's work, which can only be done by a handwheel, yet it turns the other work, and performs the labour of many hands. Whether it answers the expence or not, that is not my business.

This work was erected by one Soracule, a man expert in making mill-work, especially for raising water to supply towns for family use: But he made a very odd experiment at this place; for going to show some gentlemen the curiosity, as he called it, of his mill, and crossing the planks which lay just above the mill-wheel; regarding, it seems, what he was to show his friends more than the place where he was, and too eager in describing things, keeping his eye rather upon what he pointed at with his fingers than what he stept upon with his feet, he stepp'd awry and slipt into the river.

He was so very close to the sluice which let the water out upon the wheel, and which was then pulled up, that tho' help was just at hand, there was no taking hold of him, till by the force of the water he was carried through, and pushed just under the large wheel, which was then going round at a great rate. The body being thus forc'd in between two of the plashers of the wheel, stopt the motion for a little while, till the water pushing hard to force its way, the plasher beyond him gave way and broke; upon which the wheel went again, and, like Jonah's whale, spewed him out, not upon dry land, but into that part they call the apron, and so to the mill-tail, where he was taken up, and received no hurt at all.

Derby, as I have said, is a town of gentry, rather than trade; yet it is populous, well built, has five parishes, a large market-place, a fine town-house, and very handsome streets.

In the church of Allhallows, or, as the Spaniards call it, *De Todos los Santos*, All Saints, is the Pantheon, or Burial-place of the noble, now ducal family of Cavendish, now Devonshire, which was first erected by the Countess of Shrewsbury, who not only built the vault or sepulchre, but an hospital for eight poor men and four women, close by the church, and settled their maintenance, which is continued to this day: Here are very magnificent monuments for the family of Cavendish; and at this church is a famous tower or steeple, which for the heighth and beauty of its building, is not equalled in this county, or in any of those adjacent.

By an inscription upon this church, it was erected, or at least the steeple, at the charge of the maids and batchelors of the town; on which account, whenever a maid, native of the town, was marry'd, the bells were rung by batchelors: How long the custom lasted, we do not read; but I do not find that it is continued, at least not strictly.

The government of this town, for it is a corporation, and sends two burgesses to Parliament, is in a mayor, high-steward, nine aldermen, a recorder, fourteen brothers, fourteen capital burgesses, and a town-clerk: The trade of the town is chiefly in good malt and good ale; nor is the quantity of the latter unreasonably small, which, as they say, they dispose of among themselves, though they spare some to their neighbours too.

It is observable, that as the Trent makes the frontier or bounds of the county of Derby south, so the Dove and the Erwash make the bounds east and west, and the Derwent runs through the center; all of them beginning and ending their course in the same county; for they rise in the Peak, and end in the Trent.

I that had read Cotton's *Wonders of the Peak*, in which I always wondered more at the poetry than at the Peak; and in which there was much good humour, tho' but little good verse, could not satisfy my self to be in Derbyshire, and not see the River Dove, which that gentleman has spent so much doggerel upon, and celebrated to such a degree for trout and grailing: So from

Derby we went to Dove-Bridge, or, as the country people call it, Dowbridge, where we had the pleasure to see the river drowning the low-grounds by a sudden shower, and hastning to the Trent with a most outrageous stream, in which there being no great diversion, and travelling being not very safe in a rainy season on that side, we omitted seeing Ashbourn and Uttoxeter, the Utocetum of the antients, two market towns upon that river, and returning towards Derby, we went from thence directly up into the High Peak.

In our way we past an antient seat, large, but not very gay, of Sir Nathaniel Curson, a noted and (for wealth) over great family, for many ages inhabitants of this county. Hence we kept the Derwent on our right-hand, but kept our distance, the waters being out; for the Derwent is a frightful creature when the hills load her current with water; I say, we kept our distance, and contented our selves with hearing the roaring of its waters, till we came to Quarn or Quarden, a little ragged, but noted village, where there is a famous chalybeat spring, to which abundance of people go in the season to drink the water, as also a cold bath. There are also several other mineral waters in this part of the country, as another chalybeat near Quarden or Quarn, a hot bath at Matlock, and another at Buxton, of which in its place; besides these, there are hot springs in several places which run waste into the ditches and brooks, and are taken no notice of, being remote among the mountains, and out of the way of the common resort.

We found the wells, as custom bids us call them, pretty full of company, the waters good, and very physical, but wretched lodging and entertainment; so I resolved to stay till I came to the south, and make shift with Tunbridge or Epsom, of which I have spoken at large in the counties of Surrey and Kent.

From Quarden we advanc'd due north, and, mounting the hills gradually for four or five miles, we soon had a most frightful view indeed among the black mountains of the Peak; however, as they were yet at a distance, and a good town lay on our left called Wirksworth, we turned thither for refreshment; Here indeed we found a specimen of what I had heard before, (viz.) that however rugged the hills were, the vales were every where fruitful, well inhabited, the markets well supplied, and the provisions extraordinary good; not forgetting the ale, which every where exceeded, if possible, what was pass'd, as if the farther north the better the liquor, and that the nearer we approach'd to Yorkshire, as the place for the best, so the ale advanc'd the nearer to its perfection.

Wirksworth is a large well-frequented market town, and market towns being very thin placed in this part of the county, they have the better trade, the people generally coming twelve or fifteen miles to a market, and sometimes much more; though there is no very great trade to this town but what relates to the lead works, and to the subterranean wretches, who they call Peakrills, who work in the mines, and who live all round this town every way.

The inhabitants are a rude boorish kind of people, but they are a bold, daring, and even desperate kind of fellows in their search into the bowels of the earth; for no people in the world out-do them; and therefore they are often entertained by our engineers in the wars to carry on the sap, and other such works, at the sieges of strong fortified places.

This town of Wirksworth is a kind of a market for lead; the like not known any where else that I know of, except it be at the custom-house keys in London. The Barmoot Court, kept here to judge controversies among the miners, that is to say, to adjust subterranean quarrels and disputes, is very remarkable: Here they summon a master and twenty-four jurors, and they have power to set out the bounds of the works under ground, the terms are these, they are empowered to set off the meers (so they call them) of ground in a pipe and a flat, that is to say, twenty nine yards long in the first, and fourteen square in the last; when any man has found a vein of oar in another man's ground, except orchards and gardens; they may appoint the proprietor cartways and passage for timber, &c. This court also prescribes rules to the mines, and limits their proceedings in the works under ground; also they are judges of all their little quarrels and disputes in the mines, as well as out, and, in a word, keep the peace among them; which, by the way, may be called the greatest of all the wonders of the Peak, for they are of a strange, turbulent, quarrelsome temper, and very hard to be reconciled to one another in their subterraneous affairs.

And now I am come to this wonderful place, the Peak, where you will expect I should do as some others have, (I think, foolishly) done before me, viz. tell you strange long stories of wonders as (I must say) they are most weakly call'd; and that you may not think me arrogant in censuring so many wise men, who have wrote of these wonders, as if they were all fools, I shall give you four Latin lines out of Mr. Cambden, by which you will see there were some men of my mind above a hundred years ago.

> Mira alto Pecco tria sunt, barathrum, specus, antrum;
> Commoda tot, Plumbum, Gramen, Ovile pecus,
> Tot speciosa simul sunt, Castrum, Balnea, Chatsworth,
> Plura sed occurrunt, quæ speciosa minus.
>
> CAMBD., *Brit. Fol.*, 495.

Which by the same hand are Englished thus:

> Nine things that please us at the Peak we see; ⎫
> A cave, a den, a hole, the wonder be; ⎪
> Lead, sheep and pasture, are the useful three. ⎭
> Chatsworth the castle, and the Bath delight;
> Much more you see; all little worth the sight.

Now to have so great a man as Mr. Hobbes, and after him Mr. Cotton, celebrate the trifles here, the first in a fine Latin poem, the last in English verse, as if they were the most exalted wonders of the world: I cannot but, after wondering at their making wonders of them, desire you, my friend, to travel with me through this houling wilderness in your imagination, and you shall soon find all that is wonderful about it.

Near Wirksworth, and upon the very edge of Derwent, is, as above, a village called Matlock, where there are several warm springs, lately one of these being secured by a stone wall on every side, by which the water is brought to rise to a due heighth, is made into a very convenient bath; with a house built over it, and room within the building to walk round the water or bath, and so by steps to go down gradually into it.

This bath would be much more frequented than it is, if two things did not hinder; namely, a base, stony, mountainous road to it, and no good accommodation when you are there: They are intending, as they tell us, to build a good house to entertain persons of quality, or such who would spend their money at it; but it was not so far concluded or directed when I was there, as to be any where begun: The bath is milk, or rather blood warm, very pleasant to go into, and very sanative, especially for rheumatick pains, bruises, &c.

For some miles before we come to Matlock, you pass over the hills by the very mouths of the lead-mines, and there are melting-houses for the preparing the oar, and melting or casting it into pigs; and so they carry it to Wirksworth to be sold at the market.

Over against this warm bath, and on the other, or east side of the Derwent, stands a high rock, which rises from the very bottom of the river (for the water washes the foot of it, and is there in dry weather very shallow); I say, it rises perpendicular as a wall, the precipice bare and smooth like one plain stone, to such a prodigious heighth, it is really surprising; yet what the people believed of it surmounted all my faith too, though I look'd upon it very curiously, for they told me it was above four hundred foot high, which is as high as two of our Monuments, one set upon another; that which adds most to my wonder in it is, that as the stone stands, it is smooth from the very bottom of the Derwent to the uppermost point, and nothing can be seen to grow upon it. The prodigious heighth of this tor, (for it is called Matlock Tor) was to me more a wonder than any of the rest in the Peak, and, I think, it should be named among them, but it is not. So it must not be called one of the wonders.

A little on the other side of Wirksworth, begins a long plain called Brassington Moor, which reaches full twelve miles in length another way, (viz.) from Brassington to Buxton. At the beginning of it on this side from Wirksworth, it is not quite so much. The Peak people, who are mighty fond of having strangers shewed every thing they can, and of calling everything a wonder, told us here of another high mountain, where a giant was buried, and which they called the Giant's Tomb.

This tempted our curiosity, and we presently rod up to the mountain in order to leave our horses, dragoon-like, with a servant, and to clamber up to the top of it, to see this Giant's Tomb: Here we miss'd the imaginary wonder, and found a real one; the story of which I cannot but record, to shew the discontented part of the rich world how to value their own happiness, by looking below them, and seeing how others live, who yet are capable of being easie and content, which content goes a great way towards being happy, if it does not come quite up to happiness. The story is this:

As we came near the hill, which seemed to be round, and a precipice almost on every side, we perceived a little parcel of ground hedg'd in, as if it were a garden, it was about twenty or thirty yards long, but not so much broad, parallel with the hill, and close to it; we saw no house, but, by a dog running out and barking, we perceived some people were thereabout; and presently after we saw two little children, and then a third run out to see what was the matter. When we came close up we saw a small opening, not a door, but a natural opening into the rock, and the noise we had made brought a woman out with a child in her arms, and another at her foot. *N.B.* The biggest of these five was a girl, about eight or ten years old.

We asked the woman some questions about the tomb of the giant upon the rock or mountain: She told us, there was a broad flat stone of a great size lay there, which, she said, the people call'd a gravestone; and, if it was, it might well be called a giant's, for she thought no ordinary man was ever so tall, and she describ'd it to us as well as she could, by which it must be at least sixteen or seventeen foot long; but she could not give any farther account of it, neither did she seem to lay any stress upon the tale of a giant being buried there, but said, if her husband had been at home he might have shown it to us. I snatched at the word, at home! says I, good wife, why, where do you live. Here, sir, says she, and points to the hole in the rock. Here! says I; and do all these children live here too? Yes, sir, says she, they were all born here. Pray how long have you dwelt here then? said I. My husband was born here, said she, and his father before him. Will you give me leave, says one of our company, as curious as I was, to come in and see your house, dame? If you please, sir, says she, but 'tis not a place fit for such as you are to come into, calling him, your worship, for-sooth; but that by the by. I mention it, to shew that the good woman did not want manners, though she liv'd in a den like a wild body.

However, we alighted and went in: There was a large hollow cave, which the poor people by two curtains hang'd cross, had parted into three rooms. On one side was the chimney, and the man, or perhaps his father, being miners, had found means to work a shaft or funnel through the rock to carry the smoke out at the top, where the giant's tombstone was. The habitation was poor, 'tis true, but things within did not look so like misery as I expected. Every thing was clean and neat, tho' mean and ordinary: There were shelves with earthen ware, and some pewter and brass. There was, which I observed in particular, a whole flitch or side of bacon hanging up in the chimney, and by it a good piece of another. There was a sow and pigs running about at the door, and a little lean cow feeding upon a green place just before the door, and the little enclosed piece of ground I mentioned, was growing with good barley; it being then near harvest.

To find out whence this appearance of substance came, I asked the poor woman, what trade her husband was? She said, he worked in the lead mines. I asked her, how much he could earn a day there? she said, if he had good luck he could earn about five pence a day, but that he worked by the dish (which was a term of art I did not understand, but supposed, as I afterwards understood it was, by the great, in proportion to the oar, which they measure in a wooden bowl, which they call a dish). Then I asked, what she did? she said, when she was able to work she washed the oar: But, looking down on her children, and shaking her head, she intimated, that they found her so much business she could do but little, which I easily granted must be true. But what can you get at washing the oar, said I, when you can work? She said, if she work'd hard she could gain three-pence a day. So that, in short, here was but eight-pence a day when they both worked hard, and that not always, and perhaps not often, and all this to maintain a man, his wife, and five small children, and yet they seemed to live very pleasantly, the children look'd plump and fat, ruddy and wholesome; and the woman was tall, well shap'd, clean, and (for the place) a very well looking, comely woman; nor was there any thing look'd like the dirt and nastiness of the miserable cottages of the poor; tho' many of them spend more money in strong drink than this poor woman had to maintain five children with.

This moving sight so affected us all, that, upon a short conference at the door, we made up a little lump of money, and I had the honour to be almoner for the company; and though the sum was not great, being at most something within a crown, as I told it into the poor woman's hand, I could perceive such a surprise in her face, that, had she not given vent to her joy by a sudden flux of tears, I found she would have fainted away. She was some time before she could do any thing but cry; but after that was abated, she expressed her self very handsomely (for a poor body) and told me, she had not seen so much money together of her own for many months.

We asked her, if she had a good husband; she smiled, and said, Yes, thanked God for it, and that she was very happy in that, for he worked very hard, and they wanted for nothing that he could do for them; and two or three times made mention of how contented they were: In a word, it was a lecture to us all, and that such, I assure you, as made the whole company very grave all the rest of the day: And if it has no effect of that kind upon the reader, the defect must be in my telling the story in a less moving manner than the poor woman told it her self.

From hence enquiring no farther after the giant, or his tomb, we went, by the direction of the poor woman, to a valley on the side of a rising hill, where there were several grooves, so they call the mouth of the shaft or pit by which they go down into a lead mine; and as we were standing still to look at one of them, admiring how small they were, and scarce believing a poor man that shew'd it us, when he told us, that they went down those narrow pits or holes to so great a depth in the earth; I say, while we were wondering, and scarce believing the fact, we were agreeably surprized with seeing a hand, and then an arm, and quickly after a head, thrust up out of the very groove we were looking at. It was the more surprizing as not we only, but not the man that we were talking to, knew any thing of it, or expected it.

Immediately we rode closer up to the place, where we see the poor wretch working and heaving himself up gradually, as we thought, with difficulty; but when he shewed us that it was by setting his feet upon pieces of wood fixt cross the angles of the groove like a ladder, we found that the difficulty was not much; and if the groove had been larger they could not either go up or down so easily, or with so much safety, for that now their elbows resting on those pieces as well as their feet, they went up and down with great ease and safety.

Those who would have a more perfect idea of those grooves, need do no more than go to the church of St. Paul's, and desire to see the square wells which they have there to go down from the top of the church into the very vaults under it, to place the leaden pipes which carry the rain water from the flat of the roof to the common-shore, which wells are square, and have small iron bars placed cross the angles for the workmen to set their feet on, to go up and down to repair the pipes; the manner of the steps are thus describ'd:

When this subterranean creature was come quite out, with all his furniture about him, we had as much variety to take us up as before, and our curiosity received full satisfaction without venturing down, as we were persuaded to by some people, and as two of our company were inclined to do.

First, the man was a most uncouth spectacle; he was cloathed all in leather, had a cap of the same without brims, some tools in a little basket which he drew up with him, not one of the names of which we could understand but by the help of an interpreter. Nor indeed could we understand any of the man's discourse so as to make out a whole sentence; and yet the man was pretty free of his tongue too.

For his person, he was lean as a skeleton, pale as a dead corps, his hair and beard a deep black, his flesh lank, and, as we thought, something of the colour of the lead itself, and being very tall and very lean he look'd, or we that saw him ascend *ab inferis*, fancied he look'd like an inhabitant of the dark regions below, and who was just ascended into the world of light.

Besides his basket of tools, he brought up with him about three quarters of a hundred weight of oar, which we wondered at, for the man had no small load to bring, considering the manner of his coming up; and this indeed made him come heaving and struggling up, as I said at first, as if he had great difficulty to get out; whereas it was indeed the weight that he brought with him.

If any reader thinks this, and the past relation of the woman and the cave, too low and trifling for this work, they must be told, that I think quite otherwise; and especially considering what a noise is made of wonders in this country, which, I must needs say, have nothing in them curious, but much talked of, more trifling a great deal. See Cotton's *Wonders of the Peak*, Hobbes's *Chatsworth*, and several others; but I shall make no more apologies. I return to our subterranean apparition.

We asked him, how deep the mine lay which he came out of: He answered us in terms we did not understand; but our interpreter, as above, told us, it signified that he was at work 60 fathoms deep, but that there were five men of his party, who were, two of them, eleven fathoms, and the other three, fifteen fathoms deeper: He seemed to regret that he was not at work with those three; for that they had a deeper vein of oar than that which he worked in, and had a way out at the side of the hill, where they pass'd without coming up so high as he was obliged to do.

If we blessed ourselves before, when we saw how the poor woman and her five children lived in the hole or cave in the mountain, with the giant's grave over their heads; we had much more room to reflect how much we had to acknowledge to our Maker, that we were not appointed to get our bread thus, one hundred and fifty yards under ground, or in a hole as deep in the earth as the cross upon St. Paul's cupolo is high out of it: Nor was it possible to see these miserable people without such reflections, unless you will suppose a man as stupid and sensless as the horse he rides on. But to leave moralizing to the reader, I proceed.

We then look'd on the oar, and got the poor man's leave to bring every one a small piece of it away with us, for which we gave him two small pieces of better mettle, called shillings, which made his heart glad; and, as we understood by our interpreter, was more than he could gain at sixty fathoms under ground in three days; and we found soon after the money was so much, that it made him move off immediately towards the alehouse, to melt some of it into good Pale Derby; but, to his farther good luck, we were gotten to the same alehouse before him; where, when we saw him come, we gave him some liquor too, and made him keep his money, and promise us to carry it home to his family, which they told us lived hard by.

From hence entring upon Brassington Moor, mentioned above, we had eight mile smooth green riding to Buxton bath, which they call one of the wonders of the Peak; but is so far from being a wonder, that to us, who had been at Bath in Somersetshire, and at Aix la Chapelle in Germany, it was nothing at all; nor is it any thing but what is frequent in such mountainous countries as this is, in many parts of the world.

That which was more wonderful to me than all of it, was, that so light is made of them as to use; that the people rather wonder at them than take the benefit of them; and that, as there are several hot springs in this village of Buxton, as well as at Matlock, mentioned above, and at several other places, they are not built into noble and convenient bathing places; and, instead of a house or two, a city built here for the entertainment of company; which, if it were done, and countenance given to it, as is to the baths at Bath, I doubt not it would be as well frequented, and to as good purpose.

But though I shall not treat this warm spring as a wonder, for such it is not; I must nevertheless give it the praise due to the medicinal virtue of its waters; for it is not to be deny'd, but that wonderful cures have been wrought by them, especially in rheumatick, scorbutick and scrofulous distempers, aches of the joints, nervous pains, and also in scurfy and leprous maladies.

For a proof of this, and to give a just reputation to the waters of Buxton, I crave leave to give a brief account of what the learned say of their virtues, and the manner of their operation; and though I shall not croud this work with any thing from books, which is not more than common, and more than ordinary useful, yet I must be excused in this, as what I think excels in both: It is from the learned Dr. Leigh, in his *Natural History of Lancashire, and of the Peak*; his words are as follows:

Here, meaning at Buxton, the waters are sulphurous and saline yet not fœtid, but very palatable, because the sulphur is not united with any vitriolic particles, or but very few saline; it tinges not silver, nor is it purgative, because its saline parts are dispensed in such small proportions, which saline particles make up a compound salt, constituted of a marine salt, and the *Sal Catharticum Amarum*, which indeed is the *Nitrum Calcarium* that impregnates Epsom, Northall and Dullwich waters, and others in those parts, as at Stretham, Peckham, Shooters-Hill, &c. in the county of Kent.

These waters (Buxton) if drank, create a good appetite, open obstructions, and no doubt, if mixed with the chalybeat waters that are there also, may answer all the intentions of the Bath water in Somersetshire, and that of Sir Vincent's too at Bristol, so noted for curing the diabetes; of which I have seen several instances in these parts; and likewise for curing of bloody urines, of which I saw a most noted instance at Liverpoole.

This bath is of a temperate heat, and, without question, by a reverberating halitus might be brought to any degree of heat; but, I think, in its own natural heat, it may in general be said to be more agreeable to the constitutions of those parts; and where the hot baths cannot be safely used, this may. This last summer I saw remarkable instances of its effects in scorbutick rheumatisms in persons, that could not go before without the help of crutches, who came from thence to Manchester on foot without them, distant from Buxton full sixteen northern miles.

For the antiquity of these baths too, though there is not a King Bladud to testify for them, as at Bath in Somersetshire, whose evidence we cannot be sure is very justifiable, yet hear the same author on that article:

That these baths were eminent in the Romans time, is most certain. Lucan, and others acquaint us, they were extraordinary hot, the high road, called the Roman Bath-gate, as Mr. Cambden says, further confirms it; but it is especially evident from a Roman wall cemented with red Roman plaister, close by St. Anne's Well, where we may see the ruins of the antient bath, its dimensions and length.

The waters are temperately hot, or rather warm, and operate rather as a cold bath, without that violent attack which the cold bath makes upon all nature at once; you feel a little chilness when you first dip or plunge into the water, but it is gone in a moment; and you find a kind of an equality in the warmth of your blood and that of the water, and that so very pleasant, that far from the fainting and weakening violence of the hot baths, which makes you ready to die away if you continue above an hour, or thereabouts, in them, and will shrivel up the fingers like those of women, who have been washing cloaths; on the contrary, here you are never tired, and can hardly be persuaded to come out of the bath when you are in.

The village where the principal springs are, is called Buxton; though there are several of them, for they rise unregarded in the banks of the enclosures, and on the sides of the hill, so that the number is hardly known; there is but one bath which is walled in with stone walls, and steps made to go down into it, and a house built over it, though not so close as is fit for winter bathing.

The Duke of Devonshire is lord of the village, and consequently of the bath itself; and his grace has built a large handsome house at the bath, where there is convenient lodging, and very good provisions, and an ordinary well served for one shilling per head; but it is but one. And though some other houses in the town take in lodgers upon occasion, yet the conveniencies are not the same; so that there is not accommodation for a confluence of people, as at the bath-house it self: If it were otherwise, and that the nobility and gentry were suitably entertained, I doubt not but Buxton would be frequented, and with more effect as to health, as well as much more satisfaction to the company; where there is an open and healthy country, a great variety of view to satisfy the curious, and a fine down or moor for the ladies to take a ring upon in their coaches, all much more convenient than in a close city as the Bath is, which, more like a prison than a place of diversion, scarce gives the company room to converse out of the smell of their own excrements, and where the very city it self may be said to stink like a general common-shore.

We saw indeed a variety of objects here; some that came purely for the pleasure of bathing, taking the air, and to see the country, which has many things rare and valuable to be seen, tho' nothing, as I met with, can be called a wonder, Elden Hole excepted, of which in its place: We found others that came purely for cure, as the lame man to the pool; of which some openly applauded the virtue of the bath, as evidently working a cure upon them. One object indeed, who, whether his physician mistook his disease, or he gave his physician a wrong account, (as is most probable) was very inadvertently sent thither, found himself fatally injured by the bath: What the reason of that might be, I leave to the learned; but, upon this occasion, one of our company left the following lines written on the wall in the bathing house:

> Buxton, may all the silver streams unite,
> And be as bountiful, as they are bright:
> May every votary, diseas'd and poor,
> If chaste in blood, be certain of his cure.
> But let thy springs refuse that wretch to heal,
> Who shall a crime in his disease conceal:
> May thy chast streams quench no dishonest flame,
> But as thy fountain's pure, be pure thy fame.

South west from hence, about a quarter of a mile, or not so much, on the side, or rather at the foot of a very high ridge of mountains, is a great cave or hole in the earth, called Poole's Hole, another of the wonderless wonders of the Peak. The wit that has been spent upon this vault or cave in the earth, had been well enough to raise the expectation of strangers, and bring fools a great way to creep into it; but is ill bestowed upon all those that come to the place with a just curiosity, founded upon antient report; when these go in to see it, they generally go away, acknowledging that they have seen nothing suitable to their great expectation, or to the fame of the place.

It is a great cave, or natural vault, antient doubtless as the mountain itself, and occasioned by the fortuitous position of the rocks at the creation of all things, or perhaps at the great absorption or influx of the surface into the abyss at the great rupture of the earth's crust or shell, according to Mr. Burnet's theory; and to me it seems a confirmation of that hypothesis of the breaking in of the surface. But that by the way:

It may be deepen'd and enlarged by streams and eruptions of subterraneous waters, of which here are several, as there generally are in all such cavities; as at Castleton in this country, at Wooky Hole in Somersetshire, which I have already spoken of; and at several like caves which are now to be seen among the mountains in Swisserland, in Norway, in Hungary, and other places.

The story of one Pole or Poole, a famous giant or robber, (they might as well have called him a man eater) who harboured in this vault, and whose kitchen and lodging, or bed-chamber, they show you on your right-hand, after you have crept about ten yards upon all-four; I say, this I leave to those who such stories are better suited to, than I expect of my readers.

However, this helps among the people there, to make out the *wonder*; and indeed such things are wanting where really wonder is wanting, else there would be no wonder at all in it; as indeed there is not.

The utmost you meet with after this, is the extraordinary heighth of the arch or roof; which, however, is far from what a late flaming author has magnified it to, (viz.) a quarter of a mile perpendicular. That it is very high, is enough to say; for it is so far from a quarter of a mile, that there seems nothing admirable in it.

Dr. Leigh spends some time in admiring the spangled roof. Cotton and Hobbes are most ridiculously and outrageously witty upon it. Dr. Leigh calls it fret work, organ, and choir work. The whole of the matter is this, that the rock being every where moist and dropping, the drops are some fallen, those you see below; some falling, those you have glancing by you *en passant*; and others pendant in the roof. Now as you have guides before you and behind you, carrying every one a candle, the light of the candles reflected by the globular drops of water, dazle upon your eyes from every corner; like as the drops of dew in a sunny-bright morning reflect the rising light to the eye, and are as ten thousand rainbows in miniature; whereas were any part of the roof or arch of this vault to be seen by a clear light, there would be no more beauty on it than on the back of a chimney; for, in short, the stone is coarse, slimy, with the constant wet, dirty and dull; and were the little drops of water gone, or the candles gone, there would be none of these fine sights to be seen for wonders, or for the learned authors above to show themselves foolish about.

Let any person therefore, who goes into Poole's Hole for the future, and has a mind to try the experiment, take a long pole in his hand, with a cloth tied to the end of it, and mark any place of the shining spangled roof which his pole will reach to; and then, wiping the drops of water away, he shall see he will at once extinguish all those glories; then let him sit still and wait a little, till, by the nature of the thing, the drops swell out again, and he shall find the stars and spangles rise again by degrees, here one, and there one, till they shine with the same fraud, a meer *deceptio visus*, as they did before. As for the Queen of Scots pillar, as 'tis called, because her late unfortunate majesty, Mary, Queen of Scots, was pleased to have it be called so, it is a piece of stone like a kind of spar, which is found about the lead; and 'tis not improbable in a country where there is so much of the oar, it may be of the same kind, and, standing upright, obtained the name of a pillar; of which almost every body that comes there, carries away a piece, in veneration of the memory of the unhappy princess that gave it her name. Nor is there any thing strange or unusual in the stone, much less in the figure of it, which is otherwise very mean, and in that country very common.

As to the several stones called Mr. Cotton's, Haycock's, Poole's Chair, Flitches of Bacon, and the like, they are nothing but ordinary stones; and the shapes very little resemble the things they are said to represent; but the fruitful imagination of the country carls, who fancy to call them so, will have them to look like them; a stranger sees very little even of the similitude, any more than when people fancy they see faces and heads, castles and cities, armies, horses and men, in the clouds, in the fire, and the like.

Nor is the pertifying of the water, which appears in its pendant form like icecles in the roof aloft, or rising pyramids below, if such there were, any thing but what is frequent and natural both to water and to stone, placed thus under ground, and seems to be the way by which even stone itself, like other vegetables, fructifies and grows.

So that, in short, there is nothing in Poole's Hole to make a wonder of, any more than as other things in nature, which are rare to be seen, however easily accounted for, may be called wonderful.

Having thus accounted for two of the seven things, called wonders in this country, I pass by Elden Hole, which I shall take notice of by it self, and come to two more of them, as wonderless, and empty of every thing that may be called rare or strange, as the others; and indeed much more so.

The first of these is Mam Tor, or, as the word in the mountain jargon signifies, the Mother Rock, upon a suggestion that the soft crumbling earth, which falls from the summit of the one, breeds or begets several young mountains below. The sum of the whole wonder is this, That there is a very high hill, nay, I will add (that I may make the most of the story, and that it may appear as much like a wonder as I can) an exceeding high hill. But this in a country which is all over hills, cannot be much of a wonder, because also there are several higher hills in the Peak than that, only not just there.

The south side of this hill is a precipice, and very steep from the top to the bottom; and as the substance of this hill is not a solid stone, or rocky, as is the case of all the hills thereabouts, but a crumbling loose earth mingled with small stones, it is continually falling down in small quantities, as the force of hasty showers, or solid heavy rains, loosens and washes it off, or as frosts and thaws operate upon it in common with other parts of the earth; now as the great hill, which is thick, as well as high, parts with this loose stuff, without being sensibly diminished, yet the bottom which it falls into, is more easily perceived to swell with the quantity that falls down; the space where it is received being small, comparatively to the heighth and thickness of the mountain: Here the pretended wonder is form'd, namely, that the little heap below, should grow up into a hill, and yet the great hill not be the less for all that is fallen down; which is not true in fact, any more than, as a great black cloud pouring down rain as it passes over our heads, appears still as great and as black as before, though it continues pouring down rain over all the country. But nothing is more certain than this, that the more water comes down from it, the less remains in it; and so it certainly is of Mam

Tor, in spite of all the poetry of Mr. Cotton or Mr. Hobbes, and in spight of all the women's tales in the Peak.

This hill lies on the north side of the road from Buxton to Castleton, where we come to the so famed wonder call'd, saving our good manners, *The Devil's A——e in the Peak*; Now notwithstanding the grossness of the name given it, and that there is nothing of similitude or coherence either in form and figure, or any other thing between the thing signified and the thing signifying; yet we must search narrowly for any thing in it to make a wonder, or even any thing so strange, or odd, or vulgar, as the name would seem to import.

The short of this story is; that on the steep side of a mountain there is a large opening very high, broad at bottom, and narrow, but rounding, on the top, almost the form of the old Gothick gates or arches, which come up, not to a half circle or half oval at the top, but to a point; though this being all wild and irregular, cannot be said to be an arch, but a meer chasme, entring horizontally; the opening being upwards of thirty foot perpendicular, and twice as much broad at the bottom at least.

The arch continues thus wide but a little way, yet far enough to have several small cottages built on either side of it within the entrance; so that 'tis like a little town in a vault: In the middle, (as it were a street) is a running stream of water; the poetical descriptions of it will have this be called a river, tho' they have not yet bestow'd a name upon it, nor indeed is it worthy a name.

As you go on, the roof descends gradually, and is so far from admitting houses to stand in it, that you have not leave to stand upright your self, till stooping for a little way, and passing over another rill of water, which Mr. Cotton calls a river too, you find more room over your head. But going a little farther you come to a third water, which crosses your way; and the rock stooping, as it were, down almost to the surface of the water, forbids any farther enquiry into what is beyond.

This is the whole wonder, unless it may be called so, that our ancestors should give it so homely a sirname; and give us no reason for it, but what we must guess at from the uncouth entrance of the place, which being no guide in the case, leave us to reflect a little upon their modesty of expression; but it seems they talked broader in those days than we do now.

To conclude: If there were no such vaults and arches any where but in the Peak, or indeed if they were not frequent in such mountainous countries, as well here, as in other nations, we might call this a wonder. But as we know they are to be found in many places in England, and that we read of them in the description of other countries, and even in the Scripture, we cannot think there is any room to call it a wonder. We read of the cave of Adullam, and of the cave of Mackpelah, in the Scripture, able to receive David, and his whole troop of four hundred men. We read of the persecuted worthies in the 12th of the Hebrews, who wandered about in dens and caves of the earth. We read of a cave in the Apenine Mountains near to Florence, which was able to receive an army; there are also many such caves, as I have observed above, in the Alpes, and the hills of Dauphine and Savoy, and in other parts of the world, too many to run over; and some of them, such as this is not worthy to be named among them.

Indeed, had Gervaise of Tilbury been credited, this place had deserved all that wonder cou'd ascribe to it; for he tells us of a shepherd who, having ventured into the third river in this den, and being either carried over it or down the stream, he knew not whether, saw a beautiful heavenly country beyond it, with a spacious plain watered with many clear rivers and pleasant brooks, and several lakes of standing water. But who this shepherd was, how he got into that pleasant country; and, above all, how he came back to tell the story, our friend Gervaise forgot, it seems, to take any notice of; and so the tale is broken off before it was half told, like another of the same kind which Hudibras tells of,

> Which, like the tale o'th' bear and fiddle,
> Was told; but broke off in the middle.

The next wonder, which makes up number five, is called Tideswell, or a spring of water which ebbs and flows, as they will have it, as the sea does. A poor thing indeed to make a wonder of; and therefore most of the writers pass it over with little notice; only that they are at a loss to make up the number seven without it.

This well or spring is called Weeden Well; the basin or receiver for the water is about three foot square every way; the water seems to have some other receiver within the rock, which, when it fills by the force of the original stream, which is small, the air being contracted or pent in, forces the water out with a bubbling noise, and so fills the receiver without; but when the force is spent within, then it stops till the place is filled again; and, in the mean time, the water without runs

off or ebbs, till the quantity within swells again, and then the
same causes produce the same effects, as will always be while
the world endures. So that all this wonder is owing only to the
situation of the place, which is a meer accident in nature; and
if any person were to dig into the place, and give vent to the
air, which fills the contracted space within, they would soon
see Tideswell turned into an ordinary running stream, and a
very little one too.

So much for fictitious wonders, or indeed simple wonders.
The two real wonders which remain, are first, Elden Hole, and
secondly, the Duke of Devonshire's fine house at Chatsworth;
one a wonder of nature, the other of art. I begin with the last.

Chatsworth is indeed a most glorious and magnificent house,
and, as it has had two or three founders, may well be said to
be compleatly designed and finished. It was begun on a much
narrower plan than it now takes up, by Sir William Cavendish,
of Cavendish in Suffolk, who married the Countess Dowager
of Shrewsbury, and with her came into a noble and plentiful
fortune in this country.

Sir William died, having done little more than built one end
of the fabrick, and laid out the plan, as I have said, or ichno-
graphy of the whole. But the lady, who, it seems, was the
mover of the first design, finish'd the whole in the magnificent
manner which it appeared in, when it was first christen'd a
wonder, and ranked among the marvelleux of the Peak. But
what would the world have called it, or what would Mr. Cambden
have said of it, had it appeared in those days in the glory and
splendor its last great founder, for so we may justly call him,
left it in.

It is indeed a palace for a prince, a most magnificent building,
and, in spite of all the difficulties or disadvantages of situation,
is a perfect beauty; nay, the very obstructions and, as I called
them, disadvantages of its situation, serve to set off its beauty,
and are, by the most exquisite decoration of the place, made to
add to the lustre of the whole. But it would take up a volume
by itself to describe it. I shall only touch at those things which
other writers have omitted; for, as Mr. Hobbes has elegantly
set it off in Latin verse, Mr. Cotton, after his manner, in English,
and others, in as good a manner as they can, in history; they
have yet, all of them, left enough for me to say, and so shall
I, for many after me; and yet perhaps it shall be as many years
describing as it was in building, and the description be no more
finished than the building, which will have always an encrease

of ornament, as the noble possessors see room to add to its glory.

The front to the garden is the most regular piece of architect I have seen in all the north part of England; the pilaster seventy two foot high to the foot of the ballaster on the top; the frize under the cornish is spacious, and has the motto of the family upon it, the letters so large (and gilded) as takes up the whole front, tho' the words are but these two:

CAVENDO TUTUS

The sashes of the second story we were told are seventeen foot high, the plates polish'd looking-glass, and the woodwork double gilded; which, I think, is no where else to be seen in England.

Under this front lye the gardens exquisitely fine, and, to make a clear vista or prospect beyond into the flat country, towards Hardwick, another seat of the same owner, the duke, to whom what others thought impossible, was not only made practicable, but easy, removed, and perfectly carried away a great mountain that stood in the way, and which interrupted the prospect.

This was so entirely gone, that, having taken a strict view of the gardens at my first being there, and retaining an idea of them in my mind, I was perfectly confounded at coming there a second time, and not knowing what had been done; for I had lost the hill, and found a new country in view, which Chatsworth it self had never seen before.

The house indeed had received additions, as it did every year, and perhaps would to this day, had the duke liv'd, who had a genius for such things beyond the reach of the most perfect masters, and was not only capable to design, but to finish.

The gardens, the water-works, the cascades, the statues, vasa and painting, tho' they are but very imperfectly described by any of the writers who have yet named them, and more imperfectly by one author, who has so lately pretended to view them; yet I dare not venture to mention them here, least, for want of time, and having so long a journey to go, I should, like those who have gone before me, do it imperfectly, or leave no room to do justice to other persons and places, which I am still to mention. I shall therefore, as I said above, only touch at what others have omitted.

First, 'tis to be observed that on the east side rises a very high mountain, on the top of which they dig mill-stones, and it begins so close to, and so overlooks the house, being prodigiously high that, should they roll down a pair of those stones coupled with a wooden axis, as is the way of drawing them, they would infallibly give a shock to the building; yet this mountain is so planted, and so covered with a wood of beautiful trees, that you see no hill, only a rising wood, as if the trees grew so much higher than one another, and was only a wall of trees, whose tops join into one another so close, as nothing is seen through them.

Upon the top of that mountain begins a vast extended moor or waste, which, for fifteen or sixteen miles together due north, presents you with neither hedge, house or tree, but a waste and houling wilderness, over which when strangers travel, they are obliged to take guides, or it would be next to impossible not to lose their way.

Nothing can be more surprising of its kind, than for a stranger coming from the north, suppose from Sheffield in Yorkshire, for that is the first town of note, and wandering or labouring to pass this difficult desart country, and seeing no end of it, and almost discouraged and beaten out with the fatigue of it, (just such was our case) on a sudden the guide brings him to this precipice, where he looks down from a frightful heighth, and a comfortless, barren, and, as he thought, endless moor, into the most delightful valley, with the most pleasant garden, and most beautiful palace in the world: If contraries illustrate, and the place can admit of any illustration, it must needs add to the splendor of the situation, and to the beauty of the building, and I must say (with which I will close my short observation) if there is any wonder in Chatsworth, it is, that any man who had a genius suitable to so magnificent a design, who could lay out the plan for such a house, and had a fund to support the charge, would build it in such a place where the mountains insult the clouds, intercept the sun, and would threaten, were earthquakes frequent here, to bury the very towns, much more the house, in their ruins.

On the top of that mountain, that is to say, on the plain which extends from it, is a large pond or basin for water, spreading, as I was told, near thirty acres of ground, which, from all the ascents round it, receives, as into a cistern, all the water that falls, and from which again by pipes, the cascades, waterworks, ponds, and canals in the gardens, are plentifully supplied.

On the west side, which is the front or entrance of the house, and where the first foundress built a very august portal or gate; I say, on the west side, runs the River Derwent, which, though not many miles from its source here, is yet a terrible river, when, by hasty rains, or by the melting of the snows, the hills are pleased to pour down their waters into its channel; for the current is so rapid, and it has so many contracted passages among the rocks, and so many little cataracts amongst the stones, of which sometimes we see some of an incredible bulk come rouling down its stream; I say, there are so many of these, that the river, on the least motion of its waters above their ordinary highth, roars like the breaches on the shores of the sea.

Over this river there is a stately stone bridge, with an antient tower upon it, and in an island in the river an antient fabrick all of stone, and built like a castle. All these are the works of the first foundress, the Countess of Shrewsbury, and shew the greatness of the first design; but, except the bridge, are now, as it were, eclips'd by the modern glories of the later edifice.

In my discourse of the palace of Chatsworth, must not be forgot that fam'd compliment which the Mareschal Duke de Tallard pass'd upon it, when the Duke of Devonshire entertained him at Chatsworth, namely, "That when he should give his master the King of France the history of his seven years captivity in England, he would leave out those three days which he had spent so agreeably with his grace, in seeing the finest palace in the world."

But I must dwell no longer here, however pleasant and agreeable the place. The remaining article, and which, I grant, we may justly call a WONDER, is Elden Hole: The description of it, in brief, is thus: In the middle of a plain open field, gently descending to the south, there is a frightful chasme, or opening in the earth, or rather in the rock, for the country seems thereabouts to be all but one great rock; this opening goes directly down perpendicular into the earth, and perhaps to the center; it may be about twenty foot over one way, and fifty or sixty the other; it has no bottom, that is to say, none that can yet be heard of. Mr. Cotton says, he let down eight hundred fathoms of line into it, and that the plummet drew still; so that, in a word, he sounded about a mile perpendicular; for as we call a mile 1760 yards, and 884 is above half, then doubtless eight hundred fathoms must be 1600 yards, which is near a mile.

This I allow to be a wonder, and what the like of is not to be found in the world, that I have heard of, or believe. And would former writers have been contented with one wonder instead of seven, it would have done more honour to the Peak, and even to the whole nation, than the adding five imaginary miracles to it that had nothing in them, and which really depreciated the whole.

What Nature meant in leaving this window open into the infernal world, if the place lies that way, we cannot tell: But it must be said, there is something of horror upon the very imagination, when one does but look into it; and therefore tho' I cannot find much in Mr. Cotton, of merry memory, worth quoting, yet on this subject, I think, he has four very good lines, speaking of his having an involuntary horror at looking into this pit. The words are these:

> For he, who standing on the brink of hell,
> Can carry it so unconcern'd and well,
> As to betray no fear, is certainly
> A better Christian, or a worse than I.
>
> <div align="right">COTTON's <i>Wonders of the Peak.</i></div>

They tell a dismal story here, of a traveller, who, enquiring his way to Castleton, or to Buxton, in a dark night, two villains offer'd to guide him; but, intending to rob him, led him to the edge of this gulph, and either thrust him in, or persuaded him to believe there was a little gall of water, and bad him take a large step, which the innocent unfortunate did, not mistrusting the treachery, and stept at once into eternity; a story enough to make the blood run cold through the heart of those that hear it told, especially if they know the place too: They add, that one of these villains being hanged at Derby some years after for some other villany, confess'd this murther at the gallows.

Having then viewed those things with an impartial mind, give me leave to reduce the wonders of the Peak to a less number, and of a quite different kind.

1. Elden Hole I acknowledge to be a wonderful place, as I have said above; but to me the greatest surprise is, that, after such a real wonder, any of the trifles added to it could bear the name of wonders.

2. Of Buxton; the wonder to me is, that in a nation so full of chronical diseases as we are, such as our scorbuticks, rheumaticks, cholicks, and niphriticks, there should be such a fountain of medicine sent from heaven, and no more notice taken of it, or care to make it useful.

3. That in a nation so curious, so inquiring, and so critical

as this, any thing so unsatisfying, so foolish and so weak, should pass for wonders as those of Mam Tor, Tideswell, Poole's Hole, &c.

4. As to Chatsworth, the wonder, as I said before, seems to me; not that so noble and magnificent a palace should be built, but that it should be built in such a situation, and in such a country so out of the way, so concealed from the world, that whoever sees it must take a journey on purpose.

Having thus viewed the two counties of Nottingham and Derby, as beginning that part of England, which we call north by Trent, I resolved to go northward on the east side of the island, taking the western shore, or the Irish Sea in my return.

The Peak concludes the northern part of Derbyshire; nor are there any towns on that side worth noting. There are some other curiosities in the Peak indeed, which would deserve a fuller account, had I leisure to enlarge or descend to particulars, as the tottering stones at Byrch Over, the Roman causeway, called Bath-Gate, the several minerals found in the hills, and in the lead mines, as black lead, stibium or antimony, christal, and other things, all much more rare than the wonders they speak of.

Bakewell, is the best town in the north west side of the Peak, near which the Duke of Rutland has a very noble palace, called Haddon; but after Chatsworth no house in the same county can bear a description; so we left the Peak, and went to Chesterfield, a handsome market town at the northermost border of the county, north east from Chatsworth.

There is indeed an extended angle of this county, which runs a great way north west by Chappel in the Frith, and which they call High Peak. This, perhaps, is the most desolate, wild, and abandoned country in all England; The mountains of the Peak, of which I have been speaking, seem to be but the beginning of wonders to this part of the country, and but the beginning of mountains, or, if you will, as the lower rounds of a ladder. The tops of these hills seem to be as much above the clouds, as the clouds are above the ordinary range of hills.

Nor is this all; but the continuance of these mountains is such, that we know no bounds set to them, but they run on in a continued ridge or ledge of mountains from one to another, till they are lost in the southern parts of Scotland, and even through that to the Highlands; so that they may be said to divide Britain, as the Appennine Mountains divide Italy. Thus these hills joyning to Blackstone Edge divide Yorkshire from Lancashire, and going on north divides the Bishoprick of

Durham from Westmoreland, and so on. It is from this ridge
of mountains that all the rivers in the north of England take
their rise, I may say ALL, for it is so to a very trifle, not a considerable river north of this county, nay, and in this county
too, but begin here; those on the east side run into the German
Ocean, those on the west side into the Irish. I shall begin the
observation here; the Dove and the Derwent rise both at this
south end of them, and come away south to the Trent; but all
the rivers afterwards run, as above, east or west; and first the
Mersee rises on the west side, and the Don on the east, the
first runs to Warrington, and into the sea at Liverpoole; the
other to Doncaster, and into the sea at Humber. I shall carry
on the observation as I go, for to give an account of rivers, is
the true guide to the giving the reader the best account of the
country. But to return to my progress.

Chesterfield is a handsome populous town, well-built and well
inhabited, notwithstanding it stands in the farthest part of
this rocky country; for being on the north west side next to
Yorkshire, it enters Scarsdale, which is a rich fruitful part of
the country, though surrounded with barren moors and mountains, for such the name Scarsdale signifies, according to that
master of etymologies, Mr. Cambden. Here is, however, nothing
remarkable in this town but a free school, and a very good
market, well stored with provisions; for here is little or no
manufacture.

From hence (travelling still north) we entred the great county
of York, uncertain still which way to begin to take a full view
of it, for as 'tis a country of a very great extent, my business is
not the situation or a meer geographical description of it;
I have nothing to do with the longitude of places, the antiquities
of towns, corporations, buildings, charters, &c. nor much with
the history of men, families, cities or towns, but to give you a
view of the whole in its present state, as also of the commerce,
curiosities and customs, according to my title.

The county is divided into three ridings; as I entred it from
the south, it follows, I went in, by what they call the West
Riding, which, as it is by much the largest, so it is the wealthiest
and the most populous, has the greatest towns in it, and the
greatest number of them; the greatest manufactures, and consequently the greatest share of wealth, as it has also of people.

Two eminent towns, tho' only meer market towns, and
one of them no corporation, open the door into the West Riding
of Yorkshire; these are Sheffield and Doncaster. It is true, there

is a little market town, at the very first entrance into the county before we come to Doncaster, call'd Bautry, a town bless'd with two great conveniencies which assists to its support, and makes it a very well frequented place.

1. That it stands upon the great post highway, or road from London to Scotland; and this makes it be full of very good inns and houses of entertainment.

2. That the little but pleasant River Idle runs through, or rather just by, the side of it, which, contrary to the import of its name, is a full and quick, though not rapid and unsafe stream, with a deep channel, which carries hoys, lighters, barges, or flat-bottom'd vessels, out of its channel into the Trent, which comes within seven miles of it, to a place called Stockwith, and from thence to Burton, and from thence, in fair weather, quite to Hull; but if not, 'tis sufficient to go to Stockwith, where vessels of 200 ton burthen may come up to the town loaden as well as empty.

By this navigation, this town of Bautry becomes the center of all the exportation of this part of the country, especially for heavy goods, which they bring down hither from all the adjacent countries, such as lead, from the lead mines and smelting-houses in Derbyshire, wrought iron and edge-tools, of all sorts, from the forges at Sheffield, and from the country call'd Hallamshire, being adjacent to the towns of Sheffield and Rotherham, where an innumerable number of people are employed; as I shall speak more largely of in its place.

Also millstones and grindstones, in very great quantities, are brought down and shipped off here, and so carry'd by sea to Hull, and to London, and even to Holland also. This makes Bautry Wharf be famous all over the south part of the West Riding of Yorkshire, for it is the place whither all their heavy goods are carried, to be embarked and shipped off.

From hence to Doncaster is a pleasant road, and good ground, and never wants any repair, which is very hard to be said in any part of this lower side of the country.

Doncaster is a noble, large, spacious town, exceeding populous, and a great manufacturing town, principally for knitting; also as it stands upon the great northern post-road, it is very full of great inns; and here we found our landlord at the post-house was mayor of the town as well as post-master, that he kept a pack of hounds, was company for the best gentlemen in the town or in the neighbourhood, and lived as great as any gentleman ordinarily did.

Here we saw the first remains or ruins of the great Roman highway, which, though we could not perceive it before, was eminent and remarkable here, just at the entrance into the town; and soon after appeared again in many places: Here are also two great, lofty, and very strong stone bridges over the Don, and a long causeway also beyond the bridges, which is not a little dangerous to passengers when the waters of the Don are restrained, and swell over its banks, as is sometimes the case.

This town, Mr. Cambden says, was burnt entirely to the ground, anno 759, and is hardly recovered yet; but I must say, it is so well recovered, that I see no ruins appear, and indeed, being almost a thousand years ago, I know not how there should; and besides, the town seems as if it wanted another conflagration, for it looks old again, and many of the houses ready to fall.

I should, before I leave Doncaster, give you the famous epitaph of one Robert Byrk, a famous man of Doncaster, who lies buried in the great church here, who gave a place, call'd Rossington Wood, to the poor. On his grave is this epitaph in Old English:

> Howe, howe, who's here,
> I, Robin of Doncastere,
>   And Margaret my fere.
> That I spent, that I had;
> That I gave, that I have;
> That I left, that I lost;

Quoth Robertus Byrks, who in this world did reign threescore years and seven, but liv'd not one.

anno 1579.

Here lies also, under a plain gravestone in St. George's Church, interred, the body of one Thomas Ellis, a very memorable person. He was five times mayor of the town, founded an hospital in the town, called St. Thomas's the Apostle, and endowed it plentifully.

Strange! that of but two several authors writing a description of Yorkshire but very lately, and pretending to speak positively of the places, which they ought not to have done, if they had not been there, both of them should so strangely mistake, as one to say of Doncaster, that there was a large church with a high spire steeple; and the other to say of the cathedral at York, that from the spire of the cathedral at York, you have an unbounded prospect: Whereas neither has the tower of York, or the tower at Doncaster, any spire, unless they will pretend any of the small pinacles at the four corners of the two towers at the west end of the church at York, are to be call'd THE SPIRE of THE cathedral; so fit are such men to write descriptions of a country.

Leaving Doncaster, we turned out of the road a little way to the left, where we had a fair view of that antient whittl-making, cutlering town, called Sheffield; the antiquity, not of the town only, but of the trade also, is established by those famous lines of Geoffry Chaucer on the Miller of Trumpington, which, however they vary from the print in Chaucer, as now extant, I give you as I find it:

> At Trumpington, not far from Cambridge,
> There dwelt a miller upon a bridge;
> With a rizzl'd beard, and a hooked nose,
> And a Sheffield whittl in his hose.

This town of Sheffield is very populous and large, the streets narrow, and the houses dark and black, occasioned by the continued smoke of the forges, which are always at work: Here they make all sorts of cutlery-ware, but especially that of edged-tools, knives, razors, axes, &c. and nails; and here the only mill of the sort, which was in use in England for some time was set up, (viz.) for turning their grindstones, though now 'tis grown more common.

Here is a very spacious church, with a very handsome and high spire; and the town is said to have at least as many, if not more people in it than the city of York. Whether they have been exactly numbered one against the other, I cannot tell. The manufacture of hard ware, which has been so antient in this town, is not only continued, but much encreased; insomuch that they told us there, the hands employed in it were a prodigious many more than ever dwelt, as well in the town, as in the bounds of that they call Hallamshire; and they talked of 30000 men employed in the whole; but I leave it upon the credit of report.

There was formerly a very fine castle here, with a noble mansion-house, the seat of the Dukes of Norfolk; but it is now all demolished and decayed, though the estate or mannor remains still in the family. In the great church of this town are several very antient monuments of the family of Talbots, Earls of Shrewsbury, who once had great possessions in this and the next county.

The Queen of Scots was also for a long time detained here as prisoner, not less than sixteen or seventeen years, which was fatal afterward to the house of Norfolk; as is to be seen at large in our English history.

The River Don, with a rapid terrible current, had swelled its banks, and done a prodigious deal of damage the same year that I took this view, having carried away two or three stone bridges, ploughed up some wharfs, and drove away several mills; for this river is of kin to the Derwent for the fierceness of its streams, taking its beginning in the same western mountains, which I mentioned before; and which begin to rise first in the High Peak, and run northward to Blackstone Edge; those mountains pouring down their waters with such fury into these great rivers, their streams are so rapid, that nothing is able to stand in their way.

Here is a fine engine or mill also for raising water to supply the town, which was done by Mr. Serocoal, the same who fell into the river at the throwing-mill at Derby, as is said in its place: Here is also a very large and strong bridge over the Don, as there is another at Rotherham, a market town six miles lower. Here is also a very fine hospital, with the addition of a good revenue, settled at first by Gilbert, Earl of Shrewsbury, and confirmed afterwards by the family of Howard, Dukes of Norfolk.

George, the first Earl of Shrewsbury, who died 1538. George the second, grandson to the first, to whose custody the Queen of Scots was committed, who died 1590, and Gilbert his son, who founded the hospital above mentioned, all lie buried here.

The gift of this hospital is thus documented:

> The Hospital of the Right Hon. GILBERT, Earl of Shrewsbury, erected and settled by the Right Hon. HENRY, Earl of Norwich, Earl Marshal of ENGLAND, great grandson of the said earl, in pursuance of his last Will and Testament, An. 1673.

It is in this park that the great oak tree grew, which Mr. Evelyn gives a long account of in his book of *Forest Trees*; but as I did not see it, I refer to the said Mr. Evelyn's account. The chesnut tree near Aderclift, which Mr. Cambden's continuator mentions, the body of which could hardly be fathom'd by three men, I suppose was gone; for I could hear nothing of it.

But the remains of the Roman fortification or encampment between Sheffield and Rotherham, is there still, and very plain to be seen, and, I suppose, may remain so to the end of time.

Here is also the famous bank or trench which some call Devil's Bank, others Danes Bank; but 'tis frequent with us to give the honour of such great trenches, which they think was never worth the while for men to dig, to the devil, as if he had more leisure, or that it was less trouble to him than to a whole army of men. This bank, 'tis said, runs five mile in length; in some places 'tis called Kemp Bank, in others Temple's Bank.

Rotherham was the next town of any bulk in which, however, I saw nothing of note, except a fine stone bridge over the Don, which is here encreased by the River Rother, from whence the town, I suppose, took its name, as the famous Bishop Rotherham did his from the town: I will not say he was a foundling child in the streets, and so was sirnamed from the place, as is often suggested in such cases, though if he was so, it did not diminish his character, which was that of a great and good man. He was Archbishop of York, and was a great benefactor to this town, having founded a college here; but it seems it has been a long while ago.

From Rotherham we turned north west to Wentworth, on purpose to see the old seat of Tankersly, and the park, where I saw the largest red deer that, I believe, are in this part of Europe: One of the hinds, I think, was larger than my horse, and he was not a very small pad of fourteen hands and half high. This was antiently the dwelling of the great Thomas Wentworth, Earl of Strafford, beheaded in King Charles the First's time, by a law, *ex post facto*, voted afterward not to be drawn into a precedent. The body lies interred in Wentworth Church.

Thence over vast moors, I had almost said waste moors, we entred the most populous part of this county, I mean of the West Riding, only passing a town call'd Black Barnsley, eminent still for the working in iron and steel; and indeed the very town looks as black and smoaky as if they were all smiths that lived in it; tho' it is not, I suppose, called Black Barnsley on that account, but for the black hue or colour of the moors, which, being covered with heath, (or heather, as 'tis called in that country) look all black, like Bagshot Heath, near Windsor; after, I say, we had pass'd these moors, we came to a most rich, pleasant and populous country, and the first town of note we came to in it was Wakefield, a large, handsome, rich clothing town, full of people, and full of trade.

The Calder passes through this town under a stately stone bridge of twelve arches, upon which is a famous building, by some called a chapel, by others a castle; the former is the most likely; It was built by Edward IV. in memory of the fatal Battle of Wakefield, wherein his father, Richard, Duke of York, was killed by the Lancastrian army, under the command of Margaret, queen to Henry VI. anno 1460. It was indeed a fatal battle; but as that is not any part of this work, I leave it to the historians to give a fuller account of it; only one thing I must add, namely, that a little on this side of the town, I mean south between Wakefield, and a village called Sandal, they shewed us a little square piece of ground, which was fenced off by it self; and on which, before the late war, stood a large stone cross, in memory of that fatal battle; just upon that spot, the Duke of York fighting desperately, and refusing to yield, tho' surrounded with enemies, was kill'd. The chapel on the bridge at Wakefield, the other monument of this battle, is now made use of for civil affairs; for we do not now pray for the souls of those slain in battle, and so the intent of that building ceases.

Wakefield is a clean, large, well-built town, very populous and very rich; here is a very large church, and well filled it is, for here are very few Dissenters; the steeple is a very fine spire, and by far the highest in all this part of the country, except that at Sheffield. They tell us, there are here more people also than in the city of York, and yet it is no corporation town; and the highest magistrate, as I understand, was a constable.

Here also is a market every Friday for woollen cloaths, after the manner of that at Leeds, tho' not so great; yet as all the cloathing trade is encreasing in this country, so this market too flourishes with the rest; not but that sometimes, as foreign markets receive interruption either by wars, by a glut of the goods, or by any other incident, there are interruptions of the manufacture too, which, when it happen, the clothiers are sure to complain of loss of trade; but when the demand comes again they are not equally forward with their acknowledgments; and this, I observed, was the case every where else, as well as here.

I cannot pass by my former observation here, namely, how evidently all the great rivers take their beginning in the mountains of Blackstone Edge and High Peak, which, as I have said, part the counties of Lancaster and York, and how these rivers take all their course due east. The Don was the first; the next is the Calder, coming now to be a very large river at Wakefield; and the Aire is the next, which, running another course, of which I shall speak presently, receives the Calder into it.

The River Calder, of which I shall give an account by and by, having trac'd it from its beginning, receiving a mighty confluence of rivers into it, is now, as I have said, become a large river, and the first town it comes near of note is Huthersfield, another large cloathing place; it passes also by Eland, where there is a very fine stone bridge. This was the original seat of the Earls or Marquisses of Hallifax, when the title went in the name of Saville. Huthersfield is one of the five towns which carry on that vast cloathing trade by which the wealth and opulence of this part of the country has been raised to what it now is, and there those woollen manufactures are made in such prodigious quantities, which are known by the name of Yorkshire Kersies. Whether the scandal upon this country be just or not, (viz.) shrinking cloth and sharping k——s, that I will not take upon me to determine; at this town there is a market for kersies every Tuesday.

Nor, as I speak of their manufactures, must I forget that most essential manufacture called Yorkshire Ale, which indeed is in its perfection here, and in all this part of the county; of which I shall speak again in its place.

As the Calder rises in Blackstone Edge, so the Aire, another of the Yorkshire rivers, rises, tho' in the same ridge of hills, yet more particularly at the foot of the mountain Pennigent, on the edge of Lancashire, of which 'tis said proverbially:

> Pendle-Hill and Pennigent,
> Are the highest hills between Scotland and Trent.

As the Calder runs by Hallifax, Huthersfield, and through Wakefield; so the Aire runs by Skippon, Bradforth and thorough Leeds, and then both join at Castleford Bridge, near Pontefract, so in an united stream forming that useful navigation from this trading part of Yorkshire to Hull; to the infinite advantage of the whole country, and which, as I took a singular satisfaction in visiting and enquiring into, so I believe you will be no less delighted in reading the account of it, which will be many ways both useful and very instructive; and the more so, because none of the pretended travel-writers and journeyers thro' England, have yet thought this most remarkable part of our country worth their speaking of, or knew not how to go about it: Nor have they so much as mentioned this whole part of England, which is, on many accounts, the most considerable of all the northern division of this nation.

It is not easie to take a view of this populous and wealthy part, called the West Riding, at one, no, nor at two journies, unless you should dwell upon it, and go cross the country backward and forward, on purpose to see this or that considerable place. This is perhaps the reason why, as I hinted above, the other writers of journies and travels this way might not see how to go about it. But, as I was resolved to have a perfect knowledge of the most remarkable things, and especially of the manufactures of England, which I take to be as well worth a traveller's notice, as the most curious thing he can meet with, and which is so prodigious great in this quarter, I made no less than three journies into, and thro', this part of the country.

In my first journey I came only west from York to Wakefield, and then, turning south by Barnsley to Doncaster, went away still south to Rotherham, Sheffield, Chesterfield, Chatsworth, and the Peak, all which journey, except York, and the towns about it, and in the way to it, I have mentioned already.

The second journey, I came out of the western part of England, namely, from Cheshire thro' Lancashire, and, passing east over those Andes of England, called Blackstone Edge, and the mountains, which, as I hinted before, part Yorkshire and Lancashire, and reach from the High Peak to Scotland, I came to Hallifax, Bradforth, Huthersfield, Leeds, Wetherby, Pontefract and Burrow Bridge, and so went away into the East Riding, as you have heard.

The third journey, I went from the Peak in Derbyshire again, and, traversing the same country as I returned by the first journey as far as Wakefield, went on again north to Leeds, and thence over Harwood Bridge to Knaresborough Spaw, thence to Rippon, and thro' that old Roman street-way, called Leeming Lane, to Pier's Bridge, thence to Durham, and so into Scotland; of all which in their order.

If, by all these circuits, and traversing the country so many ways, which I name for the reasons above, I am not furnished to give a particular account of the most remarkable things, I must have spent my time very ill, and ought not to let you know how often I went through it.

In my second journey, as above, I came from Lancashire, where you are to note, that all this part of the country is so considerable for its trade, that the Post-Master General had thought fit to establish a cross-post thro' all the western part of England into it, to maintain the correspondence of merchants and men of business, of which all this side of the island is so full; this is a confirmation of what I have so often repeated, and may still repeat many times on farther occasion, of the greatness of the trade carried on in this part of the island. This cross-post begins at Plymouth, in the south west part of England, and, leaving the great western post road of Excester behind, comes away north to Taunton, Bridgwater and Bristol; from thence goes on thro' all the great cities and towns up the Severn; such as Gloucester, Worcester, Bridgenorth and Shrewsbury, thence by West-Chester to Liverpool and Warrington, from whence it turns away east, and passes to Manchester, Bury, Rochdale, Hallifax, Leeds, and York, and ends at Hull.

By this means the merchants at Hull have immediate advice of their ships which go out of the channel, and come in; by their letters from Plymouth, as readily as the merchants at London, and without the double charge of postage. The shop-keepers and manufacturers can correspond with their dealers at Manchester, Liverpool and Bristol, nay, even with Ireland directly; without the tedious interruption of sending their letters about by London, or employing people at London to forward their packets; and as the trade on this side is exceeding great, this correspondence is a mighty advantage; nor is the encrease of the revenue by it inconsiderable, the quantity of letters which pass and repass this way, being, as I was told, in all places very great.

I follow'd this post-road, from Liverpool to Bury and Rochdale, both manufacturing towns in Lancashire, and the last very considerable, for a sort of course goods, called half-thicks and kersies, and the market for them is very great, tho' otherwise the town is situated so remote, so out of the way, and so at the very foot of the mountains, that we may suppose it would be but little frequented.

Here, for our great encouragement, though we were but at the middle of August, and in some places the harvest was hardly got in, we saw the mountains covered with snow, and felt the cold very acute and piercing; but even here we found, as in all those northern countries is the case, the people had an extra-ordinary way of mixing the warm and the cold very happily together; for the store of good ale which flows plentifully in the most mountainous part of this country, seems abundantly to make up for all the inclemencies of the season, or difficulties of travelling, adding also the plenty of coals for firing, which all those hills are full of.

We mounted the hills, fortified with the same precaution, early in the morning, and though the snow which had fallen in the night lay a little upon the ground, yet we thought it was not much; and the morning being calm and clear, we had no apprehension of an uneasy passage, neither did the people at Rochdale, who kindly directed us the way, and even offered to guide us over the first mountains, apprehend any difficulty for us; so we complimented our selves out of their assistance, which we afterwards very much wanted.

It was, as I say, calm and clear, and the sun shone when we came out of the town of Rochdale; but when we began to mount the hills, which we did within a mile, or little more of the town, we found the wind began to rise, and the higher we went the more wind; by which I soon perceived that it had blown before, and perhaps all night upon the hills, tho' it was calm below; as we ascended higher it began to snow again, that is to say, we ascended into that part where it was snowing, and had, no doubt, been snowing all night, as we could easily see by the thickness of the snow.

It is not easy to express the consternation we were in when we came up near the top of the mountain; the wind blew exceeding hard, and blew the snow so directly in our faces, and that so thick, that it was impossible to keep our eyes open to see our way. The ground also was so covered with snow, that we could see no track, or when we were in the way, or when out; except when we were shewed it by a frightful precipice on one hand, and uneven ground on the other; even our horses discovered their uneasiness at it; and a poor spaniel dog that was my fellow traveller, and usually diverted us with giving us a mark for our gun, turn'd tail to it and cry'd.

In the middle of this difficulty, and as we began to call to one another to turn back again, not knowing what dangers might still be before us, came a surprizing clap of thunder, the first that ever I heard in a storm of snow, or, I believe, ever shall; nor did we perceive any lightning to precede the thunder, as must naturally be the case; but we supposed the thick falling of the snow might prevent our sight.

I must confess I was very much surprized at this blow; and one of our company would not be persuaded that it was thunder, but that it was some blast of a coal-pit, things which do sometimes happen in the country, where there are many coal mines. But we were all against him in that, and were fully satisfied that it was thunder, and, as we fancy'd, at last we were confirmed in it, by hearing more of it at a distance from us.

Upon this we made a full stop, and coming altogether, for we were then three in company, with two servants, we began to talk seriously of going back again to Rochdale; but just then one of our men called out to us, and said, he was upon the top of the hill, and could see over into Yorkshire, and that there was a plain way down on the other side.

We rode all up to him, and found it as the fellow had said, all but that of a plain way; there was indeed the mark or face of a road on the side of the hill, a little turning to the left north; but it was so narrow, and so deep a hollow place on the right, whence the water descending from the hills made a channel at the bottom, and looked as the beginning of a river, that the depth of the precipice, and the narrowness of the way, look'd horrible to us; after going a little way in it, the way being blinded too by the snow, the hollow on the right appeared deeper and deeper, so we resolved to alight and lead our horses, which we did for about a mile, though the violence of the wind and snow continuing, it was both very troublesome and dangerous.

The only reliefs we had in this track were, (1.) That we perceived some land marks, or tokens, which the honest Rochdale men had given us notice of, by which we believed we were right in the way; for till then we knew nothing where we were, or whether we were right or wrong. And, (2.) that as the road we were in descended apace, for it went very steep down, we found the lower we went the violence of the snow abated, just as on the other side of the hill the higher we went, it had encreased.

At length, to our great joy, we found too the wind abated, as well as the snow, that is to say, the hills being so high behind us, they kept back the wind, as is the case under a high wall, though you are on the windward side of it, yet the wind having no passage through, is not felt, as it would be on the top where the space is open for it to pass.

All this way the hollow on our right continued very deep, and just on the other side of it a parallel hill continued going on east, as that did which we rode on the side of; the main hill which we came down from, which is properly called Blackstone Edge, or, by the country people, the Edge, without any sirname or addition, ran along due north, crossing and shutting up those hollow gulls and vallies between, which were certainly originally formed by the rain and snow water running into them, and forcing its way down, washing the earth gradually along with it, till, by length of time, it wore down the surface to such a depth.

We continued descending still, and as the weather was

quieter, so the way seemed to mend and be broader, and, to our great satisfaction, enclining more to the hill on the left; the precipice and hollow part where the water run, as I have said, went a little off from us, and by and by, to our no small comfort, we saw an enclosed piece of ground that is enclosed with a stone wall, and soon after a house, where we asked our way, and found we were right.

Soon after this we came to the bottom, by another very steep descent, where we were obliged to alight again, and lead our horses. At the bottom, we found the hollow part, which I have so often mentioned as a precipice, was come to a level with us, that is to say, we were come down to a level with it, and it turning to the left toward us, we found a brook of water running from it, which cross'd our way to the north, you shall hear of it again presently; when we cross'd this brook, which, by reason of the snow on the hills which melted, was risen about knee deep, and run like a sluice for strength, we found a few poor houses, but saw no people, no not one; till we call'd at a door, to get directions of our way, and then we found, that though there was no body to be seen without doors, they were very full of people within, and so we found it on several occasions afterward, of which we shall speak again.

We thought now we were come into a Christian country again, and that our difficulties were over; but we soon found our selves mistaken in the matter; for we had not gone fifty yards beyond the brook and houses adjacent, but we found the way began to ascend again, and soon after to go up very steep, till in about half a mile we found we had another mountain to ascend, in our apprehansion as bad as the first, and before we came to the top of it, we found it began to snow too, as it had done before.

But, to cut short the tedious day's work, the case was this; the hill was very high, and, in our opinion, not inferior to the Edge which we came just down from; but the sun being higher, and the wind not blowing so hard, what snow fell upon the hill melted as it fell, and so we saw our way plainer, and master'd the hill, though with some labour, yet not any terror or apprehensions of losing our way, falling down precipices, and the like.

But our case was still this; that as soon as we were at the top of every hill, we had it to come down again on the other side; and as soon as we were down we had another to mount, and that immediately; for I do not remember that there was one bottom that had any considerable breadth of plain ground in it, but always a brook in the valley running from those gulls and deeps between the hills, with this remark, that they always cross'd our way in the bottoms from the right-hand to the left, the reason of which you shall see presently.

From Blackstone Edge to Hallifax is eight miles, and all the way, except from Sorby to Hallifax, is thus up hill and down; so that, I suppose, we mounted to the clouds and descended to the water level about eight times, in that little part of the journey.

But now I must observe to you, that after having pass'd the second hill, and come down into the valley again, and so still the nearer we came to Hallifax, we found the houses thicker, and the villages greater in every bottom; and not only so, but the sides of the hills, which were very steep every way, were spread with houses, and that very thick; for the land being divided into small enclosures, that is to say, from two acres to six or seven acres each, seldom more; every three or four pieces of land had a house belonging to it.

Then it was I began to perceive the reason and nature of the thing, and found that this division of the land into small pieces, and scattering of the dwellings, was occasioned by, and done for the convenience of the business which the people were generally employ'd in, and that, as I said before, though we saw no people stirring without doors, yet they were all full within; for, in short, this whole country, however mountainous, and that no sooner we were down one hill but we mounted another, is yet infinitely full of people; those people all full of business; not a beggar, not an idle person to be seen, except here and there an alms-house, where people antient, decrepid, and past labour, might perhaps be found; for it is observable, that the people here, however laborious, generally live to a great age, a certain testimony to the goodness and wholesomness of the country, which is, without doubt, as healthy as any part of England; nor is the health of the people lessen'd, but help'd and establish'd by their being constantly employ'd, and, as we call it, their working hard; so that they find a double advantage by their being always in business.

This business is the clothing trade, for the convenience of which the houses are thus scattered and spread upon the sides of the hills, as above, even from the bottom to the top; the reason is this; such has been the bounty of nature to this otherwise frightful country, that two things essential to the business, as well as to the ease of the people are found here, and that in a situation which I never saw the like of in any part of England; and, I believe, the like is not to be seen so contrived in any part of the world; I mean coals and running water upon the tops of the highest hills: This seems to have been directed by the wise hand of Providence for the very purpose which is now served by it, namely, the manufactures, which otherwise could not be carried on; neither indeed could one fifth part of the inhabitants be supported without them, for the land could not maintain them. After we had mounted the third hill, we found the country, in short, one continued village, tho' mountainous every way, as before; hardly a house standing out of a speaking distance from another, and (which soon told us their business) the day clearing up, and the sun shining, we could see that almost at every house there was a tenter, and almost on every tenter a piece of cloth, or kersie, or shalloon, for they are the three articles of that country's labour; from which the sun glancing, and, as I may say, shining (the white reflecting its rays) to us, I thought it was the most agreeable sight that I ever saw, for the hills, as I say, rising and falling so thick, and the vallies opening sometimes one way, sometimes another, so that sometimes we could see two or three miles this way, sometimes as far another; sometimes like the streets near St. Giles's, called the Seven Dials; we could see through the glades almost every way round us, yet look which way we would, high to the tops, and low to the bottoms, it was all the same; innumerable houses and tenters, and a white piece upon every tenter.

But to return to the reason of dispersing the houses, as above; I found, as our road pass'd among them, for indeed no road could do otherwise, wherever we pass'd any house we found a little rill or gutter of running water, if the house was above the road, it came from it, and cross'd the way to run to another; if the house was below us, it cross'd us from some other distant house above it, and at every considerable house was a manufactury or work-house, and as they could not do their business without water, the little streams were so parted and guided by gutters or pipes, and by turning and dividing the streams, that none of those houses were without a river, if I may call it so, running into and through their work-houses.

Again, as the dying-houses, scouring-shops and places where they used this water, emitted the water again, ting'd with the drugs of the dying fat, and with the oil, the soap, the tallow, and other ingredients used by the clothiers in dressing and scouring, &c. which then runs away thro' the lands to the next, the grounds are not only universally watered, how dry soever the season, but that water so ting'd and so fatten'd enriches the lands they run through, that 'tis hardly to be imagined how fertile and rich the soil is made by it.

Then, as every clothier must keep a horse, perhaps two, to fetch and carry for the use of his manufacture, (viz.) to fetch home his wooll and his provisions from the market, to carry his yarn to the spinners, his manufacture to the fulling mill, and, when finished, to the market to be sold, and the like; so every manufacturer generally keeps a cow or two, or more, for his family, and this employs the two, or three, or four pieces of enclosed land about his house, for they scarce sow corn enough for their cocks and hens; and this feeding their grounds still adds by the dung of the cattle, to enrich the soil.

But now, to speak of the bounty of nature again, which I but just mentioned; it is to be observed, that these hills are so furnished by nature with springs and mines, that not only on the sides, but even to the very tops, there is scarce a hill but you find, on the highest part of it, a spring of water, and a coal-pit. I doubt not but there are both springs and coal-pits lower in the hills, 'tis enough to say they are at the top; but, as I say, the hills are so full of springs, so the lower coal-pits may perhaps be too full of water, to work without dreins to carry it off, and the coals in the upper pits being easie to come at, they may chuse to work them, because the horses which fetch the coals, go light up the hill, and come loaden down.

Having thus fire and water at every dwelling, there is no need to enquire why they dwell thus dispers'd upon the highest hills, the convenience of the manufactures requiring it. Among the manufacturers houses are likewise scattered an infinite number of cottages or small dwellings, in which dwell the workmen which are employed, the women and children of whom, are always busy carding, spinning, &c. so that no hands being unemploy'd, all can gain their bread, even from the youngest to the antient; hardly any thing above four years old, but its hands are sufficient to it self.

This is the reason also why we saw so few people without doors; but if we knock'd at the door of any of the master manufacturers, we presently saw a house full of lusty fellows, some at the dye-fat, some dressing the cloths, some in the loom, some one thing, some another, all hard at work, and full employed upon the manufacture, and all seeming to have sufficient business.

*G 821

I should not have dwelt so upon this part, if there was not abundance of things subsequent to it, which will be explained by this one description, and which are needful to be understood by any one that desires a full understanding of the manner how the people of England are employed, and do subsist in these remoter parts where they are so numerous; for this is one of the most populous parts of Britain, London and the adjacent parts excepted.

Having thus described the country, and the employment of the people, I am to tell you, that this part of it which I mentioned, is all belonging to and in the parish of Hallifax, and that brings me on towards the town which I shall speak of presently.

I must only say a word or two of the River Calder, to compleat the description of the country I thus pass'd through. I hinted to you, that all the rills or brooks of water which we cross'd, one at least in every bottom, went away to the left or north side of us as we went forward east: I am to add, that following those little brooks with our eye, we could observe, that at some distance to the left there appeared a larger valley than the rest, into which not only all the brooks which we pass'd emptied themselves, but abundance more from the like hollow deep bottoms, among the hills on the north side of it, which emptied this way south, as those on our side run that way north, so that it was natural to conclude, that in this larger valley the waters of all those brooks joining, there must be some pretty large stream which received them all, and ran forward east, parallel to the way we were in.

After some time we found that great opening seemed to bend southward towards us, and that probably it would cross our road, or our road would rather cross the valley; and so it was natural to expect we should pass that larger water, either by a bridge or a ford; but we were soon convinced it was not the latter; for the snow, as is said, having poured down a quantity of water, we soon found at the next opening, that there was a considerable river in the larger valley, which, having received all those little brooks, was risen to a little flood; and at the next village we pass'd it over a stately stone bridge of several great arches. This village is called Sorby or Sowreby; and this was the main River Calder, which I mentioned at Wakefield, where it begins to be navigable, and which, without any spring or fountain, to be called the head or source of it, is formed on the declivity of these mountains, meerly by the continued fall of rains and snows, which the said mountains intercepting the clouds, are seldom free from; and this stream receiving the smaller gulls and hollows, I just now mentioned, like a common-shore, carries all away in the channel of a noble river.

This is the beginning of the Calder; and my reason for dwelling upon it, and giving so particular a description, is, because this may, once for all, shew you how all, or most of the great rivers in the north, take their rise, there being hardly any that has their beginning in any publick springs or lakes, as most of the rivers in the south of England have, as the Thames, for example, near Tring in Hertfordshire, the Vandal at Croydon and Cashalton, the Amewell at Ware, and the like.

As the Calder is thus nothing but a collection of water from the fall of these mountains, so was the Derwent, and the Don, from the High Peak, and the hills of the same range more south of the edge, and so is the Aire, the Wharf, the Swale, the Eure, the Nid, the Tees, and the Were, all in the same county of York; and so the Tyne, the Cockett, the Till, and the Tweed, farther north; and even the like of the Forth, the Tay, the Clyde, the Nyd, in Scotland; also the Mersee, the Ribble, the Rocke and the Lune, the West Calder, the Lowther and the Eden, on the other side of these mountains, in Lancashire, Westmoreland and Cumberland. And thus this description will serve for all the rest.

Having thus, I say, accounted for them all at once; I shall only mention them now as they come in my way; for you will observe, I cross'd one or other of them at every considerable town; for all the rivers as well in England as in Scotland, north of this place, run from the middle of the country where these mountains rise, either east into the German, or west into the Irish sea. None of them run like the Severn, or the Wye, or the rivers in South Wales, or the Exe in Devon, or the Avon in Wilts, or the Arun in Sussex, and others north and south. But I return to the north.

Having passed the Calder at Sorby Bridge, I now began to approach the town of Hallifax; in the description of which, and its dependencies, all my account of the commerce will come in, for take Hallifax, with all its dependencies, it is not to be equalled in England. First, the parish or vicaridge, for it is but a vicaridge; is, if not the largest, certainly the most populous in England; in short, it is a monster, I mean, for a country parish, and a parish so far out of the way of foreign trade, Courts, or sea ports.

The extent of the parish, they tell us, is almost circular, and is about twelve miles in diameter. There are in it twelve or thirteen chapels of ease, besides about sixteen meeting-houses, which they call also chapels, and are so, having bells to call the people, and burying grounds to most of them, or else they bury within them. I think they told me, the Quakers meetings, of which there are several too, are not reckoned into the number. In a word, it is some years ago that a reverend clergyman of the town of Hallifax, told me, they reckoned that they had a hundred thousand communicants in the parish, besides children.

History tells us also, that in Queen Elizabeth's time, when the inhabitants of Hallifax addressed the queen for some privileges, which I do not at present remember the particulars of, it was expressed in the petition as a moving argument, why the queen should take them into her royal care, that they were zealous Protestants, and were so loyal to her majesty, as well as so considerable, that no less than twelve thousand young men went out arm'd from this one parish, and, at her majesty's call, joined her troops to fight the Popish army, then in rebellion under the Earl of Westmorland.

If they were so populous at that time, how much must they be encreased since? and especially since the late Revolution, the trade having been prodigiously encouraged and encreased by the great demand of their kersies for clothing the armies abroad, insomuch that it is the opinion of some that know the town, and its bounds very well, that the number of people in the vicaridge of Hallifax, is encreased one fourth, at least, within the last forty years, that is to say, since the late Revolution. Nor is it improbable at all, for besides the number of houses which are encreased, they have entered upon a new manufacture which was never made in those parts before, at least, not in any quantities, I mean, the manufactures of shalloons, of which they now make, if fame does not bely them, a hundred thousand pieces a year in this parish only, and yet do not make much fewer kersies than they did before.

The trade in kersies also was so great, that I was told by very creditable, honest men, when I was there, men not given to gasconading or boasting, and less to lying, that there was one dealer in the vicaridge, who traded, by commission, for threescore thousand pounds a year in kersies only, and all that to Holland and Hamburgh.

But not to enter into particulars, it is evident that the trade must be exceeding great, in that it employs such a very great number of people, and that in this one town only; for, as I shall fully describe in my account of other places, this is not what I may call the eldest son of the cloathing trade in this county; the town of Leeds challenges a pre-eminence, and I believe, merits the dignity it claims, besides the towns of Huthersfield, Bradforth, Wakefield, and others.

But I must not leave Hallifax yet, as the vicaridge is thus far extended, and the extent of it so peopled, what must the market be, and where must this vast number of people be supplied? For, (1.) as to corn, I have observed already, they sow little and hardly enough to feed their poultry, if they were to be corn fed; and as to beef and mutton, they feed little or none; and as they are surrounded with large, populous, manufacturing towns on every side, all of them employed as these are, in the cloathing trade, they must then necessarily have their provisions from other parts of the country.

This then is a subsistence to the other part of the country, and so it is for us, the West Riding is thus taken up, and the lands occupied by the manufacture; the consequence is plain, their corn comes up in great quantities out of Lincoln, Nottingham, and the East Riding, their black cattle and horses from the North Riding, their sheep and mutton from the adjacent counties every way, their butter from the East and North Riding, their cheese out of Cheshire and Warwickshire, more black cattle also from Lancashire. And here the breeders and feeders, the farmers and country people find money flowing in plenty from the manufacturers and commerce; so that at Hallifax, Leeds, and the other great manufacturing towns so often mentioned, and adjacent to these, for the two months of September and October, a prodigious quantity of black cattle is sold.

This demand for beef is occasioned thus; the usage of the people is to buy in at that season beef sufficient for the whole year, which they kill and salt, and hang up in the smoke to dry. This way of curing their beef keeps it all the winter, and they eat this smoak'd beef as a very great rarity.

Upon this foot, 'tis ordinary for a clothier that has a large family, to come to Hallifax on a market-day, and buy two or three large bullocks from eight to ten pounds a piece. These he carries home and kills for his store. And this is the reason that the markets at all those times of the year are thronged with black cattle, as Smithfield is on a Friday; whereas all the rest of the year there is little extraordinary sold there.

Thus this one trading, manufacturing part of the country

supports all the countries round it, and the numbers of people settle here as bees about a hive.

As for the town of Hallifax it self, there is nothing extraordinary except on a market-day, and then indeed it is a prodigious thing, by reason of the multitude of people who throng thither, as well to sell their manufactures as to buy provisions; and so great is the confluence of people hither, that, except Leeds and Wakefield, nothing in all the north part of England can come near it.

The church is old, but stately and venerable, and has in it many extraordinary monuments, but most of them of great antiquity. Here is a very good hospital, and a work-house of an antient establishment, and there are several charities, of like sort, in other parts of the parish.

But I must not quit Hallifax, till I give you some account of the famous course of justice antiently executed here, to prevent the stealing of cloth. Modern accounts pretend to say, it was for all sorts of felons; but I am well assured, it was first erected purely, or at least principally, for such thieves as were apprehended stealing cloth from the tenters; and it seems very reasonable to think it was so, because of the conditions of the trial. The case was thus:

The erecting the woollen manufacture here was about the year 1480, when King Henry VII. by giving encouragement to foreigners to settle in England, and to set up woollen manufactures, caused an Act to pass prohibiting the exportation of wooll into foreign parts, unwrought, and to encourage foreign manufacturers to come and settle here, of whom several coming over settled the manufactures of cloths in several parts of the kingdom, as they found the people tractable, and as the country best suited them; as the bays at Colchester, the says at Sudbury, the broad-cloth in Wilts, and other counties; so the trade of kersies and narrow cloth fixed at this place, and other adjacent towns.

When this trade began to settle, nothing was more frequent than for young workmen to leave their cloths out all night upon the tenters, and the idle fellows would come in upon them, and tearing them off without notice, steal the cloth. Now as it was absolutely necessary to preserve the trade in its infancy, this severe law was made, giving the power of life and death so far into the hands of the magistrates of Hallifax, as to see the law executed upon them. As this law was particularly pointed against the stealing of cloth, and no other crime, so no others were capable of being punished by it, and the conditions of the law intimate as much; for the power was not given to the magistrates to give sentence, unless in one of these three plain cases:

1. Hand napping, that is, to be taken in the very fact, or, as the Scots call it in the case of murther, red hand.

2. Back bearing, that is, when the cloth was found on the person carrying it off.

3. Tongue confessing, that part needs no farther explanation.

This being the case, if the criminal was taken, he was brought before the magistrates of the town, who at that time were only a baily and the eoaldermen, how many we do not read, and these were to judge, and sentence, and execute the offender, or clear him, within so many days; I think it was three market days if the offence was committed out of the vicaridge, but within the bounds of the forest then there were frith borges also to judge of the fact, who were to be summoned of the forest holders, as they are called, who were to hold of that frith, that is, of the forest; but those were to be good and sober men, and by the magistrates of the town to be approved as such; if those acquitted him of the fact he was immediately discharged; if those censured him, no body could reprieve him but the town. The country people were, it seems, so terrified at the severity of this proceeding, that hence came that proverbial saying, which was used all over Yorkshire, (viz.)

> From Hell, Hull, and Hallifax,
> Good Lord, deliver us.

How Hull came to be included in this petition, I do not find; for they had no such law there, as I read of.

The manner of execution was very remarkable; the engine indeed is carried away, but the scaffold on which it stood is there to this time, and may continue many ages; being not a frame of wood, but a square building of stone, with stone steps to go up, and the engine it self was made in the following manner.

They tell us of a custom which prevailed here, in the case of a criminal being to be executed, (viz.) that if after his head was laid down, and the signal given to pull out the pin, he could be so nimble as to snatch out his head between the pulling out the pin and the falling down of the ax, and could get up upon his feet, jump off of the scaffold, run down a hill that lies just before it, and get through the river before the executioner could overtake him, and seize upon him, he was to escape; and though the executioner did take him on the other side the river, he was not to bring him back, at least he was not to be executed.

But as they shewed me the form of the scaffold, and the weight of the ax, it was, in my opinion, next to impossible, any man should be so quick-eyed as to see the pulling out the pin, and so quick with his head, as to snatch it out; yet they tell a story of one fellow that did it, and was so bold after he had jumpt off of the scaffold, and was running down the hill, with the executioner at his heels, to turn about and call to the people to give him his hat; that having afterwards jumpt into the river, which is but a little one, and not deep, he stopt, intending to drown the hangman, if he had come up to him; at which the poor fellow stopt too, and was afraid to go into the water to seize him. But this story is said to be too long ago to have any vouchers, though the people indeed all receive it for truth.

The force of this engine is so strong, the head of the ax being loaded with a weight of lead to make it fall heavy, and the execution is so sure, that it takes away all possibility of its failing to cut off the head; and to this purpose, the Hallifax people tell you another story of a country woman, who was riding by upon her doffers or hampers to Hallifax Market, for the execution was always on a market day (the third after the fact) and passing just as the ax was let fall upon the neck of the criminal, it chopt it thro' with such force, that the head jumpt off into one of her hampers, and that the woman not perceiving it, she carry'd it away to the market.

All the use I shall make of this unlikely story, is this, that it seems executions were so frequent, that it was not thought a sight worth the peoples running out to see; that the woman should ride along so close to the scaffold, and that she should go on, and not so much as stop to see the ax fall, or take any notice of it. But those difficulties seem to be much better solved, by saying, that 'tis as reasonable to think the whole tale is a little Yorkshire, which, I suppose, you will understand well enough.

This engine was removed, as we are told, in the year 1620, during the reign of King James the First, and the usage and custom of prosecution abolished, and criminals or felons left to the ordinary course of justice, as it is still; and yet they do not find the stealing cloth from the tenters is so frequent now as it was in those times.

But the manner of execution is preserv'd; for in the reign of the same prince, the Earl Morton, Regent or Prime Minister of

Scotland, under King James, passing thro' Hallifax, and seeing one of their executions, was so pleased with the performance, that he caused a model to be taken and carried into Scotland, where it is preserved and constantly made use of for executions to this day. But one thing must not be forgotten in this part of the story, namely, that his lordship's own head was the first that was cut off with it; and it being many years before that happened, the engine was called the Maiden, as not having so long handsell'd, and still retains the name, tho' it has cut off many a head since that.

We quitted Hallifax not without some astonishment at its situation, being so surrounded with hills, and those so high, as (except the entrance by the west) makes the coming in and going out of it exceeding troublesome, and indeed for carriages hardly practicable, and particularly the hill which they go up to come out of the town eastwards towards Leeds, and which the country people call Hallifax Bank, is so steep, so rugged, and sometimes too so slippery, that, to a town of so much business as this is, 'tis exceeding troublesome and dangerous.

From Hallifax it is twelve miles to Leeds north east, and about as many to Wakefield; due east, or a little southerly, between Hallifax and Leeds, is a little town called Burstall. Here the kersey and shalloon trade being, as it were, confined to Hallifax, and the towns already named, of Huthersfield and Bradforth, they begin to make broad cloth; I call it broad, in distinction from kersies and druggets, and such things, though the cloths in this country are called narrow, when they are spoken of in London, and compared with the broad cloths made in Wilts, Gloucester, Somerset and Devonshire, of which I have spoken in former letters.

This town is famed for dying, and they make a sort of cloths here in imitation of the Gloucester white cloths, bought for the Dutch and the Turkey trades; and though their cloths here may not be as fine, they told us their colours are as good. But that is not my business to dispute, the west country clothiers deny it; and so I leave it as I find it.

From hence to Leeds, and every way to the right hand and the left, the country appears busy, diligent, and even in a hurry of work, they are not scattered and dispersed as in the vicaridge of Hallifax, where the houses stand one by one; but in villages, those villages large, full of houses, and those houses thronged with people, for the whole country is infinitely populous.

A noble scene of industry and application is spread before

you here, and which, joined to the market at Leeds, where it chiefly centers, is such a surprising thing, that they who have pretended to give an account of Yorkshire, and have left this out, must betray an ignorance not to be accounted for, or excused; 'tis what is well worth the curiosity of a stranger to go on purpose to see; and many travellers and gentlemen have come over from Hamburgh, nay, even from Leipsick in Saxony, on purpose to see it.

And this brought me from the villages where this manufacture is wrought, to the market where it is sold, which is at Leeds.

Leeds is a large, wealthy and populous town, it stands on the north bank of the River Aire, or rather on both sides the river, for there is a large suburb or part of the town on the south side of the river, and the whole is joined by a stately and prodigiously strong stone bridge, so large, and so wide, that formerly the cloth market was kept in neither part of the town, but on the very bridge it self; and therefore the refreshment given the clothiers by the inn-keepers, of which I shall speak presently is called the Brigg-shot to this day.

The encrease of the manufacturers and of the trade, soon made the market too great to be confined to the brigg or bridge, and it is now kept in the High-street, beginning from the bridge, and running up north almost to the market-house, where the ordinary market for provisions begins, which also is the greatest of its kind in all the north of England, except Hallifax, of which I have spoken already, nay, the people at Leeds will not allow me to except Hallifax, but say, that theirs is the greatest market, and that not the greatest plenty only, but the best of all kinds of provisions are brought hither.

But this is not the case; it is the cloth market I am now to describe, which is indeed a prodigy of its kind, and is not to be equalled in the world. The market for serges at Exeter is indeed a wonderful thing, and the value sold there is very great; but then the market there is but once a week, here it is twice a week, and the quantity of goods vastly great too.

The market it self is worth describing, tho' no description can come up to the thing it self; however, take a sketch of it with its customs and usages as follows:

The street is a large, broad, fair, and well-built street, beginning, as I have said, at the bridge, and ascending gently to the north.

Early in the morning, there are tressels placed in two rows

in the street, sometimes two rows on a side, but always one row at least; then there are boards laid cross those tressels, so that the boards lie like long counters on either side, from one end of the street to the other.

The clothiers come early in the morning with their cloth; and as few clothiers bring more than one piece, the market being so frequent, they go into the inns and publick-houses with it, and there set it down.

At seven a clock in the morning, the clothiers being supposed to be all come by that time, even in the winter, but the hour is varied as the seasons advance (in the summer earlier, in the depth of winter a little later) I take it, at a medium, and as it was when I was there, at six or seven, I say, the market bell rings; it would surprize a stranger to see in how few minutes, without hurry or noise, and not the least disorder, the whole market is fill'd; all the boards upon the tressels are covered with cloth, close to one another as the pieces can lie long ways by one another, and behind every piece of cloth, the clothier standing to sell it.

This indeed is not so difficult, when we consider that the whole quantity is brought into the market as soon as one piece, because as the clothiers stand ready in the inns and shops just behind, and that there is a clothier to every piece, they have no more to do, but, like a regiment drawn up in line, every one takes up his piece, and has about five steps to march to lay it upon the first row of boards, and perhaps ten to the second row; so that upon the market bell ringing, in half a quarter of an hour the whole market is fill'd, the rows of boards cover'd, and the clothiers stand ready.

As soon as the bell has done ringing, the merchants and factors, and buyers of all sorts, come down, and coming along the spaces between the rows of boards, they walk up the rows, and down as their occasions direct. Some of them have their foreign letters of orders, with patterns seal'd on them, in rows, in their hands; and with those they match colours, holding them to the cloths as they think they agree to; when they see any cloths to their colours, or that suit their occasions, they reach over to the clothier and whisper, and in the fewest words imaginable the price is stated; one asks, the other bids; and 'tis agree, or not agree, in a moment.

The merchants and buyers generally walk down and up twice on each side of the rows, and in little more than an hour all the business is done; in less than half an hour you will perceive the cloths begin to move off, the clothier taking it up upon his shoulder to carry it to the merchant's house; and by half an hour after eight a clock the market bell rings again; immediately the buyers disappear, the cloth is all sold, or if here and there a piece happens not to be bought, 'tis carried back into the inn, and, in a quarter of an hour, there is not a piece of cloth to be seen in the market.

Thus, you see, ten or twenty thousand pounds value in cloth, and sometimes much more, bought and sold in little more than an hour, and the laws of the market the most strictly observed as ever I saw done in any market in England; for,

1. Before the market bell rings, no man shews a piece of cloth, nor can the clothiers sell any but in open market.

2. After the market bell rings again, no body stays a moment in the market, but carries his cloth back if it be not sold.

3. And that which is most admirable is, 'tis all managed with the most profound silence, and you cannot hear a word spoken in the whole market, I mean, by the persons buying and selling; 'tis all done in whisper.

The reason of this silence, is chiefly because the clothiers stand so near to one another; and 'tis always reasonable that one should not know what another does, for that would be discovering their business, and exposing it to one another.

If a merchant has bidden a clothier a price, and he will not take it, he may go after him to his house, and tell him he has considered of it, and is willing to let him have it; but they are not to make any new agreement for it, so as to remove the market from the street to the merchant's house.

By nine a clock the boards are taken down, the tressels are removed, and the street cleared, so that you see no market or goods any more than if there had been nothing to do; and this is done twice a week. By this quick return the clothiers are constantly supplied with money, their workmen are duly paid, and a prodigious sum circulates thro' the county every week.

If you should ask upon all this, where all these goods, as well here as at Wakefield, and at Hallifax, are vented and disposed of? It would require a long treatise of commerce to enter into that part: But that I may not bring you into the labyrinth, and not show you the way out, I shall, in three short heads, describe the consumption, for there are three channels by which it goes:

1. For the home consumption; their goods being, as I may

say, every where made use of, for the cloathing the ordinary people, who cannot go to the price of the fine medley cloths made, as I formerly gave you an account, in the western counties of England. There are for this purpose a set of travelling merchants in Leeds, who go all over England with droves of pack horses, and to all the fairs and market towns over the whole island, I think I may say none excepted. Here they supply not the common people by retail, which would denominate them pedlars indeed, but they supply the shops by wholesale or whole pieces; and not only so, but give large credit too, so that they are really travelling merchants, and as such they sell a very great quantity of goods; 'tis ordinary for one of these men to carry a thousand pounds value of cloth with them at a time, and having sold it at the fairs or towns where they go, they send their horses back for as much more, and this very often in a summer, for they chuse to travel in the summer, and perhaps towards the winter time, tho' as little in winter as they can, because of the badness of the roads.

2. Another sort of buyers are those who buy to send to London; either by commissions from London, or they give commissions to factors and warehouse-keepers in London to sell for them; and these drive also a very great trade: These factors and warehouse-keepers not only supply all the shop-keepers and wholesale men in London, but sell also very great quantities to the merchants, as well for exportation to the English colonies in America, which take off great quantities of those course goods, especially New England, New York, Virginia, &c. as also to the Russia merchants, who send an exceeding quantity to Petersburgh, Riga, Dantzic, Narva, and to Sweden and Pomerania.

3. The third sort of buyers, and who are not less considerable than the other, are truly merchants, that is to say, such as receive commissions from abroad to buy cloth for the merchants chiefly in Hamburgh, and in Holland, and from several other parts; and these are not only many in number, but some of them are very considerable in their dealings, and correspond as far as Nuremberg, Frankfort, Leipsick, and even to Vienna and Ausburgh, in the farthest provinces of Germany.

On account of this trade it was, that some years ago an Act of Parliament was obtained for making the Rivers Aire and Calder navigable; by which a communication by water was opened from Leeds and Wakefield to Hull, and by which means all the woollen manufactures which those merchants now export by commission, as above, is carried by water to Hull, and there shipped for Holland, Bremen, Hamburgh, and the Baltick. And thus you have a brief account, by what methods this vast manufacture is carried off, and which way they find a vent for it.

There is another trade in this part of the country, which is now become very considerable since the opening the navigation of these rivers, and that is, that from hence they carry coals down from Wakefield (especially) and also from Leeds, at both which they have a very great quantity, and such, as they told me, could never be exhausted. These they carry quite down into the Humber, and then up the Ouse to York, and up the Trent, and other rivers, where there are abundance of large towns, who they supply with coals; with this advantage too, that whereas the Newcastle coals pay four shillings per chaldron duty to the publick; these being only called river borne coal, are exempted, and pay nothing; though, strictly speaking, they are carried on the sea too, for the Humber is properly the sea. But they have been hitherto exempted from the tax, and so they carry on the trade to their very great profit and advantage.

I need not add, that by the same navigation they receive all their heavy goods, as well such as are imported at Hull, as such as come from London, and such as other counties supply, as butter, cheese, lead, iron, salt; all sorts of grocery, as sugars, tobacco, fruit, spice, hops, &c. oyl, wine, brandy, spirits, and every sort of heavy or bulky goods.

The town of Leeds is very large, and, as above, there are abundance of wealthy merchants in it. Here are two churches, and two large meeting-houses of Dissenters, and six or seven chapels of ease, besides Dissenters chapels, in the adjacent, depending villages; so that Leeds may not be much inferiour to Hallifax in numbers of people: It is really a surprising thing to see what numbers of people are thronged together in all the villages about these towns, and how busy they all are, being fully employed in this great manufacture.

Before I go forward from hence, I should tell you, that I took a little trip to see the antient town of Pontefract, with that dismal place called the Castle, a place that was really dismal on many accounts, having been a scene of blood in many several ages; for here Henry, the great Earl of Lancaster, who was at the same time lord of the castle, and whose ancestors had beautified and enlarged it exceedingly, and fortified it too, was beheaded, in King Edward the IId's time, with three or four more of the English barons. Here Richard IId, being deposed and imprisoned, was barbarously murthered, and, if history lies not, in a cruel manner; and here Anthony, Earl Rivers, and Sir Richard Gray, the first uncle, and the last brother-in-law to King Edward the Fifth, were beheaded by that tyrant Richard III. Here, in the late wars, a small party of brave fellows took the castle, by surprise, for the king, and having desperately defended it to the last extremity, and being obliged to yield, five of them attempted to break thro' the besiegers camp, three of whom perished in the attempt.

The town is large and well built, but much smaller than it has been; the castle lies in its ruins, tho' not demolished; within a mile of it is Ferry Bridge, where there is a great stone bridge over the Aire and Calder (then united) and a large stone causeway, above a mile in length, to a town call'd Brotherton, where Queen Margaret, wife of King Edward the First, was delivered of a son, being surprised as she was abroad taking the air, some histories say, a hunting; but, I must confess, it seems not very probable, that queens big with child, and within a few hours of their time, should ride a hunting. Be that as it will, here her majesty was catch'd (as the women call it) and forc'd to take up, and brought forth a son, who was christened Thomas, and sir-named from the place, De Brotherton; he afterwards was a famous man, and was made Earl of Norfolk, and Earl Marshal of England; which office is hereditary to the title of Norfolk to this day. A little on the south side of this village the road parts, and one way goes on to the right towards Tadcaster, and so to York, of which in its order; the other, being the high-post road for Scotland, goes on to Wetherby, over Bramham Moor, famous for a fight between the Royalists and the fam'd Sir Thomas Fairfax, in which the last was worsted and wounded, but made a retreat, which gain'd him as great reputation as a victory would have done.

Near the road is a noble seat of Benson, Lord Bingly, an antient family, raised to the dignity of a peer in the person of the present Lord Bingly, who was Chancellor of the Exchequer in the time of the late Queen Anne, and nominated her majesty's Ambassador Extraordinary to the Court of Spain; but the queen dying, that embassy was laid aside. It is a fine, new built, beautiful house, with very curious gardens, tho' not large. Wetherby is a small town, but being a great thoroughfare to the north, has several good inns, and a very lofty stone bridge over the River Wharfe, which comes down from the hills also, as the rest do.

But I must go back to Pontefract, to take notice, that here again the great Roman highway, which I mentioned at Doncaster, and which is visible from thence in several places on the way to Pontefract, though not in the open road, is apparent again, and from Castleford Bridge, which is another bridge over the united rivers of Aire and Calder, it goes on to Abberforth, a small market town famous for pin-making, and so to Tadcaster and York. But I mention it here on this present occasion, for otherwise these remains of antiquity are not my province in this undertaking; I say, 'tis on this occasion.

1. That in some places this causeway being cut into and broken up, the eminent care of the Romans for making firm causeways for the convenience of carriage, and for the passing of travellers, is to be seen there. The layings of different sorts of earth, as clay at the bottom, chalk upon that, then gravel upon the chalk, then stones upon the gravel, and then gravel again; and so of other kinds of earth, where the first was not to be had.

2. In some places between this bridge and the town of Abberforth, the causeway having not been used for the ordinary road, it lies as fair and untouch'd, the surface covered with turf, smooth as at its first making, not so much as the mark of a hoof or of a wheel upon it; so that it is to be seen in its full dimensions and heighth, as if it had been made but the same week; whereas 'tis very probable it had stood so fifteen or sixteen hundred years; and I take notice of it here, because I have not seen any thing like it in any other place in England, and because our people, who are now mending the roads almost every where, might take a pattern from it.

As I made this little excursion to see the town of Pontefract from Leeds, you must suppose me now returned thither, and setting out thence northward. I had no sooner pass'd out of the district of Leeds about four or five miles, and pass'd the Wharfe, at a fine stone bridge of eleven arches at a little pretty town call'd Harwood; I say, I was no sooner gotten hither, but it was easie to see we were out of the manufacturing country. Now the black moorish lands, like Black Barnsley, shew'd dismal again and frightful, the towns were thin, and thin of people too; we saw but little enclosed ground, no tenters with the cloths shining upon them, nor people busied within doors, as before; but, as in the Vicaridge, we saw inhabited mountains, here we saw waste and almost uninhabited vales.

In a word, the country look'd as if all the people were transplanted to Leeds and Hallifax, and that here was only a few just left at home to cultivate the land, manage the plough, and raise corn for the rest.

The River Wharfe seemed very small, and the water low, at Harwood Bridge, so that I was surprised to see so fine a bridge over it, and was thinking of the great bridge at Madrid over the Mansanares, of which a Frenchman of quality looking upon it, said to the Spaniards that were about him, That the King of Spain ought either to buy them some water, or they should sell their bridge. But I was afterwards satisfied that was not the case here; for coming another time this way after a heavy rain, I was convinced the bridge was not at all too big, or too long, the water filling up to the very crown of the arches, and some of the arches not to be seen at all.

From the Wharfe we went directly north, over a continued waste of black, ill looking, desolate moors, over which travellers are guided, like race horses, by posts set up for fear of bogs and holes, to a town call'd Ripley, that stands upon another river called the Nud by some, by others the Nyd, smaller than the Wharfe, but furiously rapid, and very dangerous to pass in many places, especially upon sudden rains. Notwithstanding such lofty, high built bridges as are not to be seen over such small rivers in any other place; and, on this occasion, it may be observed here, once for all, that no part of England, I may say so because I can say I have seen the whole island, a very little excepted, I say, no part can shew such noble, large, lofty, and long stone bridges as this part of England, nor so many of them; nor do I remember to have seen any such thing as a timber bridge in all the northern part of England, no not from the Trent to the Tweed; whereas in the south parts of England there are abundance, as particularly over the great river of Thames at Kingston, Chertsey, Staines, Windsor, Maidenhead, Reading, Henley, Marlow, and other places, and over the River Lea, tho' a navigable river, of thirteen bridges, we see but one built of stone, (viz.) that at Bow.

A little below Ripley, on the same River Nyd, and with a very fine bridge over it also, we saw Knaresborough; known among foreigners by the name of Knaresborough Spaw; in the south of England I have heard it call'd the Yorkshire Spaw.

I shall not enter here upon the definition of the word *spaw*, 'tis enough to speak familiarly, that here is a well of physical or mineral waters, or, to speak more exactly as one viewing the country, here are at the town, and in the adjacent lands, no less than four spaws or mineral waters.

The first thing recommended to me for a wonder, was that four springs, the waters of which are in themselves of so different a quality, should rise in so narrow a compass of ground; but I, who was surfeited with country wonders in my passing the Peak, was not so easily surprized at the wonderful strangeness of this part; and when my landlord at Knaresborough took me short, with a But is it not a strange thing, sir? I answered him with a question, Is it not as strange, sir, said I, that in Derbyshire two springs, one hot, and another cold, should rise within a hand's breadth of one another? 'Tis certain, that though the eruption of the water may be near, yet the subterranean passages may be as remote as east and west, and the mineral lying in veins may run remote also, so as to take off all the wonder.

2. The springs themselves, and indeed one of them, is nothing extraordinary, namely, that in a little cave a petrifying water drops from the roof of the cavity, which, as they say, turns wood into stone. This indeed I made light of too, because I had already been at Poole's Hole and Castleton in the Peak, and at Harwich.

But now to speak of the other two springs, they are indeed valuable rarities, and not to be equalled in England.

1. The first is the Sweet Spaw, or a vitriolick water; it was discovered by one Mr. Slingsby, anno 1630. and all physicians acknowledge it to be a very sovereign medicine in several particular distempers. *Vid*. Dr. Leigh's *Nat. Hist. of Lancashire*.

2. The Stinking Spaw, or, if you will, according to the learned, the Sulphur Well. This water is clear as chrystal, but fœtid and nauseous to the smell, so that those who drink it are obliged to hold their noses when they drink; yet it is a valuable medicine also in scorbutic, hypochondriac, and especially in hydropic distempers; as to its curing the gout, I take that, as in other cases, *ad referendum*.

The people formerly, and that for many years, only drank these waters, and used them no otherwise; but are now come into the use of bathing in them as a cold bath, and thus they must necessarily be very good for rheumatic pains, paralitic numbnesses, and many other distempers which afflict mankind.

We were surprised to find a great deal of good company here drinking the waters, and indeed, more than we found afterwards at Scarborough; though this seems to be a most desolate out-of-the-world place, and that men would only retire to it for religious mortifications, and to hate the world, but we found it was quite otherwise.

Those two bridges at Harwood and Ripley are very firm, fine, and, I assure you, very chargeable bridges; and at Rippon there are two stone bridges, whereof one of them has, I think, thirteen arches, or more, over the Eure, and is indeed a very stately and chargeable work. It is true, a bridge over the same river at Burrowbrigg, four mile lower than Rippon, has but four or five arches, but then those arches are near forty foot diameter, and one of the middlemost much more, and high in proportion, and the ends of the bridge continued by high causeways, built of stone, to keep the water in its course; and yet sometimes all is too little.

From the bridges may be observ'd, that however low these waters are in the summer, they are high and furious enough in the winter; and yet the River Aire, tho' its beginning is in the same ridge of mountains as the other, and particularly in the hill called Penigent, which overtops all its neighbours; I say this river is gentle and mild in its stream, when the other are all raging and furious; the only reason I can give for it, which however I think is a very just account, is, that it runs in a thousand windings and turnings more than any other river in those parts; and these reaches and meanders of the river greatly help to check the sharpness of the stream: The next reason is, that after it has descended from the mountains it has a deeper channel; both which, I think, put together, will sufficiently account for the abating the current.

Rippon is a very neat, pleasant, well built town, and has not only an agreeable situation on a rising ground between two rivers, but the market place is the finest and most beautiful square that is to be seen of its kind in England.

In the middle of it stands a curious column of stone, imitating the obelisks of the antients, tho' not so high, but rather like the pillar in the middle of Covent-Garden, or that in Lincoln's Inn, with dials also upon it.

But I must not omit to tell you also, however other pretended travelling writers were pleased not to see it as they went by, that here is a large collegiate church, and tho' it is not a bishoprick but a deanery only, in the diocess of York, yet it is a very handsome, antient and venerable pile of building, and shews it self a great way in the country. Mr. Cambden says, this town of Rippon owes its greatness to religion.

That here was a famous monastery built by Wilfrid, Archbishop of York, and that in the first ages of Christianity, at least in this island, is certain; but this pious gift of the bishop was swallowed up some years after, when the Danes over-running Yorkshire, rifled and burnt it to the ground, as likewise the whole town of Rippon; It afterwards flourished again as a monastery. But those being all given up in the reign of King Henry VIII. the church only was preserved. Mr. Cambden says it was built, which I conceive rather to be form'd into a church, from the ruin of the monastery, by the contribution of the gentry thereabouts.

While it was a monastery, here was a famous sanctuary, a thing however useful in some cases, yet so abused in foreign countries, by making the church a refuge of rogues, thieves and murtherers, that 'tis happy for England it is out of use here. This privilege of sanctuary was, it seems, granted to the church of Rippon by King Athelstan, an. —— and with this extraordinary sanction, that whosoever broke the rights of sanctuary of the church of Rippon, and which he extended to a mile on either side the church, should forfeit life and estate; so that, in short, not the church only, but the whole town, and a circle of two miles diameter, was like the Rules of the King's Bench here in Southwark, a refuge for all that fled to it, where they liv'd safe from all manner of molestation, even from the king, or his laws, or any person whatsoever.

Annexed to this monastery was an hospital, the intent and purposes of which are very remarkable, and would be worthy imitation in our days of Protestant charity, when indeed I see nothing come up to it. The house was called the hospital of St. Mary Magdalen, where, according to the foundation, were to be maintained two chaplains to perform divine service; and if any begging clergymen, or other needy persons, should happen to travel or stray out of their way, and call at the said hospital, they should be relieved there for one night only, with food and a bed, and to be gone in the morning; and to every poor person that came craving an alms, on St. Mary Magdalen's Day yearly, they should give one loaf, value a half penny, when corn was at the price of five shillings per quarter, and one herring.

Also 'tis recorded, that one branch of this hospital was

founded and endowed, and given to a society of religious sisters by a certain Archbishop of York, but the inquisition taken does not find his name, to the intent that they should maintain one chaplain to perform divine service, and to the farther intent that they should maintain all the lepers born and bred in Hipschire, that should come to it for maintenance; and that they should allow to each of them a garment call'd Rak, and two pair of shoes yearly, with every day a loaf fit for a poor man's sustenance, half a pitcher of beer, a sufficient portion of flesh on flesh days, and three herrings on fish days.

After this, other gifts were added to this foundation; also the sisters were removed, and a brotherhood established in their stead, which continued some time; and after that a mastership; and the maintenance of lepers finding no clients, the country proving healthy, that part was turned into a charity, to be dealt out to the poor on St. Mary Magdalen's Day, as above: At length all was demolished together, and the house, with the monastery, suppress'd, as it now stands, a collegiate church being erected on the room of it: Besides, it seems upon another inquisition, and a jury empanelled to give their verdict, it appeared in the 10th of Edward III. that the revenue of one branch of the hospital had been embezzled and squandered away by the master of the hospital, the charities interrupted, and the poor defrauded.

And so in the visitation of the church, for it seems there were frauds and embezzlements in those days, even of the goods of the church, as well as since. Mr. Dugdale, in his *Monasticon*, gives an account, that William, Archbishop of York, in a visitation of the church of Rippon, anno 1331. found it almost abandoned, notwithstanding much cure of souls depended on it; that there were good revenues belonging to it, but that they were consumed by the absent canons. *N.B.* There was then also non-residence, and the non-residents too devouring the goods of the church.

Upon this, the good archbishop took order for the future, that all the lands, meadows, revenues, and services (I give you the very words of the archbishop's decree upon his visitation) with the tithes of garbs and hay, of Nyd and Grantilaye, with a pension of twenty shillings due from the Vicar of Nyd, and the spiritual jurisdiction, and the profits of the same, should, for the future, be divided among those who should reside at the church of Rippon, and no other.

There were at that time, in this church, nine chanteries,

besides two out-chanteries in the parish, the same which we call now chapels of ease; and besides the chantery of the two priests in the hospital, the out-chanteries were one at Hutton Conyers, and one at Clotheram. *N.B.* A chantery is any consecrated place where is an oratory, and a priest allowed to sing mass, and therefore call'd a chantery or singing house.

There were in the church at that time

	l.	*s.*	*d.*	
Three deacons ——	5	10	0	each.
Three subdeacons ——	4	10	0	
Six choristers ——	3	10	0	And 1*l.* 4*s.* each for their Livery.
Six tribblers ——	2	12	6	
The organist ——	0	14	4	
The grammar school-master ——	2	0	0	

These were noble stipends in those days. How our clergy would serve at this time under such great encouragement, is left to enquiry, especially the organist's salary was notable; from whence I may, I hope without offence, suppose, that he being a layman, might get business in the town, (perhaps he was a dancing-master, or a musick-master, or both) to teach the young ladies of Rippon; and his wife might keep a boarding-school too; and so the grammar school-master might be a writing-master in the town, and the like.

Be that as it will, the church is still standing, tho' the monastery and hospital are suppress'd, and the canons and choir are maintain'd at a much better rate than as above, for they now eat as good beef, and drink as good Yorkshire ale, as their neighbours.

It is an antient building, but firm and strong, the work Gothick, according to the times, and plain; no imagry or statues of any note to be seen about it; there are three homely spires, one on the tower in the middle, and the other two on the angle towers of the west end; they are covered with lead, but not very high or handsome.

But I must not leave Rippon without giving the fam'd tale of St. Wilfrid's Needle. St. Wilfrid was the saint to whom the monastery was dedicated, and this needle was, it seems, for the trial of chastity. There was a dark vault under ground in one part of the monastery, into which there was an easy passage one way, but a narrow long entry, also dark and uneven to come out of it: If any person's chastity was suspected, it does not say whether it was not for men as well as women, but to be sure it was for the latter, they were put into this vault, and the first entrance being closed, they were at liberty to come out by the other, which was called the needle, or the eye of the needle; if they were chaste and untainted, they came out boldly, and without any difficulty; but if faulty, they were stopp'd, and could not get along in the narrow eye or passage, and, as I think the story says, were left there, unable to get out till they had confess'd their fault. Whether the priests had no craft in this case, to put some secret barrier cross the narrow passage in the dark, so to impose upon the poor girls that were put to the trial, that I am not to enquire too far into: However it was, the priests made a miracle of it; and the poor Yorkshire lasses have, no doubt, good reason to be satisfied that St. Wilfrid has left off shewing those miraculous things at this time.

In the churchyard of this minster lies a plain monument or gravestone over the remains of a generous soul, who, in charity, gave two thousand pounds to pious uses; the modest epitaph is, however, very important, as follows:

> Hic jacet Zacharias Jopson, cujus Æt. fuit 49. per paucos annos tantum vixit.

To conclude our observations of this church, be pleas'd to take the grant of King Athelstan, mentioned above, of the sanctuary of peace. I suppose all such grants were poetical.

THE CHARTER GRANTED BY KING ATHELSTAN TO ST. WILFRID OF RIPPON

> Wyt all that es an es gan,
> Yat ik King Adelstan,
> As given als frielith as i may,
> And to the capital of Seint Wilfrai,
> Of my free devotion,
> Yair pees ar Rippon
> On ylke side the kyrke a mile,
> For all ill deedys an ylke agyle,
> And within yair kyrke gate.
> At ye stan yat Grithstole hate
> Within ye kyrke dore, and ye quare,
> Yair have pees for less and mare;
> Ilkan of yis stedes sal have pees,
> Of frod mortel and ill deeds.
> Yet yair don is tol and tem,
> With iren and with water deme;
> And yat ye lond of Seint Wilfrai,
> Of alkyn geld fre sal be ay;
> Ut na man at langs me to,
> In yair herps ac sal have to do.

And for ik wil at yai be save,
I wil, at yai alkyn freedom hav;
And in all thynges be als free
As hert may thynk, or eygh may see:
At ye power of a kynge
Marts make free any thynge.
And my seal have sat yerto,
For I will yat no man it undo.

If you will have this grant speak more modern English, take
it thus:

Know all men that are or are to be,[1]
That I, King Athelstan,
Has given as freely as I am able,
To the body politick [2] of St. Wilfrid,
Of my meer bounty [3] and good-will,
Their peace that are at Rippon,[4]
For a mile on every side of the church,
For all ill deeds, and every guile,[5]
And also within the churchyard gate.[6]
He that shall stand and do pennance
Within the church door, or in the quire,
Shall be protected, let it be less or more [7];
All his goods and chattels shall have peace,[8]
Tho' guilty of mortal feud [9], or any ill deeds.
That I give them also freedom from toll
By land or by water, for themselves, horses and carts;
And that all the lands of the monastery of St. Wilfrid,
Shall be for ever free from all taxes;
So that no man that belongs to me [10]
Shall have any thing to do with their purse.[11]
And because 'tis my pleasure they shall be safe,
I will, that they every freedom have,
And in all things be as free
As heart can wish, or eye can see:
So as the power of a king
Can make free to any thing.
And my seal I have set hereto,
Because no man shall it undo.[12]

A mile from this town, or less, is a stately beautiful seat,
built a few years since by Sir Edward Blacket; the park is
extended to the bank of the River Eure, and is sometimes in
part laid under water by the river, the water of which, they
say, coming down from the western mountains, thro' a marly,
loamy soil, fructifies the earth, as the River Nile does the
Egyptian fields about Grand Cairo, tho' by their leave not
quite so much.

[1] Present and to come.   [2] Or public stock.
[3] *Devotion* here does not mean *piety* but *charity*.
[4] A place of peace or sanctuary.   [5] Every cheat or fraud.
[6] The church hatch.   [7] Be his fault what it will.
[8] His horses and cattle shall not be seized.
[9] Some think this word *frod mortel* extended to murther.
[10] None of the king's officers.   [11] Snapsack.
[12] Or that no man may dare to contradict it.

As Sir Edward spared no cost in the building, and Sir Christopher Wren laid out the design, as well as chose the ground for him, you may believe me the better, when I add, that nothing can either add to the contrivance or the situation; the building is of brick, the avenues, now the trees are grown, are very fine, and the gardens not only well laid out, but well planted, and as well kept; the statues are neat, the parterre beautiful; but, as they want fine gravel, the walks cannot shew themselves, as in this southern part of England they would. The house has a fine prospect over the country, almost to York, with the river in view most of the way; and it makes it self a very noble appearance to the great north road, which lies within two miles of it, at Burrow-bridge.

As you now begin to come into the North Riding, for the Eure parts the West Riding from it, so you are come into the place noted in the north of England for the best and largest oxen, and the finest galloping horses, I mean swift horses, horses bred, as we call it, for the light saddle, that is to say, for the race, the chace, for running or hunting. Sir Edward was a grazier, and took such delight in the breeding and feeding large siz'd black cattle, that he had two or three times an ox out of his park led about the country for a sight, and shewed as far as Newcastle, and even to Scotland, for the biggest bullock in England; nor was he very often, if ever, over-match'd.

From this town of Rippon, the north road and the Roman highway also, mentioned before, which comes from Castleford Bridge, parting at Abberforth, leads away to a town call'd Bedal, and, in a strait line (leaving Richmond about two miles on the west) call'd Leeming Lane, goes on to Piersbridge on the River Tees, which is the farthest boundary of the county of York.

But before I go forward I should mention Burrow Bridge, which is but three miles below Rippon, upon the same River Eure, and which I must take in my way, that I may not be obliged to go farther out of the way, on the next journey.

There is something very singular at this town, and which is not to be found in any other part of England or Scotland, namely, two borough towns in one parish, and each sending two members to Parliament, that is, Borough Brigg and Aldborough.

Borough Brigg, or Bridge, seems to be the modern town risen up out of Aldborough, the very names importing as much, (viz.) that Burrough at the Bridge, and the Old Borough that was before; and this construction I pretend to justify from all the antiquaries of our age, or the last, who place on the side of

Aldborough or Old Borough, an antient city and Roman colony, call'd *Isurium Brigantum*; the arguments brought to prove the city stood here, where yet at present nothing of a city is to be seen, no not so much as the ruines, especially not above ground, are out of my way for the present; only the digging up coins, urns, vaults, pavements, and the like, may be mentioned, because some of them are very eminent and remarkable ones, of which an account is to be seen at large in Mr. Cambden, and his continuator, to whom I refer. That this Old Burrough is the remain of that city, is then out of doubt, and that the Burrough at the Bridge, is since grown up, and perhaps principally by the confluence of travellers, to pass the great bridge over the Eure there; this seems too out of question by the import of the word. How either of them came to the privilege of sending members to Parliament, whether by charter and incorporation, or meer prescription, that is to say, a claim of age, which we call time out of mind, that remains for the Parliament to be satisfied in. Certain it is, that the youngest of the two, that is, Burrow Bridge, is very old; for here, in the barons wars, was a battle, and on this bridge the great Bohun, Earl of Hereford, was killed by a soldier, who lay concealed under the bridge, and wounded him, by thrusting a spear or pike into his body, as he pass'd the bridge. From whence Mr. Cambden very gravely judges, that it was not a stone bridge as is now, but a bridge of timber, a thing any man might judge without being challenged for a wizard.

I had not the curiosity so much as to go to see the four great stones in the fields on the left-hand, as you go through Burrow Bridge, which the country people, because they wonder how they could come there, will have be brought by the devil, and call them the Devil's Bolts. Mr. Cambden describes them, and they are no more than are frequent; and I have been obliged to speak of such so often, that I need say no more, but refer to other authors to describe the Romans way of setting up trophies for victory, or the dead, or places of sacrifices to their gods, and which soever it may be, the matter is the same.

From the Eure entring the North Riding, and keeping the Roman causeway, as mentioned before, one part of which went by this Isurium Brigantum from York, we come to Bedall, all the way from Hutton, or thereabout, this Roman way is plain to be seen, and is called now Leeming Lane, from Leeming Chapel, a village which it goes through.

I met with nothing at or about Bedall, that comes within the compass of my enquiry but this, that not this town only, but even all this country, is full of jockeys, that is to say, dealers in horses, and breeders of horses, and the breeds of their horses in this and the next country are so well known, that tho' they do not preserve the pedigree of their horses for a succession of ages, as they say they do in Arabia and in Barbary, yet they christen their stallions here, and know them, and will advance the price of a horse according to the reputation of the horse he came of.

They do indeed breed very fine horses here, and perhaps some of the best in the world, for let foreigners boast what they will of barbs and Turkish horses, and, as we know five hundred pounds has been given for a horse brought out of Turkey, and of the Spanish jennets from Cordova, for which also an extravagant price has been given, I do believe that some of the gallopers of this country, and of the bishoprick of Durham, which joins to it, will outdo for speed and strength the swiftest horse that was ever bred in Turkey, or Barbary, take them all together.

My reason for this opinion is founded upon those words altogether; that is to say, take their strength and their speed together; for example; match the two horses, and bring them to the race post, the barb may beat Yorkshire for a mile course, but Yorkshire shall distance him at the end of four miles; the barb shall beat Yorkshire upon a dry, soft carpet ground, but Yorkshire for a deep country; the reason is plain, the English horses have both the speed and the strength; the barb perhaps shall beat Yorkshire, and carry seven stone and a half; but Yorkshire for a twelve to fourteen stone weight; in a word, Yorkshire shall carry the man, and the barb a feather.

The reason is to be seen in the very make of the horses. The barb, or the jennet, is a fine delicate creature, of a beautiful shape, clean limbs, and a soft coat; but then he is long jointed, weak pastured, and under limb'd: Whereas Yorkshire has as light a body, and stronger limbs, short joints, and well bon'd. This gives him not speed only but strength to hold it; and, I believe, I do not boast in their behalf, without good vouchers, when I say, that English horses, take them one with another, will beat all the world.

As this part of the country is so much employed in horses, the young fellows are naturally grooms, bred up in the stable, and used to lie among the horses; so that you cannot fail of a good servant here, for looking after horses is their particular delight; and this is the reason why, whatever part of England you go to, though the farthest counties west and south, and whatever inn you come at, 'tis two to one but the hostler is a Yorkshire man; for as they are bred among horses, 'tis always the first business they recommend themselves to; and if you ask a Yorkshire man, at his first coming up to get a service, what he can do; his answer is, sir, he can look after your horse, for he handles a curry-comb as naturally as a young scrivener does a pen and ink.

Besides their breeding of horses, they are also good grasiers over this whole country, and have a large, noble breed of oxen, as may be seen at North Allerton fairs, where there are an incredible quantity of them bought eight times every year, and brought southward as far as the fens in Lincolnshire, and the Isle of Ely, where, being but, as it were, half fat before, they are fed up to the grossness of fat which we see in London markets. The market whither these north country cattle are generally brought is to St. Ives, a town between Huntingdon and Cambridge, upon the River Ouse, and where there is a very great number of fat cattle every Monday.

Richmond, which, as I said, is two or three mile wide of the Leeming Lane, is a large market town, and gives name to this part of the country, which is called after it Richmondshire, as another part of it east of this is call'd North Allertonshire.

Here you begin to find a manufacture on foot again, and, as before, all was cloathing, and all the people clothiers, here you see all the people, great and small, a knitting; and at Richmond you have a market for woollen or yarn stockings, which they make very coarse and ordinary, and they are sold accordingly; for the smallest siz'd stockings for children are here sold for eighteen pence per dozen, or three half pence a pair, sometimes less.

This trade extends itself also into Westmoreland, or rather comes from Westmoreland, extending itself hither, for at Kendal, Kirkby Stephen, and such other places in this county as border upon Yorkshire; the chief manufacture of yarn stockings is carried on; it is indeed a very considerable manufacture in it self, and of late mightily encreased too, as all the manufactures of England indeed are.

This town of Richmond (Cambden calls it a city) is wall'd, and had a strong castle; but as those things are now all slighted, so really the account of them is of small consequence, and needless; old fortifications being, if fortification was wanted, of very little signification; the River Swale runs under the wall of this castle, and has some unevenness at its bottom, by reason of rocks which intercept its passage, so that it falls like a cataract, but not with so great a noise.

The Swale is a noted river, though not extraordinary large, for giving name to the lands which it runs through for some length, which are called Swale Dale, and to an antient family of that name, one of whom had the vanity, as I have heard, to boast, that his family was so antient as not to receive that name from, but to give name to the river it self. One of the worthless successors of this line, who had brought himself to the dignity of what they call in London, a Fleeter, used to write himself, in his abundant vanity, Sir Solomon Swale, of Swale Hall, in Swale Dale, in the county of Swale in the North Riding of York.

This addition of *dale*, first given here to the low lands about the head of the Swale, is grown up into a custom or usage from all the rivers which rise in those western hills north of this, quite to and into Scotland; for example,

Teesdale for the River Tees.

Wierdale for the Wier, which runs through Durham.

Tine Dale for the Tine, which runs to Newcastle.

Tweedale for the Tweed, which passeth by Berwick.

Clydsdale, Nydsdale, and many others.

Leaving Richmond, we continue through this long Leeming Lane, which holds for about the length of six mile to the bank of Tees, where we pass'd over the River Tees at Piersbridge; the Tees is a most terrible river, so rapid, that they tell us a story of a man who coming to the ferry place in the road to Darlington, and finding the water low began to pull off his hose and shoes to wade thro', the water not being deep enough to reach to his knees, but that while he was going over, the stream swell'd so fast as to carry him away and drown him.

This bridge leads into the bishoprick of Durnam, and the road soon after turns into the great post road leading to the city of Durham. I shall dwell no longer upon the particulars found on this side except Barnard Castle, which is about four miles distant from the Tees bank west, and there I may speak of it again; as all the country round here are grooms, as is noted before; so here and hereabouts they have an excellent knack at dressing horses hides into leather, and thinking or making us think it is invulnerable, that is to say, that it will never wear out; in a word, they make the best bridle reins, belts broad or narrow, and all accoutrements for a compleat horse-master, as they do at Rippon for spurs and stirrups.

Barnard's Castle stands on the north side of the Tees, and so is in the bishoprick of Durham. 'Tis an antient town, and pretty well built, but not large; the manufacture of yarn stockings continues thus far, but not much farther; but the jockeys multiply that way; and here we saw some very fine horses indeed; but as they wanted no goodness, so they wanted no price, being valued for the stallion they came of, and the merit of the breed. One very beautiful stone-horse which they here kept, they asked two hundred guineas for; but, as I heard afterwards, tho' they carried him to London, which was no small addition to the charge of him, they sold him for much less money.

The length of the late war, it seems, caused the breeders here to run into a race or kind of horses, differing much from what they were used to raise, that is to say, from fine fleet horses for galloping and hunting, to a larger breed of charging horses, for the use of the general officers, and colonels of horse, aids du camp, and the like, whose service required strong charging horses, and yet if they were fleet horses too, they had a vast advantage of the enemy; for that if the rider was conquered and forced to fly, there was no overtaking him; and if his enemies fled they could never get away from him. I saw some of this breed, and very noble creatures they were, fit for any business whatever; strong enough for charging, fleet enough for hunting, tempered enough for travelling; and indeed, there is one thing to be said for the horse breeders in this country, their horses are all well broke, perfectly brought to hand, and to be under command, which is a thing absolutely necessary in the army, and in the hunting field also.

I was come now to the extent of the county of York northward. But as I have kept all along to the west side of the county, even from the Peak of Derby hither; and that I have all the East Riding and the eastern part of the North and West Riding to go over, I shall break off here, and conclude my first circuit; and am, with due respect,

SIR,
Your most humble servant.

THE END OF THE EIGHTH LETTER

LETTER IX

Sir,—I began my first circuit at the bank of Trent, namely, at Nottingham Bridge, and keeping the middle of the island, travelled due north into the West Riding of Yorkshire, and to the farthest part of the county to the bank of Tees, as you have seen.

I am now come back, as the French say, *sur mes pas*, to the same bank of the Trent, though lower down, towards the east, and shall gather up some fragments of Nottinghamshire and the West Riding of Yorkshire, as I go, and then hasten to the sea side, where we have not cast our eye yet.

Passing Newark Bridge, we went through the lower side of Nottinghamshire, keeping within the River Idle. Here we saw Tuxford in the Clays, that is to say, Tuxford in the Dirt, and a little dirty market town it is, suitable to its name.

Then we saw Rhetford, a pretty little borough town of good trade, situate on the River Idle; the mayor treated us like gentlemen, though himself but a tradesman; he gave us a dish of fish from the River Idle, and another from the Trent, which I only note, to intimate that the salmon of the Trent is very valuable in this country, and is oftentimes brought to London, exceeding large and fine; at Newark they have it very large, and like wise at Nottingham.

From Rhetford, the country on the right or east lies low and marshy, till, by the confluence of the Rivers Trent, Idle, and Don, they are formed into large islands, of which the first is called the Isle of Axholm, where the lands are very rich, and feed great store of cattle: But travelling into those parts being difficult, and sometimes dangerous, especially for strangers, we contented our selves with having the country described to us, as above, and with being assured that there were no towns of note, or any thing to be call'd curious, except that they dig old fir trees out of the ground in the Isle of Axholm, which they tell us have lain there ever since the Deluge; but, as I shall meet with the like more eminently in many other places, I shall content my self with speaking of it once for all, when we come into Lancashire.

There are some few market towns in these low parts between this place and the Humber, though none of great consideration, such as Thorne upon the Don, Snathe upon the Aire, Selby upon the Ouse, and Howdon near the same river; the two last are towns of good trade, the first being seated where the Ouse is navigable for large vessels, has a good share in the shipping of the river, and some merchants live and thrive here; the latter is one of the towns in England, where their annual fairs preserve the name of a mart, the other Lyn, Boston, Ganesborough, Beverley, tho' of late they begin to lose the word. The fair or mart held here is very considerable for inland trade, and several wholesale tradesman come to it from London. But I take this town to be more famous for the birth of one of our antient historians, (viz.) Roger of Hovedon or Howdon; Mr. Cambden's continuator is much in the wrong to say this town stands upon the Derwent; whereas it is above three mile east of the Derwent, and no river of any note near it but the Humber.

Having found nothing in this low part of the country but a wonderful conflux of great rivers, all pouring down into the Humber, which receiving the Aire, the Ouse, the Don and the Trent, becomes rather a sea than a river, we left it on the right; and knowing we should necessarily visit its shores again, we turned up into the post road, where, as I said, I left it before near Brotherton, and went on for Tadcaster.

On this road we pass'd over Towton, that famous field where the most cruel and bloody battle was fought between the two Houses of Lancaster and York, in the reign of Edward IV. I call it most cruel and bloody, because the animosity of the parties was so great, that tho' they were countrymen and Englishmen, neighbours, nay, as history says, relations; for here fathers kill'd their sons, and sons their fathers; yet for some time they fought with such obstinacy and such rancour, that, void of all pity and compassion, they gave no quarter, and I call it the most bloody, because 'tis certain no such numbers were ever slain in one battle in England, since the great battle between King Harold and William of Normandy, call'd the Conqueror, at Battle in Sussex; for here, at Towton, fell six and thirty thousand men on both sides, besides the wounded and prisoners (if they took any).

Tradition guided the country people, and they us, to the very spot; but we had only the story in speculation; for there remains no marks, no monument, no remembrance of the action, only that the ploughmen say, that sometimes they plough up arrow-heads and spear-heads, and broken javelins, and helmets, and the like; for we cou'd only give a short sigh to the memory of the dead, and move forward.

Tadcaster has nothing that we could see to testify the antiquity it boasts of, but some old Roman coins, which our landlord the post master shewed us, among which was one of Domitian, the same kind, I believe, with that Mr. Cambden gives an account of, but so very much defaced with age, that we could read but D O, and A V, at a distance. Here is the hospital and school, still remaining, founded by Dr. Oglethorp, Bishop of Carlisle, who, for want of a Protestant archbishop, set the crown on the head of Queen Elizabeth.

Here also we saw plainly the Roman highway, which I have mentioned, as seen at Aberforth; and, as antient writers tell us, of a stately stone bridge here, I may tell you, here was no bridge at all; but perhaps no writer after me will ever be able to say the like; for the case was this, the antient famous bridge, which, I suppose, had stood several hundred years, being defective, was just pull'd down, and the foundation of a new bridge, was laid, or rather begun to be laid, or was laying; and we were obliged to go over the river in a ferry boat; but coming that way since, I saw the new bridge finished, and very magnificent indeed it is.

Mr. Cambden gives us a little distich of a learned passenger upon this river, and the old bridge, at Tadcaster; I suppose he pass'd it in a dry summer, as the Frenchman did the bridge at Madrid, which I mentioned before.

> Nil Tadcaster habes muris vel carmine dignum,
> Præter magnifice structum sine flumine pontem.

But I can assure the reader of this account, that altho' I pass'd this place in the middle of summer, we found water enough in the river, so that there was no passing it without a boat.

From Tadcaster it is but twelve miles to York; the country is rich, fruitful and populous, but not like the western parts about Leeds, Wakefield, Hallifax, &c. which I described above; it bears good corn, and the city of York being so near, and having the navigation of so many rivers also to carry it to Hull, they never want a good market for it.

The antiquity of York, though it was not the particular enquiry I proposed to make, yet shewed it self so visibly at a distance, that we could not but observe it before we came quite up to the city, I mean the mount and high hills, where the antient castle stood, which, when you come to the city, you scarcely see, at least not so as to judge of its antiquity.

The cathedral, or the minster, as they call it, is a fine building, but not so antient as some of the other churches in the city seem to be: That mount I mentioned above, and which, at a distance, I say was a mark of antiquity, is called the old Bale, which was some ages ago fortified and made very strong; but time has eaten through not the timber and plank only, which they say it was first built with, but even the stones and mortar; for not the least footstep of it remains but the hill.

York is indeed a pleasant and beautiful city, and not at all the less beautiful for the works and lines about it being demolished, and the city, as it may be said, being laid open, for the beauty of peace is seen in the rubbish; the lines and bastions and demolished fortifications, have a reserved secret pleasantness in them from the contemplation of the publick tranquility, that outshines all the beauty of advanced bastions, batteries, cavaliers, and all the hard named works of the engineers about a city.

I shall not entertain you either with a plan of the city, or a draught of its history; I shall only say in general, the first would take up a great deal of time, and the last a great deal of paper; it is enough to tell you, that as it has been always a strong place, so it has been much contended for, been the seat of war, the rendezvous of armies, and of the greatest generals several times.

It boasts of being the seat of some of the Roman emperors, and the station of their forces for the north of Britain, being it self a Roman colony, and the like, all which I leave as I find it; it may be examined critically in Mr. Cambden, and his continuator, where it is learnedly debated. However, this I must not omit, namely, that Severus and Constantius Chlorus, father to Constantine the Great, both kept their Courts here, and both died here. Here Constantine the Great took upon him the purple, and began the first Christian empire in the world; and this is truly and really an honour to the city of York; and this is all I shall say of her antiquity.

But now things infinitely modern, compared to those, are become marks of antiquity; for even the castle of York, built by William the Conqueror, anno 1069. almost eight hundred years since Constantine, is not only become antient and decayed, but even sunk into time, and almost lost and forgotten; fires, sieges, plunderings and devastations, have often been the fate of York; so that one should wonder there should be any thing of a city left.

But 'tis risen again, and all we see now is modern; the bridge is vastly strong, and has one arch which, they tell me, was near 70 foot in diameter; it is, without exception, the greatest in England, some say it's as large as the Rialto at Venice, though I think not.

The cathedral too is modern; it was begun to be built but in the time of Edward the First, anno 1313. or thereabouts, by one John Roman, who was treasurer for the undertaking; the foundation being laid, and the whole building designed by the charitable benevolence of the gentry, and especially, as a noted antiquary there assured me, by the particular application of two eminent families in the north, namely, the Piercys and Vavasors, as is testified by their arms and portraits cut in the stone work; the first with a piece of timber, and the last with a hew'd stone in their hands; the first having given a large wood, and the latter a quarry of stone, for encouraging the work.

It was building during the lives of three archbishops, all of the Christian name of John, whereof the last, (viz.) John Thoresby, lived to see it finished, and himself consecrated it.

It is a Gothick building, but with all the most modern addenda that order of building can admit; and with much more orna- ment of a singular kind, than we see any thing of that way of building grac'd with. I see nothing indeed of that kind of structure in England go beyond it, except it be the building we call King Henry VIIth's Chapel, additional to the abbey church of Westminster, and that is not to be named with this, because it is but a chapel, and that but a small one neither.

The royal chapel at Windsor, and King's College Chapel, at Cambridge, are indeed very gay things, but neither of them can come up to the minster of York on many accounts; also the great tower of the cathedral church at Canterbury is named to match with this at York; but this is but a piece of a large work, the rest of the same building being mean and gross, compared with this at York.

The only deficiency I find at York Minster, is the lowness of the great tower, or its want of a fine spire upon it, which, doubt- less, was designed by the builders; he that lately writing a description of this church, and that at Doncaster, placed high fine spires upon them both, took a great deal of pains to tell us he was describing a place where he had never been, and that he took his intelligence grossly upon trust.

As then this church was so compleatly finished, and that so lately that it is not yet four hundred years old, it is the less to be wondered that the work continues so firm and fine, that it is now the beautifullest church of the old building that is in Britain. In a word, the west end is a picture, and so is the building, the outsides of the quire especially, are not to be equall'd.

The choir of the church, and the proper spaces round and behind it, are full of noble and magnificent monuments, too many to enter upon the description of them here, some in marble, and others in the old manner in brass, and the windows are finely painted; but I could find no body learned enough in the designs that could read the histories to us that were delineated there.

The Chapter-House is a beauty indeed, and it has been always esteemed so, witness the Latin verse which is written upon it in letters of gold.

Ur Rosa flos florum, sic est Domus ista Domorum.

But, allowing this to be a little too much of a boast, it must be own'd to be an excellent piece of work, and indeed so is the whole minster; nor does it want any thing, as I can suppose, but, as I said before, a fine spire upon the tower, such a one as is at Grantham, or at Newark. The dimensions of this church shall conclude my description of it.

	Feet.
It is in length, exclusive of the buttresses	524½
Breadth at the east end — — —	105
At the west end — — —	109
In the cross — — — —	222
Heighth of the nave of the roof — —	99
The lanthorn to the vault — —	188
To the top leads — — —	213
Of the chapter-house to the canopy —	86½
Breadth of the chapter-house — —	58¾

But to return to the city it self; there is abundance of good company here, and abundance of good families live here, for the sake of the good company and cheap living; a man converses here with all the world as effectually as at London; the keeping up assemblies among the younger gentry was first set up here, a thing other writers recommend mightily as the character of a good country, and of a pleasant place; but which I look upon with a different view, and esteem it as a plan laid for the ruin of the nation's morals, and which, in time, threatens us with too much success that way.

However, to do the ladies of Yorkshire justice, I found they did not gain any great share of the just reproach which in some other places has been due to their sex; nor has there been so many young fortunes carried off here by half-pay men, as has been said to be in other towns, of merry fame, westward and southward.

The government of the city is that of a regular corporation, by mayor, aldermen and common-council; the mayor has the honour here, by antient prescription, of being called My Lord; it is a county within its self, and has a jurisdiction extended over a small tract of land on the west suburb, called the Liberty of Ansty, which I could get no uniform account of, one pretending one thing, one another. The city is old but well built; and the clergy, I mean such as serve in, and depend upon the cathedral, have very good houses, or little palaces rather here, adjoining the cymeterie, or churchyard of the minster; the bishop's is indeed called a palace, and is really so; the deanery is a large, convenient and spacious house; and among these dwellings of the clergy is the assembly house. Whence I would infer, the conduct of it is under the better government, or should be so.

No city in England is better furnished with provisions of every kind, nor any so cheap, in proportion to the goodness of things; the river being so navigable, and so near the sea, the merchants here trade directly to what part of the world they will; for ships of any burthen come up within thirty mile of the city, and small craft from sixty to eighty ton, and under, come up to the very city.

With these they carry on a considerable trade; they import their own wines from France and Portugal, and likewise their own deals and timber from Norway; and indeed what they please almost from where they please; they did also bring their own coals from Newcastle and Sunderland, but now have them down the Aire and Calder from Wakefield, and from Leeds, as I have said already.

The publick buildings erected here are very considerable, such as halls for their merchants and trades, a large town-house or guild-hall, and the prison, which is spacious, and takes up all the ground within the walls of the old castle, and, in a building newly erected there, the assizes for the county are kept.

The old walls are standing, and the gates and posterns; but the old additional works which were cast up in the late rebellion, are slighted; so that York is not now defensible as it was then: But things lie so too, that a little time, and many hands, would put those works into their former condition, and make the city able to stand out a small siege. But as the ground seems capable by situation, so an ingenious head, in our company, taking a stricter view of it, told us, he would undertake to make it as strong as Tourney in Flanders, or as Namure, allowing him to add a citadel at that end next the river. But this is a speculation; and 'tis much better that we should have no need of fortified towns than that we should seek out good situations to make them.

While we were at York, we took one day's time to see the fatal field called Marston Moor, where Prince Rupert, a third time, by his excess of valour, and defect of conduct, lost the royal army, and had a victory wrung out of his hands, after he had all the advantage in his own hands that he could desire: Certain it is, that charging at the head of the right wing of horse with that intrepid courage that he always shewed, he bore down all before him in the very beginning of the battle, and not only put the enemies cavalry into confusion, but drove them quite out of the field.

Could he have bridled his temper, and, like an old soldier, or rather an experienced general, have contented himself with the glory of that part, sending but one brigade of his troops on in the pursuit, which had been sufficient to have finished the work, and have kept the enemies from rallying, and then with the rest of his cavalry, wheeled to the left, and fallen in upon the croup of the right wing of the enemies cavalry, he had made a day of it, and gained the most glorious victory of that age; for he had a gallant army. But he followed the chace clear off, and out of the field of battle; and when he began to return, he had the misfortune to see that his left wing of horse was defeated by Fairfax and Cromwell, and to meet his friends flying for their lives; so that he had nothing to do but to fly with them, and leave his infantry, and the Duke, then Marquis of Newcastle's, old veteran soldiers to be cut in pieces by the enemy.

I had one gentleman with me, an old soldier too, who, though he was not in the fight, yet gave us a compleat account of the action from his father's relation, who, he said, had served in it, and who had often shew'd him upon the very post every part of the engagement where every distinct body was drawn up, how far the lines extended, how the infantry were flank'd by the cavalry, and the cavalry by the woods, where the artillery were planted, and which way they pointed; and he accordingly described it in so lively a manner to me, that I thought it was as if I had just now seen the two armies engaging.

His relation of Prince Rupert's ill conduct, put me in mind of the quite different conduct of old General Tilly, who commanded the imperial army at the great Battle of Leipsick in Germany, against that glorious Prince Gustavus Adolphus.

Upon the first charge, the cavalry of the right wing of Tilly's army, commanded by the Count of Furstemburgh, fell on with such fury, and in such excellent order, being all old troops, and most of them cuirassers, upon the Saxon troops, which had the left of the Swedish army, and made twenty two thousand men, that, in short, they put them into confusion, and drove them upon their infantry of the main battle, so that all went off together except General Arnheim, who commanded the Saxon right wing, and was drawn up next to the Swedes.

The Saxons being thus put into confusion, the Imperialists cried *Victoria, the enemy fly,* and their general officers cry'd out to Tilly to let them follow. No, says Tilly, let 'em go, let 'em go; but let us beat the Swedes too, or we do nothing; and immediately he ordered the cavalry that had performed so well, should face to the left, and charge the rest of the army in flank. But the King of Sweden, who saw the disorder, and was ready at all places to encourage and direct his troops, ordered six thousand Scots, under Sir John Hepburn, who made his line of reserve, to make a front to the left, and face the victorious troops of the Imperialists, while, in the mean time, with a fury not to be resisted, he charg'd, in person, upon the Imperial left wing, and bore down all before him.

Then it appeared that Count Tilly was in the right; for though he had not let his right wing pursue the Saxons, who, notwithstanding being new men, never rallied, yet with his whole army he was not able to beat the rest; but the King of Sweden gained the most glorious victory that ever a Protestant army had till then obtain'd in the world over a Popish. This was 1632.

I came back extremely well pleased with the view of Marston Moor, and the account my friend had given of the battle; 'twas none of our business to concern our passions in the cause, or regret the misfortunes of that day; the thing was over beyond our ken; time had levelled the victors with the vanquished, and the royal family being restored, there was no room to say one thing or other to what was pass'd; so we returned to York the same night.

York, as I have said, is a spacious city, it stands upon a great deal of ground, perhaps more than any city in England out of Middlesex, except Norwich; but then the buildings are not close and throng'd as at Bristol, or as at Durham, nor is York so populous as either Bristol or Norwich. But as York is full of gentry and persons of distinction, so they live at large, and have houses proportioned to their quality; and this makes the city lie so far extended on both sides the river. It is also very magnificent, and, as we say, makes a good figure every way in its appearance, even at a distance; for the cathedral is so noble and so august a pile, that 'tis a glory to all the rest.

There are very neat churches here besides the cathedral, and were not the minster standing, like the Capitol in the middle of the city of Rome, some of these would pass for extraordinary, as the churches of St. Mary's and Allhallows, and the steeples of Christ-Church, St. Mary's, St. Pegs, and Allhallows.

There are also two fine market-houses, with the town-hall upon the bridge, and abundance of other publick edifices, all which together makes this city, as I said, more stately and magnificent, though not more populous and wealthy, than any other city in the king's dominions, London and Dublin excepted. The reason of the difference is evidently for the want of trade.

Here is no trade indeed, except such as depends upon the confluence of the gentry: But the city, as to lodgings, good houses, and plenty of provisions, is able to receive the King, Lords and Commons, with the whole Court, if there was occasion; and once they did entertain King Charles I. with his whole Court, and with the assembly of Peers, besides a vast confluence of the gentry from all parts to the king, and at the same time a great part of his army.

We went out in a double excursion from this city, first to see the Duke of Leeds's house, and then the Earl of Carlisle's, and the Earl of Burlington's in the East Riding; Carlisle House is by far the finest design, but it is not finished, and may not, perhaps, in our time; they say his lordship sometimes observes noblemen should only design, and begin great palaces, and leave posterity to finish them gradually, as their estates will allow them; it is called Castle Howard. The Earl of Burlington's is an old built house, but stands deliciously, and has a noble prospect towards the Humber, as also towards the Woulds.

At Hambledon Down, near this city, are once a year very great races, appointed for the entertainment of the gentry, and they are the more frequented, because the king's plate of a hundred guineas is always run for there once a year; a gift designed to encourage the gentlemen to breed good horses.

Yorkshire is throng'd with curiosities, and two or three constantly attend these races, namely, First, That (as all horse matches do) it brings together abundance of noblemen and gentlemen of distinction, and a proportion of ladies; and, I assure you, the last make a very noble appearance here, and, if I may speak my thoughts without flattery, take the like number where you will, yet, in spite of the pretended reproach of country breeding, the ladies of the north are as handsome and as well dress'd as are to be seen either at the Court or the Ball.

From York we did not jump at once over the whole country, and, like a late author, without taking notice of any thing, come out again sixty or seventy miles off, like an apparition, without being seen by the way. The first thing we did, we took a view of the suburb of York over the river, opposite to the city, and then entring the East Riding, took our audience *de conge* in form, and so stood over that division towards Hull.

In our road we had a clear view of the Earl of Burlington's noble and magnificent house, mentioned just now, soon after our passing the River Derwent, on a very high rising ground, very advantageously situated.

The River Derwent, contrary to the course of all the rivers in Yorkshire, (as I have observed) runs north and south, rising in that part of the country called Cleveland, and running through, or hard by, several market towns, as Pickering, Pocklington, North Malton, and others, and is, by the course, a good guide to those who would take a view of the whole country.

I observed the middle of this riding or division of Yorkshire is very thin of towns, and consequently of people, being overspread with Woulds, that is to say, plains and downs, like those of Salisbury; on which they feed great numbers of sheep, and breed also a great many black cattle and horses; especially in the northern part, which runs more mountainous, and makes part of the North Riding of York. But the east and west part is populous and rich, and full of towns, the one lying on the sea coast, and the other upon the River Derwent, as above; the sea coast or west side, is call'd Holderness.

After passing the Derwent we saw little of moment, but

keeping under the woulds or hills mentioned above, we came to your old acquaintance John a Beverley, I mean the famous monastery at that town.

It is a large and populous town, though I find no considerable manufacture carried on there. The great collegiate church is the main thing which ever did, and still does, make the town known in the world. The famous story of John of Beverley, is, in short, this: That one John, Archbishop of York, a learned and devout man, out of meer pious zeal for religion, and contempt of the world, quitted or renounced his honours and superiority in the Church, and, laying aside the pall, and the mitre, retired to Beverley, and liv'd here all the rest of his time a recluse.

This story will prompt you to enquire how long ago 'twas, for you know as well as I, and will naturally observe, that very few such bishops are to be found now; it was indeed a long time ago, for it is this very year just five year above a thousand year ago that this happened; for the good man died Anno Dom. 721. you may soon cast up the rest to 1726.

The memory of this extraordinary man has been much honoured; and had they gone no farther, I should have join'd with them most heartily. But as to sainting him, and praying to him, and offering at his shrine, and such things, that we Protestants must ask their leave to have nothing to say to.

However, King Athelstan, after making a vow to him if he got the victory over the Danes, made him his tutelar saint, and gave great gifts and immunities to this place on his account; among the rest, the king granted his peace to it, as was the word in those days; that is to say, made it a sanctuary, as he did much about the same time to the church at Rippon; and I shall here give you the copy of his grant in the old English rhimes, as I did of the other.

As to this privilege of sanctuary, Mr. Cambden gives us the description of a stone chair, with a Latin inscription upon it in capital letters, which he Englishes also.

Here on the 13th of September, anno 1664, upon opening a grave they met with a vault of square free stone fifteen foot long, and two foot broad; within it was a sheet of lead four foot long, and in that the ashes, six beads (whereof three crumbled to dust with a touch; of the three remaining two were supposed to be Cornelian) with three great brass pins, and four large iron nails. Upon the sheet laid a leaden plate, with this inscription:

✠

Cross over this there lay a box of lead about seven inches
long, six broad, and five high, wherein were several pieces of
bones mixed with a little dust, and yielding a sweet smell. All
these things were carefully re-interred in the middle alley of the
body of the minster, where they were taken up: This circumstance does not by any means agree with what Bishop Godwin
has left us about this saint, namely, that he was buried in the
church porch; for though what is mentioned in the inscription
was only a reinterment upon the inquisition made; yet it looks
a little odd they should not lay the relicks in the same place
where they found them, unless one should solve it this way,
that but part of the church was then standing, and they might
lay him there with a design to remove him when it should be
rebuilt, but afterwards either neglected or forgot it.

The minster here is a very fair and neat structure; the roof
is an arch of stone, in it there are several monuments of the
Piercy's, Earls of Northumberland, who have added a little
chapel to the choir, in the windows of which are the pictures
of several of that family drawn in the glass at the upper end
of the choir. On the right side of the altar-place stands the freed
stool, mentioned by our author, made of one entire stone, and
said to have been removed from Dunbar in Scotland, with a
well of water behind it. At the upper end of the body of the
church, next the choir, hangs an antient table with the picture
of St. John (from whom the church is named) and of King
Athelstan the founder of it, and between them this distich:

> Als free make I thee,
> As heart can wish, or egh can see.

Hence the inhabitants of Beverley pay no toll or custom in any
port or town in England; to which immunity (I suppose) they
owe, in great measure, their riches and flourishing condition;
for indeed, one is surprised to find so large and handsome a
town within six miles of Hull: In the body of the church stands
an antient monument, which they call the Virgins Tomb,

because two virgin sisters lay buried there who gave the town
a piece of land, into which any freeman may put three milch
kine from Ladyday to Michaelmas. At the lower end of the
body of the church, stands a fair, large font of agat stone.

Near the minster, on the south side of it, is a place nam'd
Hall Garth, wherein they keep a court of record, called the
Provost's Court. In this may be try'd causes for any sum
arising within its liberties; (which are very large, having about
a hundred towns and parts of towns in Holderness, and other
places of the East Riding belonging to it). It is said to have
also a power in criminal matters, though at present that is
not used.

But to come to the present condition of the town, it is above
a mile in length, being of late much improv'd in its buildings,
and has pleasant springs running quite through its streets. It is
more especially beautified with two stately churches, and has a
free-school that is improved by two fellowships, six scholarships, and three exhibitions in St. John's College, in Cambridge,
belonging to it; besides six alms-houses, the largest whereof
was built lately by the executors of Michael Warton, Esq; who,
by his last will, left one thousand pounds for that use; the
mayor and aldermen having sometimes been deceived in their
choice, admit none into their alms-houses but such as will give
bond to leave their effects to the poor when they die; a good
example to other places.

The principal trade of the town is making malt, oatmeal,
and tann'd leather; but the poor people mostly support themselves by working bone-lace, which of late has met with particular encouragement, the children being maintain'd at school
to learn to read, and to work this sort of lace. The cloathing
trade was formerly follow'd in this town, but Leland tells us,
that even in his time it was very much decay'd.

They have several fairs, but one more especially remarkable,
called the Mart, beginning about nine days before Ascension
Day, and kept in a street leading to the Minster Garth, called
Londoners Street, for then the Londoners bring down their
wares, and furnish the country tradesmen by wholesale.

About a mile from Beverly to the east, in a pasture belonging
to the town, is a kind of spaw, though they say it cannot be
judg'd by the taste whether or no it comes from any mineral;
yet taken inwardly it is a great drier, and wash'd in, dries
scorbutick scurf, and all sorts of scabs, and also very much
helps the king's evil.

It is easie to conceive how Beverley became a town from this very article, namely, that all the thieves, murtherers, house-breakers and bankrupts, fled hither for protection; and here they obtained safety from the law whatever their crimes might be.

After some time, the town growing bigger and bigger, the church was also enlarged; and though it fell into the king's hands, King Henry VIII. having done by this as he did by others; and the monks of Beverley were suppress'd, yet the town continues a large, populous town; and the River Hull is made navigable to it for the convenience of trade.

I remember, soon after the Revolution, when the late King William hired six thousand Danish auxiliaries to assist him in his wars in Ireland, they landed at Hull, and, marching from thence for West-Chester, in order to embark for Carrickfergus, they came thro' this town, and halted here a few days for refreshment. Here two of their foot soldiers quarrelled and fought a duel, in which one of them was kill'd. The other being taken, was immediately tried and sentenced to a court marshal of their own officers, and by the rules of war, such as were in force among them, was sentenced and put to death, and was then buried in the same grave with the man he had kill'd; and upon their grave is set up a stone with an English inscription thus:

Under this stone two Danish soldiers lie.

There are other lines mentioning the story, as above, but I do not remember them, it being some years since I made this observation. But to return to St. John of Beverley, and King Athelstan's merry grant, which I shall make speak English as well as I can; it is as follows:

The Charter of Privileges granted by King Athelstan to St. John of Beverley, in the Year of our Lord 925

> Yat witen alle yat ever been,
> Yat yis Charter heren and seen,
> Yat j ye King Adelstan,
> Has yaten and given to Seint John
> Of Beverlike; yat sai know
> Tol and theam, yet wit ye now,
> Sok and sake over all yat land
> Yat is given into his hand:
> On ever ilks kinges gai,
> Be it all free yon znd ay.
> Be it almousend, be all free
> Wit ilke man, and ekke wit mee.
> Yat will j (be him yat me scop)
> Bot till an ercebiscop,
> And til ye seven minstre prestes,

Yat serves God ther Saint John restevs
Yat give j God and Saint John,
Her before you ever ilkan,
All my herst corn in eldeel,
To uphold his minstre weel;
Ya four threve (be Heven kinge)
Of ilka plough of Estriding.
    If it swa betid or swa gaas,
Yat ani man her again taas,
Be he baron, be he erle,
Clare, prest, parson, or cherel;
Na, be he na yet ilke gome,
I will forsaye yat he come:
(Yat wit ye weel, (or and or)
Till Saint John minstre dor.
And yar i will (swa Christ me red)
Yat he bet his misdeed,
Or he be cursed for on on.
Wit at yat servis Saint John.
    Yit hit swa betid and swa es,
Yat ye man in mansing es,
J say, you over fourty daghes,
Swilke yan be Saint John laghes,
Yat the Chapitel of Beverlike
Till ye Scirif of Everwike.
Send yair writ son anon,
Yat yis man sed man becan.
Ye the scirif yan say I ye,
Witout en any writ one me,
Sal minen him (swa Christ me red)
And into my prison lede
And hald him, (yat is my will)
Till he bet his misgilt.
    If men rise new laghes
In any oyer kinges daghes,
Be yay framed, be yay yemed,
Wit yham of the mynstree demed,
Ye mercy of the misdeed,
Gif j Saint John (swa Crist me red)
Yif man be cald of limes or lif,
Or men challenges land in strife,
Wit my bodlack wit writ of right,
Y will Saint John have ye might,
Yat man yer for nought fight in feeld,
Now yet wit staf no with sheeld;
Bot twelve men will j yat it telle,
Swo sall it be, swo her ibelle.
And he yat him swo werne may
Overcomen be he ever and ay,
Als he in feeld war overcomen.
Ye cravantise of him be nomen,
Yat yat j God, and Saint John;
Her before iow ever ilkon.
If men be founden than I drunkened,
Sterved on Saint John, rike his agmen men.
Without en swike his akkend bailife make ye sight,
Nad oyer coroner have ye might:
Swa milkel freedom give I ye,
Swa hert may think, or eghe see,

Yat have j thought and forbiseen,
Y will yat yar ever been,
Samenyng, and mynstre life.
Last follike witout en strife.
God helpe alle that ilk men
Yat helpes to ye thowen. Amen.

The same in modern English:

Let all men know that e'er have been,
That this Charter have heard and seen;
That I, King Athelstan,
Have taken and given to Saint John
Of Beverley, I say again (or now)
Toll and team, that know ye too,
Sok and sake o'er all that land
That is given into his hand;
As ever as any kings whatever,
It shall be all free then and for ever
As my alms are all free;
Witness every man, and witness me.
I will also (in spite of any that shall hinder me),
That as well an archbishop
As seven ministers of priests orders,
Shall serve God there where Saint John lies;
And that I give to God, and to Saint John,
Here, in all your presence ever one,
All my last crop of corn in Erdale,
To maintain his ministers very well,
And four trave,[1] (by the King of Heaven)
Of every plough land in the East Riding.[2]
 If it shall happen, or so fall out,
That any man with-holds it, or takes it away.
Be he lord, or be he earl,
Clerk, priest, parson, or layman;
Nay, be he never so great a person,
I will forbid that he shall touch it:
(That pray observe over and over)
Till St. John's ministers have their due:
And moreover I will (so Christ hear me)
That he shall pay for the trespass,
Or be he curs'd from son to son;
Know ye this all that serve St. John,
(Witness all you servants of St. John).
 If it should so happen, or so is,
That any man is secured in or fled to a house,
I command, that in forty days,
According to St. John's laws,
That the Chapter of Beverley
Shall send out his writ with all speed
To the Sheriff of Everwick,
That the man may be apprehended:
And to the sheriff I hereby say,
Without any farther warrant from me,
Shall carry him (so Christ me bless)
Into my prison directly;

[1] A trave is a shock, or twelve sheaves of corn in the ear.
[2] Beverley is in the East Riding of Yorkshire.

And shall keep him there, such is my will,
Till he make satisfaction for the trespass.
　If other men make other laws,
In any other king's reign;
Be they made or intended to be made,
Witness those then in trust,
The amends or fines of every such trespass
I give St. John (as Christ me help).
　If any man be accused for life or limb,
Or titles of land be disputed at law,
Taken in execution or legal process;
I will, that St. John shall have the decision;
And no man shall combat for any cause whatever
Neither with weapon, or with armour,
But twelve men shall decide the cause,
That so it shall be well and fairly tried;
And he that is cast by their sentence
Shall be so for ever,
As much as if he were overcome in fight:
And the estate shall be called his
As if 'twas given him by Me, God, and St. John,
In presence of you every one.
　If any man be found kill'd, or dead with drink,
Or starv'd with hunger, or cold in St. John's bounds,
His next doers shall be told thereof;
Ye shall have no other coroner to judge.
　As much freedom give I to you,
As heart can think, or eye can see.
　That I have thought or have foreseen;
I will also that there shall always be,
Peaceable and quiet living among ye,
To the last, without any strife.
And God help every man
That gives to you his help. Amen.

From Beverley I came to Hull, distance six miles. If you would expect me to give an account of the city of Hamburgh or Dantzick, or Rotterdam, or any of the second rate cities abroad, which are fam'd for their commecre, the town of Hull may be a specimen. The place is indeed not so large as those; but, in proportion to the dimensions of it, I believe there is more business done in Hull than in any town of its bigness in Europe; Leverpool indeed of late comes after it apace; but then Leverpool has not the London trade to add to it.

In the late war, the fleets from Hull to London were frequently a hundred sail, sometimes including the other creeks in the Humber, a hundred and fifty to a hundred and sixty sail at a time; and to Holland their trade is so considerable, that the Dutch always employ'd two men of war to fetch and carry, that is, to convoy the trade, as they call'd it, to and from Hull, which was as many as they did to London.

In a word, all the trade at Leeds, Wakefield and Hallifax, of which I have spoken so justly and so largely, is transacted here, and the goods are ship'd here by the merchants of Hull; all the lead trade of Derbyshire and Nottinghamshire, from Bautry Wharf, the butter of the East and North Riding, brought down the Ouse to York: The cheese brought down the Trent from Stafford, Warwick and Cheshire, and the corn from all the counties adjacent, are brought down and shipp'd off here.

Again, they supply all these countries in return with foreign goods of all kinds, for which they trade to all parts of the known world; nor have the merchants of any port in Britain a fairer credit, or fairer character, than the merchants of Hull, as well for the justice of their dealings as the greatness of their substance or funds for trade. They drive a great trade here to Norway, and to the Baltick, and an important trade to Dantzick, Riga, Narva and Petersburgh; from whence they make large returns in iron, copper, hemp, flax, canvas, pot-ashes, Muscovy linnen and yarn, and other things; all which they get vent for in the country to an exceeding quantity. They have also a great importation of wine, linen, oil, fruit, &c. trading to Holland, France and Spain; the trade of tobacco and sugars from the West-Indies, they chiefly manage by the way of London. But besides all this, their export of corn, as well to London as to Holland and France, exceeds all of the kind, that is or can be done at any port in England, London excepted.

Their shipping is a great article in which they outdo all the towns and ports on the coast except Yarmouth, only that their shipping consists chiefly in smaller vessels than the coal trade is supplied with, tho' they have a great many large vessels too, which are employed in their foreign trade.

The town is situated at the mouth of the River Hull, where it falls into the Humber, and where the Humber opens into the German Ocean, so that one side of their town lies upon the sea, the other upon the land. This makes the situation naturally very strong; and, were there any occasion, it is capable of being made impregnable, by reason of the low situation of the grounds round it.

King Charles II. on occasion of the frequent Dutch wars in that reign, had once resolved to appoint a station for a squadron of men of war here; with a yard and dock, for building men of war (ships) in the Humber; and, on this occasion, resolved to make the place strong, in proportion to the necessity of those affairs; upon which a large citadel was marked out on the other side the river; but it was never finished.

The greatest imperfection, as to the strength of Hull in case of a war, is, that, lying open to the sea, it is liable to a bombardment; which can only be prevented by being masters at sea, and while we are so, there's no need of fortifications at all; and so there's an end of argument upon that subject.

The town is exceeding close built, and should a fire ever be its fate, it might suffer deeply on that account; 'tis extraordinary populous, even to an inconvenience, having really no room to extend it self by buildings. There are but two churches, but one of them is very large, and there are two or three very large meeting-houses, and a market stored with an infinite plenty of all sorts of provision.

They shew us still in their town-hall the figure of a northern fisherman, supposed to be of Greenland, that is to say, the real Greenland, being the continent of America to the north of those we call the north west passages; not of Spiltbergen, where our ships go a whale fishing, and which is, by mistake, called Greenland. He was taken up at sea in a leather boat, which he sate in, and was covered with skins, which drew together about his waste, so that the boat could not fill, and he could not sink; the creature would never feed nor speak, and so died.

They have a very handsome exchange here, where the merchants meet as at London, and, I assure you, it is wonderfully filled, and that with a confluence of real merchants, and many foreigners, and several from the country; for the navigation of all the great rivers which fall into the Humber centers here, such as the Trent, the Idle, the Don, the Aire and Calder, and the Ouse; and consequently the commerce of all the great towns on those rivers is managed here, from Gainsborough and Nottingham on the Trent, York and Selby on the Ouse, and so of the rest.

There is also a fine free-school, over which is the merchant's hall. But the Trinity-House here is the glory of the town: It is a corporation of itself, made up of a society of merchants: It was begun by voluntary contribution for relief of distressed and aged seamen, and their wives or widows; but was afterwards approved by the government, and incorporated: They have a very good revenue, which encreases every day by charities, and bounties of pious minded people.

They maintain thirty sisters now actually in the house, widows of seamen; they have a government by twelve elder brethren and six assistants; out of the twelve they chuse annually two wardens, but the whole eighteen vote in electing them, and two stewards. These have a power to decide disputes between masters of ships and their crews, in matters relating to the sea affairs only; and with this limitation, that their judgment be not contrary to the laws of the land; and, even in trials at law, in such affairs they are often called to give their opinions.

They have a noble stone bridge here over the River Hull, consisting of fourteen arches. They had once set up a Greenland fishery, and it went on with success for a time; but it decayed in the time when the Dutch wars were so frequent, and the house built by the Greenland merchants is now turned into granaries for corn, and warehouses for other goods.

The old hospital, call'd God's House, stands near it, with a chapel rebuilt since the late war, and the arms of Michael de la Pole, the first founder, set up again; so that the foundation is restored, the building is nobly enlarged, and an entire new hospital built as an addition to the old one. The story of this De la Pole may not be unwelcome, because, though it be a piece of antiquity, 'tis a piece of honour both to the merchants of Hull, and to the town it self. Sir Michael de la Pole was a merchant of Hull, but first at a place called Raven's Rood in Brabant, where, growing rich, he advanced to King Richard II. several thousand pounds in gold for his urgent occasions in his wars; upon which the king invited him to come and live in England, which he did; here the king knighted him, made his son, Michael de la Pole, Earl of Suffolk, and gave him several lordships in Holderness; and Mr. Cambden observes, he is stiled by the king in those grants, William de la Pole, Dilectus Valectus & Mercator Noster, so that he was called the King's Merchant.

This De la Pole founded a monastery of Carthusians, and an hospital, which, when that was suppress'd, remain'd; and this they call God's House.

Farther east from Hull there is a little pleasant town call'd Headon, handsome, well built, and having a little haven from the sea, which threatens Hull, that it will in time grow up to be a great place, for it indeed increases daily; but I fear for them, that their haven will do nothing considerable for them, unless they can do something very considerable for that.

They tell us at Headon, that the sea encroaches upon the land on all that shore, and that there are many large fields quite eaten up; that several towns were formerly known to be there, which are now lost; from whence they may suppose, that as the sea by encroachment had damnified their harbour, so if it grows upon them a little more they shall stand open to the sea, and so need no harbour at all, or make a mole, as 'tis called abroad, and have a good road without it. But this is a view something remote.

The Spurn Head, a long promontory thrusting out into the sea, and making the north point of Humber, is a remarkable thing. But I leave that to the description of the sea coasts, which is none of my work; the most that I find remarkable here, is, that there is nothing remarkable upon this side for above thirty miles together; not a port, not a gentleman's seat, not a town of note; Bridlington or Burlington is the only place, and that is of no note, only for a bay or road for shipping, which is of use to the colliers on this coast to defend them, in case of extremity of weather.

The country people told us a long story here of gipsies which visit them often in a surprising manner. We were strangely amused with their discourses at first, forming our ideas from the word, which, in ordinary import with us, signifies a sort of strolling, fortune-telling, hen-roost-robbing, pocket-picking vagabonds, called by that name. But we were soon made to understand the people, as they understood themselves here, namely, that at some certain seasons, for none knows when it will happen, several streams of water gush out of the earth with great violence, spouting up a huge heighth, being really natural *jette d'eaus* or fountains; that they make a great noise, and, joining together, form little rivers, and so hasten to the sea. I had not time to examine into the particulars; and as the irruption was not just then to be seen, we could say little to it: That which was most observable to us, was, that the country people have a notion that whenever those *gipsies*, or, as some call 'em, *vipseys*, break out, there will certainly ensue either famine or plague. This put me in mind, that the very same thing is said to happen at Smitham Bottom in Surrey, beyond Croydon, and that the water gushing out of the chalky hills about eight miles from Croydon, on the road to Ryegate, fills the whole bottom, and makes a large river running just to the towns end of Croydon; and then turning to the left runs into the river which rises in the town, and runs to Cashalton; and I name it, because the country people here have exactly the same notion, that this water never breaks out but against a famine; and as I am sure it has not now broken out for more than fifty years, it may, for ought I know, be true.

Scarborough next presents it self, a place formerly famous for the strong castle, situate on a rock, as it were hanging over the sea, but now demolish'd, being ruined in the last wars. The town is well built, populous and pleasant, and we found a great deal of good company here drinking the waters, who came not only from all the north of England, but even from Scotland. It is hard to describe the taste of the waters; they are apparently ting'd with a collection of mineral salts, as of vitriol, allom, iron, and perhaps sulphur, and taste evidently of the allom. Here is such a plenty of all sorts of fish, that I have hardly seen the like, and, in particular, here we saw turbets of three quarters of a hundred weight, and yet their flesh eat exceeding fine when taken new.

To describe the herring, the mackrel, the cod, the whiting, is only to repeat what is said in other places, and what we shall have occasion to repeat more than once, now we begin to go far north.

At the entrance of a little nameless river, scarce indeed worth a name, stands Whitby, which, however, is an excellent harbour, and where they build very good ships for the coal trade, and many of them too, which makes the town rich.

From hence the North Riding holds on to the bank of Tees, the northern bounds of Yorkshire, and where there are two good towns, (viz.) Stockton and Yarum, towns of no great note; but what they obtain by the river and adjacent sea, but are greatly encreased of late years, especially the first, by being the chiefest place in the North Riding of York, or in the county of Cumberland, for the shipping off lead, and butter for London.

I began now to consider the long journey I had to go, and that I must not stop at small matters: We went from Stockton to Durham. North Allerton, a town on the post road, is remarkable for the vast quantity of black cattle sold there, there being a fair once every fortnight for some months, where a prodigious quantity are sold.

I have not concern'd this work at all in the debate among us in England, as to Whig and Tory. But I must observe of this town, that, except a few Quakers, they boasted that they had not one Dissenter here, and yet at the same time not one Tory, which is what, I believe, cannot be said of any other town in Great Britain.

I must now leave Yorkshire, which indeed I might more fully have described, if I had had time; for there are abundance of rarities in nature spoken of in this North Riding, which I had not leisure to enquire into; as the allom mines or pits near Moultgrave or Musgrave, from whence the Lord Musgrave now Duke of Buckinghamshire, has his title, as he has also a great part of his estate from the allom works not far off. Next here are the snake stones, of which nothing can be said but as one observes of them, to see how nature sports her self to amuse us, as if snakes could grow in those stones. Then the glates or gargates, that is, in short jett, a black smooth stone found in Cleveland; also a piece of ground, which, if the wild geese attempt to fly over, they fall down dead. But I cannot dwell any longer here.

Darlington, a post town, has nothing remarkable but dirt, and a high stone bridge over little or no water, the town is eminent for good bleaching of linen, so that I have known cloth brought from Scotland to be bleached here. As to the Hell Kettles, so much talked up for a wonder, which are to be seen as we ride from the Tees to Darlington, I had already seen so little of wonder in such country tales, that I was not hastily deluded again. 'Tis evident, they are nothing but old coal pits filled with water by the River Tees.

Durham is next, a little compact neatly contriv'd city, surrounded almost with the River Wear, which with the castle standing on an eminence, encloses the city in the middle of it; as the castle does also the cathedral, the bishop's palace, and the fine houses of the clergy, where they live in all the magnificence and splendour imaginable.

I need not tell you, that the Bishop of Durham is a temporal prince, that he keeps a court of equity, and also courts of justice in ordinary causes within himself. The county of Durham, like the country about Rome, is called St. Cuthbert's Patrimony. This church, they tell us, was founded by David, King of Scots; and afterward Zouch, the valiant bishop, fought the Scots army at Nevil's Cross, where the Scots were terribly cut in pieces, and their king taken prisoner.

But what do I dip into antiquity for, here, which I have avoided as much as possible every where else? The church of Durham is eminent for its wealth; the bishoprick is esteemed the best in England; and the prebends and other church livings, in the gift of the bishop, are the richest in England. They told me there, that the bishop had thirteen livings in his gift, from five hundred pounds a year to thirteen hundred pounds a year; and the living of the little town of Sedgfield, a few miles south of the city, is said to be worth twelve hundred pounds a year, beside the small tithes, which maintain a curate, or might do so.

Going to see the church of Durham, they shewed us the old

Popish vestments of the clergy before the Reformation, and which, on high days, some of the residents put on still. They are so rich with embroidery and emboss'd work of silver, that indeed it was a kind of a load to stand under them.

The town is well built but old, full of Roman Catholicks, who live peaceably and disturb no body, and no body them; for we being there on a holiday, saw them going as publickly to mass as the Dissenters did on other days to their meeting-house.

From hence we kept the common road to Chester in the Street, an old, dirty, thorowfare town, empty of all remains of the greatness which antiquaries say it once had, when it was a Roman colony. Here is a stone bridge, but instead of riding over it we rode under it, and riding up the stream pass'd under or through one of the arches, not being over the horse hoofs in water; yet, on enquiry, we found, that some times they have use enough for a bridge.

Here we had an account of a melancholy accident, and in it self strange also, which happened in or near Lumley Park, not long before we pass'd through the town. A new coal pit being dug or digging, the workmen workt on in the vein of coals till they came to a cavity, which, as was supposed, had formerly been dug from some other pit; but be it what it will, as soon as upon the breaking into the hollow part, the pent up air got vent, it blew up like a mine of a thousand barrels of powder, and, getting vent at the shaft of the pit, burst out with such a terrible noise, as made the very earth tremble for some miles round, and terrify'd the whole country. There were near three-score poor people lost their lives in the pit, and one or two, as we were told, who were at the bottom of the shaft, were blown quite out, though sixty fathom deep, and were found dead upon the ground.

Lumley Castle is just on the side of the road as you pass between Durham and Chester, pleasantly seated in a fine park, and on the bank of the River Were. The park, besides the pleasantness of it, has this much better thing to recommend it, namely, that it is full of excellent veins of the best coal in the country, (for the Lumley coal are known for their goodness at London, as well as there). This, with the navigable river just at hand, by which the coals are carried down to Sunderland to the ships, makes Lumley Park an inexhaustible treasure to the family.

They tell us, that King James the First lodg'd in this castle, at his entrance into England to take possession of the crown, and seeing a fine picture of the antient pedigree of the family, which carried it very far beyond what his majesty thought credible, turn'd this good jest upon it to the Bishop of Durham, who shewed it him, viz. That indeed he did not know that Adam's sirname was Lumley before.

From hence the road to Newcastle gives a view of the in-exhausted store of coals and coal pits, from whence not London only, but all the south part of England is continually supplied; and whereas when we are at London, and see the prodigious fleets of ships which come constantly in with coals for this encreasing city, we are apt to wonder whence they come, and that they do not bring the whole country away; so, on the contrary, when in this country we see the prodigious heaps, I might say mountains, of coals, which are dug up at every pit, and how many of those pits there are; we are filled with equal wonder to consider where the people should live that can consume them.

Newcastle is a spacious, extended, infinitely populous place; 'tis seated upon the River Tyne, which is here a noble, large and deep river, and ships of any reasonable burthen may come safely up to the very town. As the town lies on both sides the river, the parts are join'd by a very strong and stately stone bridge of seven very great arches, rather larger than the arches of London Bridge; and the bridge is built into a street of houses also, as London Bridge is.

The town it self, or liberty, as it is a corporation, extends but to part of the bridge, where there is a noble gate built all of stone, not much unlike that upon London Bridge, which so lately was a safeguard to the whole bridge, by stopping a terrible fire which otherwise had endangered burning the whole street of houses on the city side of the bridge, as it did those beyond it.

There is also a very noble building here, called the Exchange: And as the wall of the town runs parallel from it with the river, leaving a spacious piece of ground before it between the water and the wall, that ground, being well wharf'd up, and fac'd with free-stone, makes the longest and largest key for landing and lading goods that is to be seen in England, except that at Yarmouth in Norfolk, and much longer than that at Bristol.

Here is a large hospital built by contribution of the keel men, by way of friendly society, for the maintenance of the poor of their fraternity, and which, had it not met with dis-couragements from those who ought rather to have assisted so good a work, might have been a noble provision for that numerous and laborious people. The keel men are those who manage the lighters, which they call keels, by which the coals are taken from the steaths or wharfs, and carryed on board the ships, to load them for London.

Here are several large publick buildings also, as particularly a house of state for the mayor of the town (for the time being) to remove to, and dwell in during his year: Also here is a hall for the surgeons, where they meet, where they have two skeletons of humane bodies, one a man and the other a woman, and some other rarities.

The situation of the town to the landward is exceeding unpleasant, and the buildings very close and old, standing on the declivity of two exceeding high hills, which, together with the smoke of the coals, makes it not the pleasantest place in the world to live in; but it is made amends abundantly by the goodness of the river, which runs between the two hills, and which, as I said, bringing ships up to the very keys, and fetching the coals down from the country, makes it a place of very great business. Here are also two articles of trade which are particularly occasioned by the coals, and these are glass-houses and salt pans; the first are at the town it self, the last are at Shields, seven miles below the town; but their coals are brought chiefly from the town. It is a prodigious quantity of coals which those salt works consume; and the fires make such a smoke, that we saw it ascend in clouds over the hills, four miles before we came to Durham, which is at least sixteen miles from the place.

Here I met with a remark which was quite new to me, and will be so, I suppose, to those that hear it. You well know, we receive at London every year a great quantity of salmon pickled or cured, and sent up in the pickle in kits or tubs, which we call Newcastle salmon; now when I came to Newcastle, I expected to see a mighty plenty of salmon there, but was surprized to find, on the contrary, that there was no great quantity, and that a good large fresh salmon was not to be had under five or six shillings. Upon enquiry I found, that really this salmon, that we call Newcastle salmon, is taken as far off as the Tweed, which is three-score miles, and is brought by land on horses to Shields, where it is cur'd, pickl'd, and sent to London, as above; so that it ought to be called Berwick salmon, not Newcastle.

There are five or six churches in Newcastle, I mean on the town side, being north by Tine, besides meeting-houses, of

which, I was told, there are also five or six, (including the
Quakers) some of which are throng'd with multitudes of people,
the place, as has been said, being exceeding populous. It is not
only enriched by the coal trade; but there are also very considerable merchants in it, who carry on foreign trade to divers
parts of the world, especially to Holland, Hamburgh, Norway,
and the Baltick.

They build ships here to perfection, I mean as to strength,
and firmness, and to bear the sea; and as the coal trade occasions
a demand for such strong ships, a great many are built here. This
gives an addition to the merchants business, in requiring a supply
of all sorts of naval stores to fit out those ships.

Here is also a considerable manufacture of hard ware, or
wrought iron, lately erected after the manner of Sheffield, which
is very helpful for employing the poor, of which this town has
always a prodigious number.

West of this town lies the town of Hexham, a pass upon the
Tine, famous, or indeed infamous, for having the first blood
drawn at it, in the war against their prince by the Scots in King
Charles the First's time, and where a strong detachment of
English, tho' advantageously posted, were scandalously defeated
by the Scots. Whether the commanders were in fault, or the
men, I know not, but they gave way to an inferior number of
Scots, who gain'd the pass, fought through the river, and killed
about four hundred men, the rest basely running away; after
which, the town of Newcastle was as easily quitted also, without
striking a stroke; the country round this town is vulgarly
call'd Hexamshire.

I was tempted greatly here to trace the famous Picts Wall,
built by the Romans, or rather rebuilt by them, from hence to
Carlisle; of the particulars of which, and the remains of antiquity
seen upon it, all our histories are so full; and I did go to several
places in the fields thro' which it passed, where I saw the
remains of it, some almost lost, some plain to be seen. But
antiquity not being my business in this work, I omitted the
journey, and went on for the north.

Northumberland is a long coasting county, lying chiefly on
the sea to the east, and bounded by the mountains of Stainmore
and Cheviot on the west, which are in some places inaccessible,
in many unpassable. Here is abundant business for an antiquary;
every place shews you ruin'd castles, Roman altars, inscriptions,
monuments of battles, of heroes killed, and armies routed, and
the like: The towns of Morpeth, Alnwick, Warkworth, Tickill,

and many others, shew their old castles, and some of them still in tolerable repair, as Alnwick in particular, and Warkworth; others, as Bambrough, Norham, Chillingham, Horton, Dunstar, Wark, and innumerable more, are sunk in their own ruins, by the meer length of time.

We had Cheviot Hills so plain in view, that we could not but enquire of the good old women every where, whether they had heard of the fight at Chevy Chace: They not only told us they had heard of it, but had all the account of it at their fingers end; and, taking a guide at Wooller to shew us the road, he pointed out distinctly to us the very spot where the engagement was, here, he said Earl Piercy was killed, and there Earl Douglas, here Sir William Withington fought upon his stumps, here the Englishmen that were slain were buried, and there the Scots.

A little way off of this, north, he shewed us the field of battle, called Flodden Field, upon the banks of the Till, where James IV. King of Scotland, desperately fighting, was killed, and his whole army overthrown by the English, under the noble and gallant Earl of Surrey, in the reign of King Henry VIII. upon their perfidiously invading England, while the king was absent on his wars in France.

I must not quit Northumberland without taking notice, that the natives of this country, of the antient original race or families, are distinguished by a shibboleth upon their tongues, namely, a difficulty in pronouncing the letter *r*, which they cannot deliver from their tongues without a hollow jarring in the throat, by which they are plainly known, as a foreigner is, in pronouncing the *th*: This they call the Northumbrian *r*, and the natives value themselves upon that imperfection, because, forsooth, it shews the antiquity of their blood.

From hence lay a road into Scotland, by the town of Kelso, which I after pass'd thro', but at present not willing to omit seeing Berwick upon Tweed, we turn'd to the east, and visited that old frontier, where indeed there is one thing very fine, and that is, the bridge over the Tweed, built by Queen Elizabeth, a noble, stately work, consisting of sixteen arches, and joining, as may be said, the two kingdoms. As for the town it self, it is old, decay'd, and neither populous nor rich; the chief trade I found here was in corn and salmon.

I am now on the borders of Scotland, and must either enter upon it now, and so mix it with other parts of England, or take up short, and call to mind that I have not yet taken the western coast of England in my way, I mean, the three north west counties of Lancaster, Westmoreland and Cumberland.

I cannot but say, that since I entred upon the view of these northern counties, I have many times repented that I so early resolved to decline the delightful view of antiquity, here being so great and so surprizing a variety, and every day more and more discovered; and abundance since the tour which the learned Mr. Cambden made this way, nay, many since his learned continuator; for as the trophies, the buildings, the religious, as well as military remains, as well of the Britains, as of the Romans, Saxons, and Normans, are but, as we may say, like wounds hastily healed up, the calous spread over them being remov'd, they appear presently; and though the earth, which naturally eats into the strongest stones, metals, or whatever substance, simple or compound, is or can be by art or nature prepared to endure it, has defaced the surface, the figures and inscriptions upon most of these things, yet they are beautiful, even in their decay, and the venerable face of antiquity has some thing so pleasing, so surprizing, so satisfactory in it, especially to those who have with any attention read the histories of pass'd ages, that I know nothing renders travelling more pleasant and more agreeable.

But I have condemn'd my self (unhappily) to silence upon this head, and therefore, resolving however to pay this homage to the dust of gallant men and glorious nations, I say therefore, I must submit and go on; and as I resolve once more to travel through all these northern countries upon this very errand, and to please, nay, satiate my self with a strict search into every thing that is curious in nature and antiquity. I mortify my self now with the more ease, in hopes of letting the world see, some time or other, that I have not spent those hours in a vain and barren search, or come back without a sufficient reward to all the labours of a diligent enquirer; but of this by the way, I must, for the present, make this circuit shorter than usual, and leave the description of the other three counties to my next.

I am, &c.

THE END OF THE NINTH LETTER

LETTER X

Sir,—Having thus finished my account of the east side of the north division of England, I put a stop here, that I may observe the exact course of my travels; for as I do not write you these letters from the observations of one single journey, so I describe things as my journies lead me, having no less than five times travelled through the north of England, and almost every time by a different rout; purposely that I might see every thing that was to be seen, and, if possible, know every thing that is to be known, though not (at least till the last general journey) knowing or resolving upon writing these accounts to you. Now as by my exact observations on all these several traverses of the country, I hope I am not the less able, so I am sure I am much the better furnished, as well to tell you wherein others have ignorantly or superficially represented things, as to give you such other and fuller accounts, as in your own intended travels you will find confirmed, and by which you will be able the better to guide your farther enquiries.

I entred Lancashire at the remotest western point of that county, having been at West-Chester upon a particular occasion, and from thence ferry'd over from the Cestrian Chersonesus, as I have already call'd it, to Liverpoole. This narrow slip of land, rich, fertile and full of inhabitants, tho' formerly, as authors say, a meer waste and desolate forest, is called Wirall, or by some Wirehall. Here is a ferry over the Mersee, which, at full sea, is more than two miles over. We land on the flat shore on the other side, and are contented to ride through the water for some length, not on horseback but on the shoulders of some honest Lancashire clown, who comes knee deep to the boat side, to truss you up, and then runs away with you, as nimbly as you desire to ride, unless his trot were easier; for I was shaken by him that I had the luck to be carry'd by more than I car'd for, and much worse than a hard trotting horse would have shaken me.

Liverpoole is one of the wonders of Britain, and that more, in my opinion, than any of the wonders of the Peak; the town was, at my first visiting it, about the year 1680, a large, hand-

some, well built and encreasing or thriving town; at my second
visit, anno 1690, it was much bigger than at my first seeing it,
and, by the report of the inhabitants, more than twice as big
as it was twenty years before that; but, I think, I may safely
say at this my third seeing it, for I was surpriz'd at the view,
it was more than double what it was at the second; and, I am
told, that it still visibly encreases both in wealth, people, business
and buildings: What it may grow to in time, I know not.

There are no fortifications either to landward or seaward,
the inhabitants resting secure under the protection of the
general peace; though when the late northern insurrection
spread down their way, and came to Preston, they could have
been glad of walls and gates; and indeed, had the rebel party
had time to have advanced to Warrington, seized the pass
there, and taken Manchester, as they would certainly have
done in three days more, it would have fared but very ill with
Liverpoole; who could have made but little resistance against
an arm'd and desperate body of men, such as they appeared
to be, and by that time would have been: Besides, the invaders
would here have found not the sweets of plunder only, but
arms, ammunition, powder and lead, all which they extreamly
wanted; they would have had ships also to have facilitated a
communication with their fellows in Ireland, who would have
throng'd over upon the least view of their success, if it had been
only in hopes of plunder.

But heaven had Liverpoole in its particular protection, as
well as the whole kingdom; the rebels were met with, fought
and defeated, before they gat leave to get so far, or to make
any offer that way. The story of which, as it does not belong
to this work, so it is too recent in memory, to need any account
of it here, other than in general.

The town has now an opulent, flourishing and encreasing
trade, not rivalling Bristol, in the trade to Virginia, and the
English island colonies in America only, but is in a fair way to
exceed and eclipse it, by encreasing every way in wealth and
shipping. They trade round the whole island, send ships to
Norway, to Hamburgh, and to the Baltick, as also to Holland
and Flanders; so that, in a word, they are almost become like
the Londoners, universal merchants.

The trade of Liverpoole is not my particular province, so
I shall be short in that part; it consists not only in merchandizing
and correspondencies beyond seas; but as they import almost
all kinds of foreign goods, they have consequently a great

inland trade, and a great correspondence with Ireland, and with Scotland, for their consumption, exactly as it is with Bristol; and they really divide the trade with Bristol upon very remarkable equalities.

Bristol lies open to the Irish Sea, so does Liverpoole: Bristol trades chiefly to the south and west parts of Ireland; from Dublin in the east, to Galloway west; Liverpoole has all the trade of the east shore and the north from the harbour of Dublin to London Derry.

Bristol has the trade of South Wales; Liverpoole great part of the trade of North Wales; Bristol has the south west counties of England, and some north of it, as high as Bridge North, and perhaps to Shrewsbury; Liverpoole has all the northern counties, and a large consumption of goods in Cheshire and Staffordshire are supplied from Liverpoole. It is some advantage to the growing commerce of this town, that the freemen of it are, in consequence of that freedom, free also of Bristol; and they are free also of the corporations of Waterford and Wexford in the kingdom of Ireland. Not that these corporation privileges are of any great value to Liverpoole in its foreign trade, but in particular cases it may be some advantage, as in town duties, in admitting them to set up trades in those corporations, and the like.

The people of Liverpoole seem to have a different scene of commerce to act on from the city of Bristol, which to me is a particular advantage to both, namely, that though they may rival one another in their appearances, in their number of shipping, and in several particulars, yet they need not interfere with one another's business, but either of them seem to have room enough to extend their trade, even at home and abroad, without clashing with one another. One has all the north, and the other all the south of Britain to correspond in. As for Wales, 'tis, as it were, divided between them by nature it self. Bristol lies open to South Wales, and into the very heart of it, by the navigation of the Rivers Wye and Lug, and by the many open harbours all the way to Milford and St. David's, and into all the east side of Wales, and the counties of Monmouth, Hereford and Salop, by the Severn; Liverpoole has the same with North Wales, by the water of Dee, the Cluyd, the Conway, Canal of the Mona, and all the rivers in Carnarvon Bay.

Ireland is, as it were, all their own, and shared between them, as above; and for the northern coast of it, if the Liverpoole men have not the whole fishery, or, at least, in company with the merchants of London Derry, the fault is their own. The situation of Liverpoole gives it a very great advantage to improve their commerce, and extend it in the northern inland counties of England, particularly into Cheshire and Staffordshire, by the new navigation of the Rivers Mersee, the Weaver, and the Dane, by the last of which they come so near the Trent with their goods, that they make no difficulty to carry them by land to Burton, and from thence correspond quite through the kingdom, even to Hull; and they begin to be very sensible of the advantage of such a commerce. But I must not dwell here; I might otherwise take up great part of the sheets I have left in describing the commerce of this town, and some of its neighbours.

I return therefore to the description of it as a town; the situation being on the north bank of the river, and with the particular disadvantage of a flat shore. This exposed the merchants to great difficulties in their business; for though the harbour was good, and the ships rode well in the offing, yet they were obliged to ride there as in a road rather than a harbour. Here was no mole or haven to bring in their ships and lay them up, (as the seamen call it) for the winter; nor any key for the delivering their goods, as at Bristol, Biddiford, Newcastle, Hull, and other sea ports: Upon this, the inhabitants and merchants have, of late years, and since the visible encrease of their trade, made a large basin or wet dock, at the east end of the town, where, at an immense charge, the place considered, they have brought the tide from the Mersee to flow up by an opening that looks to the south, and the ships go in north; so that the town entirely shelters it from the westerly and northerly winds, the hills from the easterly, and the ships lye, as in a mill-pond, with the utmost safety and convenience. As this is so great a benefit to the town, and that the like is not to be seen in any place in England but here, I mean London excepted, it is well worth the observation and imitation of many other trading places in Britain who want such a convenience, and, for want of it, lose their trade.

The new church built on the north side of the town is worth observation. 'Tis a noble, large building, all of stone, well finish'd; has in it a fine font of marble placed in the body of the church, surrounded with a beautiful iron pallisado; the gift of the late Mr. Heysham, a merchant of London, but considerably concerned in trade on this side, and for many years Member of Parliament for Lancaster. There is a beautiful tower to this church, and a new ring of eight very good bells.

The town-house is a fine modern building, standing all upon pillars of free-stone; the place under it is their Tolsey or Exchange, for the meeting of their merchants; but they begin to want room, and talk of enlarging it or removing the Exchange to the other part of the town, where the ships and the merchants business is nearer hand.

In a word, there is no town in England, London excepted, that can equal Liverpoole for the fineness of the streets, and beauty of the buildings; many of the houses are all of free stone, and compleatly finished; and all the rest (of the new part I mean) of brick, as handsomely built as London it self.

Mr. Cambden says, it was a neat and populous town in his time; his reverend continuator confirms what I have said thus, that it was more than doubly encreased in buildings and people in twenty eight years, and that the customs were augmented tenfold in the same time; to which I am to add, that they are now much greater, that being written about two and thirty years ago, before the new church, or the wet dock, mentioned above, were made, and we know they have gone on encreasing in trade, buildings and people, to this day. I refer the reader therefore to judge of the probable greatness of it now.

From hence the Mersee opening into the Irish Sea, we could see the great and famous road of Hile Lake, made famous for the shipping off, or rather rendezvous of the army and fleet under King William, for the conquest of Ireland, an. 1689, for here the men of war rode as our ships do in the Downs, till the transports came to them from Chester and this town.

The sea coast affords little remarkable on the west side of this port, till we come farther north; so we left that part of the county, and going east we came to Warrington. This is a large market town upon the River Mersee, over which there is a stately stone bridge, which is the only bridge of communication for the whole county with the county of Chester; it is on the great road from London leading to Carlisle and Scotland, and, in case of war, has always been esteemed a pass of the utmost importance. It was found to be so upon several extraordinary occasions in the time of the late civil war; and had the rebels advanced thus far in the late Preston affair, so as to have made themselves masters of it, it would have been so again; and, on that account, the king's forces took special care, by a speedy advance to secure it.

Warrington is a large, populous old built town, but rich and full of good country tradesmen. Here is particularly a weekly market for linnen, as I saw at Wrexham in Wales, a market for flannel. The linnen sold at this market, is, generally speaking, a sort of table linnen, called huk-a-back or huk-a-buk; 'tis well known among the good housewives, so I need not describe it. I was told there are generally as many pieces of this linnen sold here every market day as amounts to five hundred pounds value, sometimes much more, and all made in the neighbourhood of the place.

From hence, on the road to Manchester, we pass'd the great bog or waste call'd Chatmos, the first of that kind that we see in England, from any of the south parts hither. It extends on the left-hand of the road for five or six miles east and west, and they told us it was, in some places, seven or eight miles from north to south. The nature of these mosses, for we found there are many of them in this country, is this, and you will take this for a description of all the rest.

The surface, at a distance, looks black and dirty, and is indeed frightful to think of, for it will bear neither horse or man, unless in an exceeding dry season, and then not so as to be passable, or that any one should travel over them.

The substance of the surface seems to be a collection of the small roots of innumerable vegetables matted together, interwoven so thick, as well the bigger roots as the smaller fibres, that it makes a substance hard enough to cut out into turf, or rather peat, which, in some places, the people cut out, and piling them up in the sun, dry them for their fewel. The roots I speak of are generally small and soft not unlike the roots of asparagus or of bearbind, they have no earth among them, except what they contract from the air, and dust flying in it, but the rain keeps them, as it were, always growing, though not much encreasing.

In some places the surface of this kind lies thicker, in some not very thick. We saw it in some places eight or nine foot thick, and the water that dreins from it look'd clear, but of a deep brown, like stale beer. What nature meant by such a useless production, 'tis hard to imagine; but the land is entirely waste, except, as above, for the poor cottagers fuel, and the quantity used for that is very small.

Under this moss, or rather in the very body of it, not here only, but in several like places, and perhaps in all of them, those antient fir trees are found, of which so much dispute has been what they are or were, but especially how they should come there. Much mob-learning is sometimes expended upon these questions, which, in my weak judgment, amounts to no more than this; That nature, whose works are all directed by a superior hand, has been guided to produce trees here under ground, as she does in other places above ground; that these live rather than grow, though 'tis manifest they encrease too, otherwise they would not be found of so great a bulk; that as the trees above the surface grow erect and high, these lie prone and horizontal; those shoot forth branches and leaves; these shoot forth no branches or leaves, yet have a vegetation by methods directed by nature, and particularly to that kind; and 'tis remarkable, that as if they lie buried they will grow and encrease, so if you take them up, and plant them in the air, they will wither and die; and why should this be more strange than that a fish will strangle in the air, and a bird drown in the water, or than that every thing lives in its proper element, and will not live, or at least not thrive out of it.

It is observable, that these trees are a kind of fir, and are very full of turpentine. Whether there is any tar in them I am not positive, but I suppose there is. And yet I do not see, that for this reason they should not be a natural ordinary product, as other vegetables are.

If it be enquired, why no kind of trees should grow thus but fir; it may be as well ask'd, why no stone grows in such or such quarries, or countries, but marble, or in others than free stone, nature alone can resolve that part.

As to their being brought hither by the general convulsion of the globe at the deluge, the thought is so mean, and the thing so incongruous, that I think it neither needs or deserves any other notice.

From hence we came on to Manchester, one of the greatest, if not really the greatest meer village in England. It is neither a wall'd town, city, or corporation; they send no members to Parliament; and the highest magistrate they have is a constable or headborough; and yet it has a collegiate church, several parishes, takes up a large space of ground, and, including the suburb, or that part of the town called —— over the bridge; it is said to contain above fifty thousand people; and though some people may think this strange, and that I speak by guess, and without judgment, I shall justify my opinion so well, that I believe, it will convince you my calculation is at least very probable, and much under what fame tells us is true.

The Manchester trade we all know; and all that are concerned in it know that it is, as all our other manufactures are, very much encreased within these thirty or forty years especially beyond what it was before; and as the manufacture is encreased, the people must be encreased of course. It is true, that the encrease of the manufacture may be by its extending itself farther in the country, and so more hands may be employed in the county without any encrease in the town. But I answer that though this is possible, yet as the town and parish of Manchester is the center of the manufacture, the encrease of that manufacture would certainly encrease there first, and then the people there not being sufficient, it might spread itself further.

But the encrease of buildings at Manchester within these few years, is a confirmation of the encrease of people; for that within very few years past, here, as at Liverpoole, and as at Froom in Somersetshire, the town is extended in a surprising manner; abundance, not of new houses only, but of new streets of houses, are added, a new church also, and they talk of another, and a fine new square is at this time building; so that the town is almost double to what it was a few years ago, and more than double to what it was at the time I am to mention.

Now to go back to the last age, the right reverend continuator of Mr. Cambden tells us positively, that sixty years before his writing, and that is now thirty-two years ago, there were computed twenty thousand communicants in Manchester parish, for then the whole town was but one parish. Now if there were twenty thousand communicants, we may be allowed to suppose ten thousand children, from fifteen years old down wards, which is thirty thousand people; and if the town is since more than doubled in buildings, and the trade manifestly encreased, as I believe every one will grant; and also that I take in the suburb or village of —— to it, which is another parish, I think my computation of fifty thousand people to be not reasonable only, but much within compass; and some of the antient inhabitants are of the opinion there are above sixty thousand.

If then this calculation is just, as I believe it really is, you have here then an open village, which is greater and more populous than many, nay, than most cities in England, not York, Lincoln, Chester, Salisbury, Winchester, Worcester, Gloucester, no not Norwich it self, can come up to it; and for lesser cities, two or three put together, would not equal it, such as Peterborough, Ely, and Carlisle, or such as Bath, Wells and Litchfield, and the like of some others.

I must not quit Manchester without giving some account of the college there, which has been very famous for learning and learned men, even in our age; and has just now given a bishop to the church in the person of the late master Dr. Peploe, now Lord Bishop of Chester.

The town of Manchester boasts of four extraordinary foundations, viz. a college, an hospital, a free-school, and a library, all very well supported.

The college was the charity of Thomas, Lord Delaware, who being but the cadet of the family, was bred a scholar, and was in orders; afterwards became rector of the parish, and enjoy'd the same many years, succeeding to that honour by the decease of his elder brother without heirs.

He founded the college anno 1421, after he was come to the honour and estate of his brother. By the foundation it was dedicated to the Virgin Mary, and the two patron saints of France and England, St. Dennis and St. George.

The foundation escaped the general ruin in the time of Henry VIII. but was dissolved in the reign of his successor Edward VI. and the revenues fell to the Crown; but they were restored by Queen Mary, and the house re-established upon the first foundation, though with several additions.

Queen Elizabeth enquiring into the nature of the gift, and having a favourable representation of it as a seminary not of Popery but of learning and true religion, founded it anew, at the same time as she did the great free-school at Shrewsbury. This was anno 1578. and as, I say, she refounded it, so she new christen'd it, gave it the name it still enjoys, of Christ's College in Manchester, and settled its antient revenues as far as they could be recovered; but there had been great dilapidations in the time of the former unsettled governours of it by several former foundations, as follows:

The college was first founded, A.D. 1421, by Thomas de la Ware, at first, rector of the said parish church, and brother to the Lord De la Ware, whom he succeeded in the estate and honour; and then himself founded a college there, consisting of one master or keeper, eight fellows chaplains, four clerks, and six choristers, in honour of St. Mary, (to whom the said parish church was formerly dedicated) St. Dennis of France, and St. George of England.

This foundation was dissolved 1547, in the first year of King Edward VI. the lands and revenues of it taken into the king's hands, and by him demised to the Earl of Derby, and the college-house, and some lands sold to the said earl.

After this, the college was refounded by Queen Mary, who restored most of the lands and revenues, only the college it self, and some of its revenues, remained still in the hands of the Earl of Derby.

It was also founded anew by Queen Elizabeth, A.D. 1578. by the name of Christ's College, in Manchester, consisting of one warden, four fellows, two chaplains, four singing men, and four choristers, the number being lessened, because the revenues were so; chiefly by the covetousness and base dealing of Thomas Herle, then warden, and his fellows, who sold away, or made such long leases of the revenues, as could never yet, some of them, be retrieved.

It was last of all refounded by King Charles the First, A.D. 1636, consisting then of one warden, four fellows, two chaplains, four singing-men, and four choristers, and incorporating them, as before, by the name of the Warden and Fellows of Christ's College in Manchester, the statutes for the same being drawn up by Archbishop Laud.

The hospital was founded by Humphry Cheetham, Esq; and incorporated by King Charles the Second, designed by the said bountiful benefactor for the maintenance of forty poor boys out of the town and parish of Manchester, and some other neighbouring parishes; but since 'tis enlarged to the number of sixty, by the governours of the said hospital, to be taken in between the age of six and ten, and there maintain'd with meat, drink, lodging and cloaths, to the age of fourteen, and then to be bound apprentices to some honest trade or calling, at the charge of the said hospital; for the maintenance of which he endowed it with the yearly revenue of 420l. which is since improved by the care and good husbandry of the feoffees or governours, to the yearly sum of 517l. 8s. 4d. they having laid out in the purchase of lands the sum of 1825l. which was saved out of the yearly income, over and above the maintenance of the poor children, and others, belonging to the said hospital, wherein there are annually near seventy persons provided for.

By the bounty of the said founder, is also erected a very fair and spacious library, already furnished with a competent stock of choice and valuable books, to the number of near four thousand, and daily increasing with the income of 116l. per annum, settled upon the same by the said worthy benefactor, to buy books for ever, and to afford a competent salary for a library keeper. There is also a large school for the hospital boys, where they are daily instructed, and taught to read and write.

The publick school was founded, A.D. 1519. by Hugh Oldham, D.D. and Bishop of Exeter, who bought the lands on which the school stands, and took the mills there in lease on the Lord De la Ware, for sixty years; afterwards, with the bishop's money, Hugh Benwick, and Joan his sister, purchased of the Lord De la Ware, his land in Awcoates, and the mills upon right and left of them in feoffment to the said free-school for ever, which revenues are of late very much encreased by the feoffees of the schools; who, out of the improvements, have as well considerably augmented the masters salaries, as the exhibitions annually allowed to the maintenance of such scholars at the university, as the warden of the college and the high master shall think requisite, and have besides, for some years past, added a third master, for whom they have lately erected a new and convenient school at the end of the other.

Besides these publick benefactions and endowments, there have been several other considerable sums of money, and annual revenues, left and bequeathed to the poor of the said town, who are thereby, with the kindness and charity of the present inhabitants, competently provided for, without starving at home, or being forced to seek relief abroad.

As for the antiquity of the place, I have no room to mention it here, though the authors who have mentioned it say much of that part too; nor is it my business, the antiquity of the manufacture indeed is what is of most consideration; and this, though we cannot trace it by history, yet we have reason to believe it began something earlier than the great woollen manufactures in other parts of England, of which I have spoken so often, because the cotton might it self come from the Mediterranean, and be known by correspondents in those countries, when that of wooll was not push'd at, because our neighbours wrought the goods, and though they bought the wool from England, yet we did not want the goods; whereas, without making the cotton goods at home, our people could not have them at all; and that necessity, which is the mother of invention, might put them upon one; whereas having not the same necessity, ignorance and indolence prevented the other.

I am the rather of this opinion too, because Mr. Cambden speaks of this manufacture too, by the name of Manchester Cottons, and that being written in Queen Elizabeth's time, when the woollen manufacture was, though much improved, yet, as we may say, in its infancy, or, at least, not at full age; we may reasonably believe, that cotton was the elder manufacture of the two, and that by some considerable time. This manufacture of Manchester Cottons, as it seems they were then call'd, I suppose is the same that is now call'd fustian or dimity, or that both these are but different kinds of the other.

I cannot doubt but this encreasing town will, some time or other, obtain some better face of government, and be incorporated, as it very well deserves to be.

The River Irwell runs close by this town, and receives the little River Irke just above the town, on the north and north east side. There is a very firm, but antient stone bridge over the Irwell, which is built exceeding high, because this river, though not great, yet coming from the mountainous part of the country, swells sometimes so suddenly, that in one night's time they told me the waters would frequently rise four or five yards, and the next day fall as hastily as they rose.

The author of the *Geographical Dictionary* places this town upon the bank of the River Spolden, which Mr. Cambden's continuator, mentioned so often, takes notice of as a mistake, and so it is; but I suppose 'twas occasioned by this: There is a river named Spodden, not Spolden, which rising under Blackstone Edge, runs into the Roch at Rochdale, and so losing its name in the Roch, runs into the Irwell, about Ratcliff, six or seven miles above Manchester, and, in some maps, they have made not the Spodden lose its name in the Roch, but the Roch in the Spodden, and so give it yet its own name after it joins the Irwell, and on to Manchester.

About eight mile from Manchester, north west, lies Bolton, the town which gives title to the noble family of Powlet, Dukes of Bolton, raised to the heighth of duke by the late King William, at the same time, or near it, with the Dukes of Bedford, Devonshire, Rutland and Newcastle. We saw nothing remarkable in this town, but that the cotton manufacture reach'd hither; but the place did not, like Manchester, seem so flourishing and encreasing.

On the left hand of this town, west, even to the sea-shore, there are not many towns of note, except Wiggan, on the high post road, and Ormskirk, near which we saw Latham House, famous for its being not only gallantly defended in the times of the late fatal wars, but that it was so by a woman; for the Lady Charlotte, Countess of Derby, defended the house to the last extremity against the Parliament forces; nor could she ever be brought to capitulate, but kept the hold till Prince Rupert, with a strong body of the King's army, came to her relief, and obliged the enemy to raise their siege, anno 1644: It was indeed ruin'd in a second siege, and is not yet fully recovered from the calamity of it.

In this town of Bolton the old Earl of Derby was beheaded by the Parliament, or by the army rather, in the time of those fatal wars, October 15. 1651.

In the neighbourhood of this town, that is to say, between Wiggan and Bolton, in the estate of Sir Roger Bradshaw, is found that kind of coal they call Canell or Candle Coal, which, tho' they are found here in great plenty, and are very cheap, are yet very singular; for there are none such to be seen in Britain, or perhaps in the world besides: They so soon take fire, that, by putting a lighted candle to them, they are presently in a flame, and yet hold fire as long as any coals whatever, and more or less, as they are placed in the grate or hearth, whether flat or edg'd, whether right up and down, and polar, or level and horizontal.

They are smooth and slick when the pieces part from one anoiher, and will polish like alabaster; then a lady may take them up in a cambrick handkerchief and they will not soil it, though they are as black as the deepest jet. They are the most pleasant agreeable fuel that can be found, but they are remote; and though some of them have been brought to London, yet they are so dear, by reason of the carriage, that few care to buy them; we saw some of them at Warrington too, but all from the same pits.

We saw nothing remarkable in Ormskirk but the monuments of the antient family of the Stanly's, before they came to the title of Earls of Derby. Here they are all buried, and have some very fine, tho' antient, and even decayed remains of monuments; and here they continue to bury the family still, whose seat of Latham, as I said before, is but hard by. Mr. Cambden gives a full account how Latham House, and a great estate with it, came to the Earls of Derby by marriage, and has continued in the family to this day.

It is not to be forgot that Warrington is near Winnick, a small town, but a large parish, and great benefice; but though it might be the greatest in England in those days, 'tis very far from being now so; for we never heard that it was worth above 800l. per annum, whereas Sedgfield, near Durham, is valued at this time at 1200l. per annum at least.

I must not pass over here the Burning Well, as 'tis called, near Wiggan, though I must acknowledge, that being turned from Bolton towards Rochdale, before I heard any thing of it that I gave any credit to, I did not go back to see it; not that I had not curiosity enough, if I had been satisfied it was valuable, but the country people, who usually enlarge upon such things rather than lessen them, made light of this; and so I cool'd in my curiosity.

But the account given in publick of it is also so particular, that it abundantly makes amends to me for my not seeing it. Mr. Cambden's continuator gives the following account of it:

Within a mile and a half of Wiggan is a well, which does not appear to be a spring but rather rain water, at first sight. There is nothing about it that seems extraordinary, but, upon emptying it, there presently breaks out a sulphureous vapour, which makes the water bubble up as if it boiled; a candle being put to it, it presently takes fire, and burns like brandy; the flame, in a calm season, will continue a whole day, by the heat whereof they can boil eggs, meat, &c. though the water it self be cold By this bubbling the water does not encrease, but is only kept in motion by the constant halitus of the vapours breaking out; the same water taken out of the well will not burn, as neither the mud upon which the halitus has beat.

Dr. Leigh, in his *Natural History of Lancashire,* not only describes it, but accounts very judiciously for the thing it self, and by it for the warmth of all hot baths.

As I have noted above, we turned east here, and came to Bury, a small market town on the River Roch, mentioned above, where we observed the manufacture of cotton, which are so great at Manchester, Bolton, &c. was ended, and woollen manufacture of coarse sorts, called half-thicks and kersies, began, on which the whole town seemed busy and hard at work; and so in all the villages about it.

From thence we went on to Rochdale, a larger and more populous town than Bury, and under the hills, called Blackstone Edge, of which I have spoken sufficiently in my former letter having travelled this way to Hallifax, &c.

But I must now look northward. This great county, as we advance, grows narrow, and not only so, but mountainous, and not so full of towns or inhabitants as the south part, which I have been over; Preston and Lancaster are the only towns of note remaining.

Preston is a fine town, and tolerably full of people, but not like Liverpoole or Manchester; besides, we come now beyond the trading part of the county. Here's no manufacture; the town is full of attorneys, proctors, and notaries, the process of law here being of a different nature than they are in other places, it being a dutchy and county palatine, and having particular privileges of its own. The people are gay here, though not perhaps the richer for that; but it has by that obtained the name of Proud Preston. Here is a great deal of good company, but not so much, they say, as was before the late bloody action with the northern rebels; not that the battle hurt many of the immediate inhabitants, but so many families there and thereabout, have been touched by the consequences of it, that it will not be recovered in a few years, and they seem to have a kind of remembrance of things upon them still.

Lancaster is the next, the county town, and situate near the mouth of the River Lone or Lune. The town is antient; it lies, as it were, in its own ruins, and has little to recommend it but a decayed castle, and a more decayed port (for no ships of any considerable burthen); the bridge is handsome and strong, but, as before, here is little or no trade, and few people. It surprized me to hear that there is not above sixty parishes in all this large county, but many of them are necessarily very large.

This part of the country seemed very strange to us, after coming out of so rich, populous and fruitful a place, as I have just now described; for here we were, as it were, lock'd in between the hills on one side high as the clouds, and prodigiously higher, and the sea on the other, and the sea it self seemed desolate and wild, for it was a sea without ships, here being no sea port or place of trade, especially for merchants; so that, except colliers passing between Ireland and Whitehaven with coals, the people told us they should not see a ship under sail for many weeks together.

Here, among the mountains, our curiosity was frequently moved to enquire what high hill this was, or that; and we soon were saluted with that old verse which I remembered to have seen in Mr. Cambden, viz.

> Inglebrough, Pendle-hill and Penigent,
> Are the highest hills between Scotland and Trent.

Indeed, they were, in my thoughts, monstrous high; but in a country all mountainous and full of innumerable high hills, it was not easy for a traveller to judge which was highest.

Nor were these hills high and formidable only, but they had a kind of an unhospitable terror in them. Here were no rich pleasant valleys between them, as among the Alps; no lead mines and veins of rich oar, as in the Peak; no coal pits, as in the hills about Hallifax, much less gold, as in the Andes, but all barren and wild, of no use or advantage either to man or beast. Indeed here was formerly, as far back as Queen Elizabeth, some copper mines, and they wrought them to good advantage; but whether the vein of oar fail'd, or what else was the reason, we know not, but they are all given over long since, and this part of the country yields little or nothing at all.

But I must not forget Winander Meer, which makes the utmost northern bounds of this shire, which is famous for the char fish found here and hereabout, and no where else in England; it is found indeed in some of the rivers or lakes in Swisserland among the Alps, and some say in North Wales; but I question the last. It is a curious fish, and, as a dainty, is potted, and sent far and near, as presents to the best friends; but the quantity they take also is not great. Mr. Cambden's continuator calls it very happily the Golden Alpine Trout.

Here we entred Westmoreland, a country eminent only for

being the wildest, most barren and frightful of any that I have passed over in England, or even in Wales it self; the west side, which borders on Cumberland, is indeed bounded by a chain of almost unpassable mountains, which, in the language of the country, are called Fells, and these are called Fourness Fells, from the famous promontory bearing that name, and an abbey built also in antient times, and called Fourness.

But 'tis of no advantage to represent horror, as the character of a country, in the middle of all the frightful appearances to the right and left; yet here are some very pleasant, populous and manufacturing towns, and consequently populous.

Such as Kirby Launsdale, or Lunedale, because it stands on the River Lune, which is the boundary of the county, and leaves the hills of Mallerstang Forest, which are, in many places, unpassable. The manufacture which the people are employed in here, are chiefly woollen cloths, at Kirkby Launsdale, and Kendal, and farther northward, a security for the continuance of the people in the place; for here is a vast concourse of people. In a word, I find no room to doubt the hills above mentioned go on to Scotland, for from some of the heighths hereabouts, they can see even into Scotland it self.

The upper, or northern part of the county, has two manufacturing towns, called Kirkby Stephen, and Appleby; the last is the capital of the county, yet neither of them offer any thing considerable to our observation, except a great manufacture of yarn stockings at the former.

My Lord Lonsdale, or Lonsdown, of the antient family of Louther, has a very noble and antient seat at Louther, and upon the River Louther; all together add a dignity to the family, and are tests of its antiquity. The house, as now adorned, is beautiful; but the stables are the wonder of England, of which, having not taken an exact view of them my self, I am loth to say, at second-hand, what fame has said; but, in general, they are certainly the largest and finest that any gentleman or nobleman in Britain is master of.

When we entred at the south part of this county, I began indeed to think of Merionethshire, and the mountains of Snowden in North Wales, seeing nothing round me, in many places, but unpassable hills, whose tops, covered with snow, seemed to tell us all the pleasant part of England was at an end. The great Winander Meer, like the Mediterranean Sea, extends it self on the west side for twelve miles and more, reckoning from North Bridge on the south, where it contracts it self again into a river up to Grasmere North, and is the boundary of the county, as I have said, on that side; and the English Appenine, as Mr. Cambden calls them, that is, the mountains of Yorkshire North Riding, lie like a wall of brass on the other; and in deed, in one sense, they are a wall of brass; for it is the opinion of the most skilful and knowing people in the country, that those mountains are full of inexhaustible mines of copper, and so rich, as not only to be called brass, copper being convertible into brass, but also to have a quantity of gold in them also: It is true, they do at this time work at some copper mines here, but they find the oar lies so deep, and is so hard to come at, that they do not seem to go cheerfully on.

But notwithstanding this terrible aspect of the hills, when having passed by Kendal, and descending the frightful mountains, we began to find the flat country show it self; we soon saw that the north and north east part of the county was pleasant, rich, fruitful, and, compared to the other part, populous. The River Eden, the last river of England on this side, as the Tyne is on the other, rises in this part out of the side of a monstrous high mountain, called Mowill Hill, or Wildbore Fell, which you please; after which, it runs through the middle of this vale, which is, as above, a very agreeable and pleasant country, or perhaps seems to be so the more, by the horror of the eastern and southern part.

In this vale, and on the bank of this river, stands Appleby, once a flourishing city, now a scattering, decayed, and half-demolished town, the fatal effects of the antient inroads of the Scots, when this being a frontier county, those invasions were frequent, and who several times were masters of this town, and at length burnt it to the ground, which blow it has not yet recovered.

The searchers after antiquity find much more to recreate their minds, and satisfy their curiosity, in these northern countries than in those farther south, which are more populous and better inhabited, because the remains of antient things have met with less injury here, where there are not so many people, or so many buildings, or alterations, enclosings and plantings, as in other places; but, for my purpose, who am to give the present state of things, here is not much to observe; nor are there many houses or seats of the nobility in this part, tho' many antient families dwell here, as particularly Strickland, from the lands of Strickland, Wharton from Wharton Hall, Louther from the River Louther, as above, Warcop of Warcop,

Langdale of Langdale, Musgrave from Musgrave, and many others.

The Roman highway, which I have so often mentioned, and which, in my last letter, I left at Leeming Lane and Peers Brigg, in the North Riding of York, enters this county from Rear Cross upon Stanmore, and crossing it almost due east and west, goes through Appleby, passing the Eden a little north from Perith, at an antient Roman station call'd Brovoniacam, where there was a large and stately stone bridge; but now the great road leads to the left-hand to Perith, in going to which we first pass the Eden, at a very good stone bridge call'd Louther Bridge, and then the Elnot over another.

Perith, or Penrith, is a handsome market town, populous, well built, and, for an inland town, has a very good share of trade. It was unhappily possessed by the late party of Scots Highland rebels, when they made that desperate push into England, and which ended at Preston; in the moor or heath, on the north part of this town, the militia of the county making a brave appearance, and infinitely out-numbering the Highlanders, were drawn up; yet, with all their bravery, they ran away, as soon as the Scots began to advance to charge them, and never fired a gun at them, leaving the town at their mercy. However, to do justice even to the rebels, they offered no injury to the town, only quartered in it one night, took what arms and ammunition they could find, and advanced towards Kendal.

From hence, in one stage, through a country full of castles, for almost every gentleman's house is a castle, we came to Carlisle, a small, but well fortified city, the frontier place and key of England on the west sea, as Berwick upon Tweed is on the east; and in both which there have, for many years, I might say ages, been strong garrisons kept to check the invading Scots; from below this town the famous Picts Wall began, which cross'd the whole island to Newcastle upon Tyne, where I have mentioned it already.

Here also the great Roman highway, just before named, has its end, this being the utmost station of the Roman soldiers on this side.

But before I go on to speak of this town, I must go back, as we did for our particular satisfaction, to the sea coast, which, in this northern county, is more remarkable than that of Lancashire, though the other is extended much farther in length; for here are some towns of good trade; whereas in Lancashire,

Liverpoole excepted, there is nothing of trade to be seen upon the whole coast.

I enquired much for the pearl fishery here, which Mr. Cambden speaks of, as a thing well known about Ravenglass and the River Ire, which was made a kind of bubble lately: But the country people, nor even the fishermen, could give us no account of any such thing; nor indeed is there any great quantity of the shell-fish to be found here (now) in which the pearl are found, I mean the large oyster or muscle. What might be in former times, I know not.

The cape or head land of St. Bees, still preserves its name; as for the lady, like that of St. Tabbs beyond Berwick, the story is become fabulous, viz. about her procuring, by her prayers, a deep snow on Midsummer Day, her taming a wild bull that did great damage in the country; these, and the like tales, I leave where I found them, (viz.) among the rubbish of the old women and the Romish priests.

In the little town, which bears her name there, is a very good free-school, founded by that known and eminent benefactor to, and promoter of pious designs, Archbishop Grindal; it is endowed very well by him, and the charity much encreased by the late Dr. Lamplugh, Archbishop of York: The library annexed to this foundation is very valuable, and still encreasing by several gifts daily added to it; and they show a list of the benefactors, in which are several persons of honour and distinction. The master is put in by the Provost and Fellows of Queen's College in Oxon.

Under this shore, the navigation being secured by this cape of St. Bees, is the town of Whitehaven, grown up from a small place to be very considerable by the coal trade, which is encreased so considerably of late, that it is now the most eminent port in England for shipping off coals, except Newcastle and Sunderland, and even beyond the last, for they wholly supply the city of Dublin, and all the towns of Ireland on that coast; and 'tis frequent in time of war, or upon the ordinary occasion of cross winds, to have two hundred sail of ships at a time go from this place for Dublin, loaden with coals.

They have of late fallen into some merchandizing also, occasioned by the great number of their shipping, and there are now some considerable merchants; but the town is yet but young in trade, and that trade is so far from being ancient, that Mr. Cambden does not so much as name the place, and his continuator says very little of it.

About ten miles from Whitehaven north east, lies Cockermouth, upon the little River Cocker, just where it falls into the Derwent. This Derwent is famous for its springing out of those hills, call'd Derwent Fells, where the ancient copper mines were found in Queen Elizabeth's time, and in which, it was said, there was a large quantity of gold. But they are discontinued since that time, for what reason, I know not; for there are several copper mines now working in this county, and which, as they told me, turn to very good account.

Some tell us, the copper mines on Derwent Fells were discontinued, because there being gold found among the oar, the queen claimed the royalty, and so no body would work them; which seems to be a reason why they shou'd have been applied to the search with more vigor; but be that how it will, they are left off, and the more probable account is, what a gentleman of Penrith gave us, namely, that the charge of working them was too great for the profits.

Here are still mines of black lead found, which turn to very good account, being, for ought I have yet learned, the only place in Britain where it is to be had.

Here we saw Skiddaw, one of those high hills of which, wherever you come, the people always say, they are the highest in England. Skiddaw indeed is a very high hill, but seems the higher, because not surrounded with other mountains, as is the case in most places where the other hills are, as at Cheviot, at Penigent, and at other places. From the top of Skiddaw they see plainly into Scotland, and quite into Dumfries-shire, and farther.

Cockermouth stands upon the River Derwent, about twelve miles from the sea, but more by the windings of the river, yet vessels of good burthen may come up to it. The Duke of Somerset is chief lord of this town, in right of his lady, the only heiress of the ancient family of the Piercy's, Earls of Northumberland, and which the duke of Somerset enjoys now in right of marriage.

The castles and great houses of this estate go every where to ruin, as indeed all the castles in this county do; for there being no more enemy to be expected here, the two kingdoms being now united into one, there is no more need of strong holds here, than in any other part of the kingdom. At Cockermouth there is a castle which belongs to the same family, and, I think they told us, the duke has no less than thirteen castles in all, here and in Northumberland.

This River Derwent is noted for very good salmon, and for a very great quantity, and trout. Hence, that is, from Workington at the mouth of this river, and from Carlisle, notwithstanding the great distance, they at this time carry salmon (fresh as they take it) quite to London. This is perform'd with horses, which, changing often, go night and day without intermission, and, as they say, very much out-go the post; so that the fish come very sweet and good to London, where the extraordinary price they yield, being often sold at two shillings and sixpence to four shillings per pound, pay very well for the carriage.

They have innumerable marks of antiquity in this county, as well as in that of Westmoreland, mentioned before; and if it was not, as I said before, that antiquity is not my search in this work, yet the number of altars, monuments, and inscriptions, is such, that it would take up a larger work than this to copy them, and record them by themselves; yet, passing these, I could not but take notice of two or three more modern things, and which relate to our own nation: Such as,

1. That of Hart-Horn Tree, where they shew'd us the head of a stag nail'd up against a tree, or rather shew'd us the tree where they said it was nail'd up, in memory of a famous chase of a stag by one single dog. It seems the dog (not a greyhound, as Mr. Cambden's continuator calls it, but a stanch buckhound, to be sure) chas'd a stag from this place, (Whitfield Park) as far as the Red Kirk in Scotland, which, they say, is sixty miles at least, and back again to the same place, where, being both spent, and at the last gasp, the stag strain'd all its force remaining to leap the park pales, did it, and dy'd on the inside; the hound, attempting to leap after him, had not strength to go over, but fell back, and dy'd on the outside just opposite; after which the heads of both were nail'd up upon the tree, and this distich made on them; the hound's name, it seems, was Hercules.

> Hercules kill'd Hart a Greese,
> And Hart a Greese kill'd Hercules.

2. Another thing they told us was in the same park, viz. three oak trees which were call'd the Three Brether, the least of which was thirteen yards about; but they own'd there was but one of them left, and only the stump of that; so we did not think it worth going to see, because it would no more confirm the wonder, than the peoples affirming it by tradition only. The tree or stump left, is call'd the Three Brether Tree, that is to say, one of the three brothers, or brethren.

3. West of this Hart-horn Tree, and upon the old Roman way, is the famous column, call'd the Countess Pillar, the best and most beautiful piece of its kind in Britain. It is a fine

column of free-stone, finely wrought, encha'd, and in some places painted. There is an obelisk on the top, several coats of arms, and other ornaments in proper places all over it, with dials also on every side, and a brass-plate with the following inscription upon it:

THIS PILLAR WAS ERECTED ANNO MDCLVI, BY THE RIGHT HONOR-ABLE ANNE COUNTESS DOWAGER OF PEMBROKE, AND SOLE HEIR OF THE RIGHT HONORABLE GEORGE EARL OF CUMBERLAND, ETC. FOR A MEMORIAL OF HER LAST PARTING IN THIS PLACE WITH HER GOOD AND PIOUSE MOTHER THE RIGHT HONORABLE MARGARETE COUNTESS DOWAGER OF CUMBERLAND, THE SECOUND OF APRIL, MDCXVI, IN MEMORY WHEREOF SHE ALSO LEFT AN ANNUITY OF FOUR POUNDS, TO BE DISTRIBUTED TO THE POOR WITHIN THIS PARISH OF BROUGHAM EVERY SECOND DAY OF APRIL FOR EVER UPON THE STONE TABLE HERE BY.

This Countess of Pembroke had a noble and great estate in this county, and a great many fine old seats or palaces, all which she repaired and beautified, and dwelt sometimes at one, and sometimes at another, for the benefits of her tenants, and of the poor, who she always made desirous of her presence, being better'd constantly by her bounty, and her noble house-keeping. But those estates are all since that time gone into other families.

This lady was of the family of Clifford; she had no less than four castles in this county, of which Pendragon Castle was the chief, which is a fine building to this day.

4. At Penrith also we saw several remarkable things, some of which I find mentioned by the right reverend continuator of Mr. Cambden, and which I was glad to see, so confirm'd my observation, viz. (1.) Two remarkable pillars fourteen or fifteen foot asunder, and twelve foot high the lowest of them, though they seem equal. The people told us, they were the monument of Sir Owen Cæsar, the author above-nam'd calls him, Sir Ewen Cæsarius, and perhaps he may be right; but we have no inscription upon them. This Sir Owen, they tell us, was a champion of mighty strength, and of gygantick stature, and so he was, to be sure, if, as they say, he was as tall as one of the columns, and could touch both pillars with his hand at the same time.

They relate nothing but good of him, and that he exerted his mighty strength to kill robbers, such as infested the borders much in those days, others related wild boars; but the former is most probable. (2.) On the north side of the vestry of this church is erected in the wall an ancient square stone, with a memorial, intimating, that in the year 1598 there was a dreadful plague in those parts, in which there dy'd;

Persons.

In Kendal,	2500
In Penrith,	2266
In Richmond,	2200
In Carlisle,	1196

8162

N.B. By this account it should seem that every one of those towns had separately more people than the city of Carlisle, and that Kendal, which is the only manufacturing town of them, was the most populous. We did not go into the grotto on the bank of the River Eden, of which mention is made by Mr. Cambden's continuator; the people telling us, the passage is block'd up with earth, so I must be content with telling you, that it seems to have been a lurking place, or retreat of some robbers in old time; as to its being a place of strength, I do not see any possibility of that; but its strength seems to be chiefly in its being secret and concealed; it had certainly been worth seeing, if it had been passable, the entry is long and dark, but whether strait or crooked, I cannot say, the iron gates leading to it are gone, nor is there any sign of them, or what they were hung to.

But though I am backward to dip into antiquity, yet no English man, that has any honour for the glorious memory of the greatest and truest hero of all our kings of the English or Saxon race, can go to Carlisle, and not step aside to see the monument of King Edward I. at Burgh upon the Sands, a little way out of the city Carlisle, where that victorious prince dy'd. Indeed I cannot wonder that two writers, both Scots, viz. Ridpath and Mr. Kay, should leave it, as it were, not worth their notice, that prince being the terror of Scotland, and the first compleat conqueror of their country, who brought away the sacred stone at Scone Abbey, on which their kings were crowned, also the regalia, and, in a word, made their whole country submit to his victorious arms.

Near this town, and, as the inhabitants affirm, just on the spot where the king's tent stood in which he expired, for he died in the camp, is erected a pillar of stone near thirty foot high, besides the foundation. On the west side is the following inscription:

Memoriæ Æternæ Edvardi I. Regis Angliæ longe Clarissimi, qui in Belli apparatu contra Scotos occupatus. Hic in Castris obiit. 7 Julii, A.D. 1307.

On the south side:

Nobilissimus Princeps Henricus Howard, Dux Norfolciæ, Comes Marshal Angliæ, Comes Arund. &c......ab Edvardo I, Rege Angliæ oriundus P. 1685.

On the north side:

Johannes Aglionby, J. C. F. i.e. Juris-consultus fieri fecit. *Beneath,* Tho. Langstone fecit. 1685.

It is not to be ask'd why Mr. Cambden takes no notice of this because it was not erected till near an hundred years after his survey of the country, only the place was marked by the country people, or perhaps by the soldiers of his army, by a great heap of stones rolled together upon the place; but this monument was erected, as is said above, by a private gentleman, for the eternal memory of a prince, who, when he lived, was the darling of the world, both for virtue and true fame.

But I return to Carlisle: The city is strong, but small, the buildings old, but the streets fair; the great church is a venerable old pile, it seems to have been built at twice, or, as it were, rebuilt, the upper part being much more modern than the lower.

King Henry VIII fortify'd this city against the Scots, and built an additional castle to it on the east side, which Mr. Cambden, though I think not justly, calls a cittadel; there is indeed another castle on the west, part of the town rounds the sea, as the wall rounds the whole, is very firm and strong. But Carlisle is strong by situation, being almost surrounded with rivers. On the east it has the River Poterell, on the north Eden, and on the south the Cande, or Canda, or Calda, which all fall into the arm of the sea, which they call the Solway, or Solway Firth.

Here is a bridge over the Eden, which soon lets you into Scotland; for the limits are not above eight miles off, or thereabout. The south part of Scotland on this side, coming at least fifty miles farther into England, than at Berwick. There is not a great deal of trade here either by sea or land, it being a meer frontier. On the other side the Eden we saw the Picts Wall, of which I have spoken already, and some remains of it are to be seen farther west, and of which I shall perhaps have occasion to speak again in my return. But being now at the utmost extent of England on this side, I conclude also my letter, and am,

Sir, &c.

THE END OF THE TENTH LETTER

INDEX

ABBOTSBURY, famous for the ruins of a great monastery, i. 214

Ackemanstreet (the ancient Saxon road leading to Bath), whence its name is derived, ii. 32

Ailesbury, its famous Vale, ii. 14. One enclos'd pasture field rented by a grazier for 1400*l*. per annum, *ibid*. Annual horse races near it. *See* Quainton

Alarm of an Irish massacre at the Revolution, described, and accounted for, i. 292–8

(St.) Albans, its ancient church, ii. 9. Good Duke Humphrey's vault and corps found there, *ibid*.

Aldborough, an ancient city and Roman colony, ii. 219

Alresford, a happy circumstance attending it, i. 181. Consum'd by fire and re-edify'd, *ibid*. The noted Batterd'eau, *ibid*. Roman highway there, *ibid*.

Althorp, the beautiful seat of the Earl of Sunderland, ii. 87

Amesbury, a meadow there let for 12*l*. per annum only for grass, i. 211

Ampthill, grac'd and enrich'd by the noble family of Bruce, Earls of Ailesbury, ii. 114

Andover, a thriving, populous town, i. 289. Prodigious fair for sheep near it, *ibid*.

Anglesea, Isle of, monumental stones there, surpassing those of Stonehenge, ii. 63. Its castle, and town of Baumaris, ii. 64

Ankaster, famous for its remains of antiquity and the title of duke it now gives to the Lindsey family, ii. 102. Formerly a Roman city, but now a poor village, *ibid*.

Arundel, excellent timber shipped off there for the King's Yards, etc., i. 131. Noted for the best mullets in England, i. 132

(St.) Asaph, a good bishoprick, but a poor town, ii. 65. Though situated in a rich and pleasant country, *ibid*.

Assemblies, their pernicious tendency, i. 186. Though none of them in Dorsetshire, yet the ladies more polite, and sooner married, than where they are set up, i. 217

Atherstone, a great cheese fair, ii. 88

Avon, several rivers of that name, ii. 41. That in Warwickshire greatly advantageous to the country, ii. 42

Badminton, a noble palace of the Dukes of Beaufort, ii. 36

Bangor, antiquity of its cathedral, ii. 64. A poor bishoprick, *ibid*. Its decay'd condition, ii. 74. Pelagius the heresiarch, a monk of it, *ibid*. For nothing now remarkable but a fine stone bridge, *ibid*.

Banstead Downs, its beautiful situation, and splendid appearance at the races there, i. 159

Barking, in Essex, its great trade in fishing, i. 8

Barnard-Castle, many horse-breeders there, and particularly of charging horses, ii. 224

Barnsley, called Black Barnsley, ii. 185

Barnstaple and Biddiford, two great trading towns in one port, i. 260. Advantageous situation of both, *ibid*. Barnstable the most ancient, Biddiford the most flourishing, *ibid*. Particular description of both, *ibid*., *et seq*. Ridiculous mistake of a certain author relating to their bridge, i. 161

Barrington, Lord Viscount, his great fortune, etc., i. 15

Barrows, in Wiltshire, what, i. 198–9

Barton, its dangerous ferry over the Humber, ii. 94

Basing House, its brave defence in the late Civil Wars, i. 180

Basingstoke, its corn-market, and present trade in druggets, etc., i. 180

EVERYMAN'S LIBRARY

A Selected List

In each of the thirteen classifications in this list (except BIO-GRAPHY) the volumes are arranged alphabetically under the authors' names, but Anthologies, etc., are listed under titles. Where authors appear in more than one section, a cross-reference is given. The number at the end of each item is the number of the volume in the series.

EVERYMAN'S LIBRARY

BIOGRAPHY

CLASSICAL

ESSAYS AND BELLES-LETTRES

FICTION

HISTORY

ORATORY

PHILOSOPHY AND THEOLOGY

POETRY AND DRAMA

REFERENCE

The following volumes in this section are now in the special edition of
Everyman's Reference Library:

ROMANCE

SCIENCE

TRAVEL AND TOPOGRAPHY

FOR YOUNG PEOPLE

EVERYMAN'S LIBRARY was founded in 1906, and for all the changes and chances in the book world during its long life the series stands strong to-day as the most comprehensive, inexpensive collection of books of classic measure. It is, indeed, still what its publisher intended it to be. J. M. Dent conceived it as a library arranged to cover the whole field of English literature, including translations of the ancient classics and outstanding foreign works; a series to make widely available those great books which appeal, as he says in his Memoirs, 'to every kind of reader: the worker, the student, the cultured man, the child, the man, and the woman.' The aim and scope of the series was crystallized in the title *Everyman's Library*, a title which has justified itself by the worldwide sales, totalling in 1958 some forty-five millions.

There were, of course, other popular series of reprints already in being in 1906, but none on the scale proposed for *Everyman*. One hundred and fifty-five volumes were published in three batches in the Library's first year; they comprised a balanced selection from many branches of literature and set the standard on which the Library has been built up. By early 1915 the 733rd volume had been issued; and, in spite of the interruptions of two world wars and their aftermath, the total had reached 980 by the end of the Second World War. The founder-publisher aimed at a library of a thousand volumes, and that goal was achieved at the jubilee of the Library in 1956.

A rough and ready pointer to the representative character of the Library is the number of volumes in each of the broad classifications into which the Library is divided—Biography has some 80 volumes; the Greek and Latin classics, about 40; Essays and Belles-lettres, 100; Fiction, 300; History, 80; Poetry and Drama, 100; Romance, 30; Science, 25; Religion and Philosophy, 60; Travel and Topography, 45. (The reference section is now being published separately as Everyman's Reference Library, and the Young People's Section is in the process of transference to our Children's Illustrated Classics Series.) Most of these volumes are in print now; some absent ones are works which changing taste has ruled out; but the classified sections of the Library are maintained in the original proportions, and to-day there are available in the Library the works of some five hundred authors of all times and all lands, the honoured names that stand for great literature. Moreover, many 'temporarily out of print' volumes are now being reinstated.

In March 1953 a fresh development of the Library began;

new volumes and all new issues of established volumes in *Everyman's Library* began to be produced in the larger size of crown octavo. The larger volumes have new title-pages, bindings, and wrappers, and the text pages have generous margins. Three hundred and forty volumes in this improved format have been issued in the first five years of its inauguration.

Editorially the Library is under constant survey; all volumes are re-examined and brought up to date, with new introductions, annotations, and additional matter wherever desirable; often a completely new translation or newly edited text is substituted when transferring an old volume to the new format, such as the new editions of *Pepys's Diary*, *Caesar's War Commentaries*, *The Anglo-Saxon Chronicle*, and the *Canterbury Tales*. New titles are still added: Manzoni's *Betrothed*, Aristotle's *Metaphysics*, Conrad's *Nostromo*, Jerome's *Three Men in a Boat* are all recent accessions.

The new larger volumes are in keeping with the reader's own collection in his home, for which the Library is planned, and they are also in the suitable size for the shelves of all public, institutional, university, and school libraries. Many important works in *Everyman's Library* are unobtainable in any other edition, while over 250 are *unobtainable in any other reprint series*, and they are as essential to the comprehensiveness of the Library as are the masterpieces of fiction, some of which are in one *Everyman* volume of anything up to 800 or 900 pages. The new *Everyman's Library* in crown octavo is published at four prices (except in the U.S.A.), according to the length and nature of the work. Volumes at the lowest price are in red wrapper, marked * in catalogues; the second price in blue wrapper †; the third price in green wrapper §; the highest price in yellow wrapper ‡.

This development entails no break in the continuity of the Library; there are at this writing some two hundred and eighty volumes in the original format, and they will be obtainable in the old size and at the old price until they are reissued in the new. At intervals the Publishers issue a prospectus of the volumes to be issued in the larger format during the next few months: this will be sent free to all applicants. A descriptive catalogue of all volumes is also freely available, the annotations giving the year of birth and death of the author, the date of first publication of the work, and a brief description, or details of the contents, of the last revised *Everyman's Library* edition.

J. M. DENT & SONS LTD.